DATE DUE

THE
COMING
REVOLUTION
IN
SOCIAL SECURITY

THE
COMING
REVOLUTION
IN
SOCIAL SECURITY

A. HAEWORTH ROBERTSON

Security Press
McLean, Virginia

For further information and to place purchase orders please address:

Security Press, Inc.
Box 854
McLean, Virginia
22101

This publication is designed to provide accurate and authoritative information in regard to the subject matter covered. It is sold with the understanding that the publisher is not engaged in rendering legal, accounting, or other professional service. If legal advice or other expert assistance is required, the services of a competent professional person should be sought.

From a Declaration of Principles jointly adopted by a Committee of the American Bar Association and a Committee of Publishers and Associations.

In this book, the masculine pronoun "he" has occasionally been used to refer to both sexes for the sake of simplicity.

Manufactured in the United States of America
Composed and printed by Science Press, Ephrata, Pennsylvania

Library of Congress Cataloging in Publication Data

Robertson, A. Haeworth, 1930–
   The coming revolution in social security.

   Includes bibliographical references and index.
   1. Social security—United States. I. Title.
HD7125.R62   1981   368.4'3'00973   81-4700
                                          AACR2

ISBN 0-939568-00-4

To
my parents
Al and Bonnie Robertson
and my children
Valerie, Alan, and Mary
two distinct generations
with immeasurable influence
on the preparation of this book

1981
CONGRESSIONAL
EDITION

A
special edition
dedicated
to the
97th Congress of the United States
as it
seeks to resolve
the
tangle of problems
confronting
Social Security

Contents

List of Charts   xiii

List of Tables   xv

Preface   xix

PART ONE
INTRODUCTION

1. The Slumbering Giant Awakens   3

PART TWO
BASIC BACKGROUND INFORMATION

2. Social Security — An Overview   13

3. Social Security Benefits   25

4. How Much Do Social Security Benefits Cost?   41

5. How Is the Money Obtained to Pay for Social
   Security Benefits?   57

6. When Do We Pay for Social Security Benefits?   69

7. Trillion Dollar "Actuarial Deficits" and
   "Accrued Liabilities"   81

CONTENTS

PART THREE
COMMENTARY ON SELECTED TOPICS

8. *Public Understanding of Social Security*   **107**

9. *The Need for a Periodic Benefit Statement*   **111**

10. *A Program of Future Promises — Fulfilled or Broken?*   **121**

11. *Do We Get Our Money's Worth from Social Security?*   **127**

12. *The Earnings Test*   **139**

13. *Sex and Social Security*   **145**

14. *Integration of Private Benefit Plans with Social Security*   **153**

15. *Inflation and Automatic Benefit Increases*   **161**

16. *Should Social Security Cover Everyone?*   **167**

17. *Should You Opt Out of Social Security If You Can?*   **175**

18. *Should You Opt Into Social Security If You Can?*   **191**

19. *The Fortunate Eight Percent*   **195**

20. *Is Social Security Enough?*   **227**

21. *How to Take Advantage of Social Security*   **247**

22. *Social Security as a Determinant of Behavior*   **269**

23. *The Great American Retirement Dream*   **283**

24. *What Is the Outlook for Social Security?*   **289**

25. *Can Social Security Be Abolished or Changed Drastically?*   **295**

CONTENTS

PART FOUR
THE FREEDOM PLAN

26. Social Insurance in Perspective   301

27. Provision for Old Age   309

28. Provision for Illness   323

29. Provision for Death and Disability   327

30. Cost and Financing of Proposed Social
    Insurance Program   331

31. Conclusion   343

Appendix — Summary of Principal Actuarial
            Assumptions Used in Cost
            Projections   347

Notes   353

Index   361

About the Author   375

List of Charts

		Page
2.A	Workers in Covered and Noncovered Employment, 1940 and 1978	15
2.B	Principal Groups Not Covered by Social Security as of March 1978	16
2.C	OASDI Beneficiaries as of June 30, 1979 and Amount of Benefits in Fiscal Year 1979, by Type of Beneficiary	22
4.A	Projected Expenditures for Benefits and Administration of the Social Security Program under Alternative Demographic and Economic Assumptions	52
4.B	Past, Present, and Projected Retired Workers and Other Social Security Beneficiaries, and Covered Workers	54
5.A	Federal Government Income by Source, Fiscal Year 1979	58
7.A	Projected Expenditures and Legislated Tax Income for Old-Age, Survivors, and Disability Insurance Program	83
7.B	Projected Expenditures and Legislated Tax Income for Hospital Insurance Program	87
7.C	Projected Expenditures for Old-Age, Survivors, Disability, and Hospital Insurance Programs Combined under Alternative Demographic and Economic Assumptions, and Legislated Tax Income	90

xiii

LIST OF CHARTS

7.D Projected Expenditures and Premium Income for Supplementary Medical Insurance Program 94

7.E Projected Expenditures for Supplementary Medical Insurance Program under Alternative Demographic and Economic Assumptions 96

22.A The Effect of One Beneficiary's Marriage to Another Beneficiary 274

30.A Projected Expenditures for Benefits and Administration of Existing Social Security Program and Proposed Social Insurance Program 333

30.B Projected Expenditures for Benefits and Administration of Proposed Social Insurance Program— Proportion Financed by Payroll Taxes and by General Revenue 336

30.C Comparison of Projected Expenditures for Benefits and Administration of Proposed Social Insurance Program Based upon Alternative Assumptions 338

List of Tables

		Page
4.1	Social Security Beneficiaries at End of Selected Calendar Years	42
4.2	Amount of Benefits and Administrative Expenses Paid during Calendar Year	43
4.3	Amount of Benefits and Administrative Expenses as a Percentage of Effective Taxable Payroll during Past Calendar Years	44
4.4	Percentage of Total Earnings in Covered Employment That Is Subjected to Social Security Payroll Tax	45
4.5	Projected Expenditures for Benefits and Administration as a Percentage of Effective Taxable Payroll during Future Calendar Years	47
4.6	Projected Expenditures for Benefits and Administration of the Social Security Program under Alternative Demographic and Economic Assumptions	51
5.1	Social Security Taxes Payable in 1980 with Respect to Selected Individuals	60
5.2	Projected Tax Rates Necessary to Finance Present Social Security Program	63
5.3	Projected Supplementary Medical Insurance Expenditures and Proportion Financed by General Revenue	65

LIST OF TABLES

6.1 Expenditures for Benefits and Administration under the Old-Age, Survivors, Disability, and Hospital Insurance Program for Selected Years 70

6.2 History of Increases in the Maximum Taxable Earnings Base 72

6.3 Comparison of Current Costs and Tax Rates, and Trust Fund Levels, under the Old-Age, Survivors, Disability, and Hospital Insurance Program for Selected Years 73

7.1 Projected Expenditures and Legislated Tax Income for Old-Age, Survivors, and Disability Insurance Program 84

7.2 Projected Expenditures and Legislated Tax Income for Hospital Insurance Program 88

7.3 Projected Expenditures, Tax Income, and Deficits for Old-Age, Survivors, Disability, and Hospital Insurance Programs Combined, under Alternative Demographic and Economic Assumptions 92

7.4 Projected Expenditures, Premium Income, and General Revenue Requirements for Supplementary Medical Insurance Program 95

11.1 Summary of Cumulative Income and Outgo under the Old-Age, Survivors, Disability, and Hospital Insurance Programs, 1937–1979 128

11.2 Summary of Cumulative Income and Outgo under the Supplementary Medical Insurance Program, 1966–1979 129

11.3 Theoretical Tax Rate Payable by Workers and Employers, Each, If Taxes Are to Be Equivalent to Benefits for Selected Workers Entering the Work Force in 1978 132

15.1 Automatic Increases in Social Security Benefits 162

15.2 Comparison of Yearly Increase in Consumer Price Index and Average Earnings of Social Security Taxpayers 164

17.1 State and Local Government Groups and Employees—Comparison of Number Newly Covered and Terminated during the Period 1973–1979 177

xvi

LIST OF TABLES

19.1 Contribution and Benefit Base, Tax Rate, and Maximum Tax for Selected Years   196

19.2 Maximum Cumulative Taxes Paid during Selected Periods by Employees and Self-Employed Persons   199

19.3 Estimated Social Security Retirement Benefits for Workers Retiring at Age 65 in January 1980, Having Had Maximum Career Earnings   205

19.4 Estimated Social Security Disability Benefits for Workers Becoming Eligible for Disability Benefits in January 1980 at Various Ages, Having Had Maximum Career Earnings   211

19.5 Estimated Amount and Value of Social Security Survivors Benefits for Survivors of Workers Dying in January 1980 at Various Ages, Having Had Maximum Career Earnings   215

20.1 Ratio of Initial Social Security Disability Benefits to Average Earnings Prior to Disability for Illustrative Workers   234

20.2 Ratio of Initial Social Security Survivors Benefits to Deceased Worker's Average Earnings Prior to Death for Illustrative Surviving Families   238

20.3 Ratio of Initial Social Security Retirement Benefits to Average Earnings Prior to Retirement for Illustrative Workers   242

A.1 Selected Economic Assumptions under Optimistic, Intermediate, and Pessimistic Alternatives, Calendar Years 1979–2055   349

A.2 Selected Demographic Assumptions under Optimistic, Intermediate, and Pessimistic Alternatives, Calendar Years 1979–2055   351

Preface

In 1975, only six months after becoming Chief Actuary of the United States Social Security Administration, I concluded that the most important problem confronting Social Security in the immediate future was the widespread lack of understanding of the program—its basic rationale, the type and level of benefits it provides, the method of financing, the significance of its high future cost, and the tenuous relationship between taxes paid and benefits received by an individual. For the most part, people's ideas about Social Security were wrong. It was natural, therefore, that the program could not satisfy their expectations. Furthermore, it was evident that as taxes continued their inexorable rise this frustration and disenchantment would get worse and not better.

Immediately I began trying to clarify these issues by talking with anyone who would listen to me—inside or outside the government. People were thirsting for knowledge about Social Security, yet there was no single source of written information concerning the many questions being asked. As time went by and I developed simplified answers to these never-ending questions, I decided the most effective way to communicate with a broad audience would be to write a book on the subject—a book that could be read and understood by nontechnicians.

At first I thought a mere explanation of what Social Security really is would suffice. In fact, that is all I could do while working as an actuary responsible for estimating the future costs of Social Security. It was not appropriate for me to criticize Social Security or propose major changes. One night in

Atlanta, however, after I had addressed a group of actuaries and other businesspeople, the audience was almost frantic in asking, "What do we do to resolve these problems?" They virtually demanded a solution. This experience, repeated over and over, demonstrated that any book on Social Security should also include suggestions for change—and a new dimension was added to my mission. I soon developed a personal sense of urgency about my "outreach project," as the Commissioner of Social Security used to call it, and in 1978 left the Social Security Administration to have the time and freedom to prepare this book.

Some of the material in the book is an elaboration of ideas advanced orally while serving as the William Elliott Lecturer, College of Business Administration, The Pennsylvania State University, in April 1978, and presented in writing in a commentary entitled *Social Security—Prospect for Change,* prepared for the National Chamber Foundation and presented at the Sixty-sixth Annual Meeting of the Chamber of Commerce of the United States on May 1, 1978.

Many people encouraged and assisted me. I am grateful to the consulting firm with which I am associated, William M. Mercer, Incorporated, for the many accommodations necessary to develop and write the book. Chapter 3, in particular, draws heavily upon a summary of the Social Security Act published semi-annually by Mercer. I wish to acknowledge the cooperation of the actuarial staff of the Social Security Administration, headed by Chief Actuary Dwight K. Bartlett and Deputy Chief Actuaries Harry C. Ballantyne and Francisco R. Bayo, and the actuarial staff of the Health Care Financing Administration, headed by Roland E. King, Acting Director, Office of Financial and Actuarial Analysis. The actuarial work performed by these staffs is crucial to ensure that we are able to honor our commitments to future generations.

Although it is not practical to acknowledge everyone who helped me with this particular work as well as with prior endeavors that made this book possible, I would mention a few individuals who were of particular assistance: Richard S. Foster, Actuary, Social Security Administration; Maynard I. Kagen, Director of Research, Railroad Retirement Board; and Robert W. Kalman, Consultant/Public Employee Benefits,

William M. Mercer, Incorporated. Valerie L. Robertson, my daughter, provided the invaluable talent needed to prepare an accurate and consistent manuscript. The views expressed herein are strictly mine, of course, and not necessarily those of my employer or anyone else who helped me.

It is unfortunate that the public perception of Social Security has been allowed to grow so far apart from the reality. This has created a serious dilemma for Social Security. If public misunderstanding is allowed to persist, confusion and disappointment will worsen because Social Security will continue its failure to match most of the public's expectations; and this will result in a frenzied cry for change. On the other hand, if the misunderstanding is eliminated it is probable that the public will not like what it sees and thus will demand significant revision. In either event, therefore, a big change is on the horizon. *There is a coming revolution in Social Security.*

This book is dedicated to the premise that any new Social Security system should arise from a clearheaded appraisal of our existing system and not from our present state of bewilderment. This should permit a more reasoned transition, even if it is no less traumatic.

Washington, D.C.   A. Haeworth Robertson
January 20, 1981

THE
COMING
REVOLUTION
IN
SOCIAL SECURITY

Part One
Introduction

"What you don't know won't hurt you" may be an appropriate maxim in many situations, but Social Security is not one of them. There is widespread misunderstanding about Social Security, an institution having a pervasive effect on our lives and the lives of our children. Part One raises questions to heighten the awareness of the need to learn more about Social Security—before it is too late.

1
The Slumbering Giant Awakens

Social Security, a slumbering giant for the last forty years, is finally awakening—rapidly and noisily. Is it friend or foe? Without a closer examination we cannot be sure.

Most of us don't understand what Social Security is all about. The general purposes of Social Security, the types and levels of benefits it provides, how it is financed, the relation between an individual's taxes and benefits—all of these areas are sources of confusion or uncertainty to many people.

Most of us don't realize how large Social Security has become or how rapidly it will grow in the future. In 1940 the Social Security program paid out less than $1 billion in benefits and administrative expenses; in 1979 it paid out $138 billion; in 1990 it will pay out an estimated $387 billion. During the next ten years, 1981 through 1990, it is estimated that about $2,734 billion will be paid out in benefits and administrative expenses.[1] In December 1979 Social Security monthly cash benefits were paid to 35 million persons, one out of every seven Americans.

But what Social Security pays out in benefits it must first collect in taxes.

In 1979, 114 million workers paid about $65 billion in Social Security taxes, an average of roughly $570 per person. For approximately 50 percent of all American workers, their Social Security tax is greater than their federal income tax. Ten years ago (1970) the average Social Security tax paid by each taxpayer was about $220; ten years from now (1990) it is estimated that it will be $1,450.

In addition to these taxes paid directly by individuals, an approximately equal amount was paid by their employers.[2] Total income to the Social Security program in 1979, most of it from taxes of one kind or another, was some $138 billion ($138,455,480,515.72 to be precise).

Some Questions

What do we get for our money? What do you know about your own Social Security benefits? How much, if anything will you receive if today you become disabled and are unable to work any longer? Can you work part time and still collect disability benefits? Are your benefits higher if you are married? And have children? If Social Security benefits are not adequate to support you and your family, and if your spouse goes to work to supplement your income, will any of these benefits be forfeited?

If you die tomorrow will any benefits be paid to your spouse, children, parents? If so, how much? How long will the benefits be paid? Will this be enough to support your family? Will your spouse be able to work without forfeiting these benefits? Should you buy life insurance to supplement your Social Security benefits? If so, how much should you buy?

If you stay in good health and work until age 65, will you be eligible for a retirement benefit from Social Security? If so, how much will it be? Are there any strings attached to its payment? Can you continue working after age 65 and still receive your Social Security benefits? Can you collect the benefits if you move to another country when you retire? Will these benefits be enough to support you and your family? Should you have your own private savings program in order to supplement your Social Security benefits?

How much will you personally pay in Social Security taxes this year? Did you know that your employer will also pay this same amount? To get an idea of how much you and your employer pay in Social Security taxes, examine the following figures which show the amount of such taxes paid in 1980 for three employees with different levels of pay.

| | Social Security Taxes | | |
Earnings in 1980	Paid by Employee	Paid by Employer	Total
$ 6,000	$ 367.80	$ 367.80	$ 735.60
$12,000	$ 735.60	$ 735.60	$1,471.20
$25,900 or more	$1,587.67	$1,587.67	$3,175.34

The maximum tax paid by the employee and employer combined is estimated by the Social Security Administration to rise from $3,175.34 in 1980 to $8,078 by 1990, just ten years from now. This increase is due in part to a scheduled increase in the tax rate and in part to a projected increase in the maximum amount of earnings subject to tax (an estimated $52,800 in 1990).[3]

A person who is self-employed and thus doesn't have an employer to share the cost pays somewhat higher taxes than those paid by an employee (but lower than the total taxes paid by employees and employers combined). The following figures show the Social Security taxes paid in 1980 by three self-employed persons with different levels of earnings.

Self-Employment Earnings in 1980	Social Security Taxes
$ 6,000	$ 486.00
$12,000	$ 972.00
$25,900 or more	$2,097.90

The maximum tax paid by self-employed persons is estimated by the Social Security Administration to rise from $2,097.90 in 1980 to $5,676 by 1990.

Do you spend this much money for anything else and know so little about what you get for your money? Whose fault is it that you do not know more about your Social Security benefits? Did you know that there are millions of people in the United States who do not participate in Social Security and thus do not pay its taxes and receive its benefits?

Is Social Security going bankrupt? Will there be enough money to pay your benefits when you retire? In 1950 the Social Security Trust Funds had enough money to pay benefits for twelve years (at the rate benefits were being paid in 1950); in 1960 there was enough money to pay benefits for about two years; at the beginning of 1980 there was enough money left to pay benefits for only about three months. What happened to all the money you and your employers paid into the Social Security Trust Funds?

If you don't know the answers to any or all of these questions, don't feel left out. Not many people know the answers. Social Security is one of the least understood, perhaps I should say most misunderstood, programs around. This misunderstanding of Social Security is not unique to us in America. In my travels and work with social insurance programs around the world, I have found this confusion everywhere—in sophisticated industrial economies as well as in emerging agricultural economies.

The Problem

Social Security has been roundly criticized in recent months. Complaints are heard about its financial condition, the inadequacy of its benefits, the overadequacy of its benefits, the fact that some persons receive more in benefits than they pay in taxes, the fact that some people receive less in benefits than they pay in taxes, and so on. Although some of these criticisms are valid, many are not. And none of them poses a real threat to Social Security at this time.

The most serious threat to Social Security in the immediate future is the widespread misunderstanding of the program. Why is this misunderstanding a threat? Because the very survival of Social Security depends upon our continued ability and willingness to pay the taxes necessary to support the benefit payments. It is not reasonable to expect this support to continue if we do not understand and approve of the Social Security program.

The Social Security program is not what most people think it is. It is not what many critics think it is. Because of this, it does not always behave the way we think it should. Therefore, it is natural for us to resent the program, the Congressmen who adopted it, the Social Security Administration and the Health Care Financing Administration which administer it, and most of all the tax collectors who take our hard-earned money and use it in ways that are different from the ways we thought it would be used.

The Social Security program does not have a chance of being successful until we understand it. Once we know what the program is and we decide what we believe our income security needs are, we can compare what we have with what we want. If they are the same, then we can congratulate ourselves and our leaders who designed Social Security over the years and be content. If they are different, we can set about to change the program to better suit our needs. Until then—until we really understand what the present Social Security program is—all discussions of the program will be chaotic and most of the proposed changes will be nonsensical.

The Solution—The First Step

Part Two of this book presents basic background information on Social Security and has one purpose: to help you understand the Social Security program in its present form. This is the first step toward accepting the program as it is or revising the program to make it what you want it to be.

This book is intended to be constructive. It is intended to be based on facts and objective analysis, not on fantasies and uninformed opinions. It is intended to explain the Social Security program as it is, not as others would like us to believe it is.

Many of you will not like what you read. Some people have been shocked at the explanations in this book. Some will consider the book an exposé of Social Security. The book will probably be looked upon with disfavor by certain special interest groups and by some planners and administrators of social insurance. Some will view the book's publication as heresy and not in the best interest of the public.

Why would anyone object to this book? In some cases, because "they" know what is best for you; because you (the public) do not know enough to decide what is best for you; and because, in order to enact and perpetuate a social insurance program which "they" believe is best for you, it is acceptable to do whatever is necessary to sell the program to you—the consumer—and to the Congress which must enact it. If half-truths, omissions, or misleading statements are necessary, some will use them on the theory that the end justifies the means.

Does the End Justify the Means?

In our complicated and technical society, there are undoubtedly issues that can be fully understood and evaluated only by a small group of informed experts. In these cases, the public must place substantial trust in its leaders.

For example, how is an average person to know for certain how much money should be spent for defense in order for America to remain a free and independent nation? What is the real threat to our freedom from other countries with different ideologies, food shortages, land shortages, or demagogic leaders?

How is an average person to know what our national energy policy should be if we are to avoid crippling shortages in the future? Should we have gasoline rationing, higher gasoline taxes, restrictions on oil imports, improved public transportation facilities, smaller cars, increased nuclear and solar energy capabilities, or should we take some other action?

What about the current debate over environmentalism? How do we balance the trade-off between continued industrial growth and a less healthful environment? How much is our increasingly crowded and polluted environment threatening our physical, emotional, and spiritual health?

In all these and many other areas we must rely heavily upon experts, people who study these matters full time. But we ourselves should also be as fully informed as possible. We must not leave important decisions exclusively to the experts or to the politicians who act, sometimes solely, on their advice. This would seem obvious from recent revelations concerning activities by the government and its various agencies where decisions were made by individuals and select groups of experts who did not think they were accountable to the public and who did not think the public knew what was best for it.

But what about the Social Security program? Is it so difficult a subject that only the experts can understand it? Is it so complex that we have no choice but to leave it to the experts and politicians to decide what is best for us without our being told the facts? I don't think so.

Certainly, Social Security is complicated. Many aspects of Social Security are neither fully understood nor agreed upon by experts who have spent years studying it. Despite its complexity, there is no excuse for the failure to explain in plain words as much as possible about the program. It is time for us all to stop hiding behind the mystique created by the double-talk explanations that make it so difficult to understand Social Security. Let's tell it like it is. Let's make as many people as fully informed as possible about the Social Security program. Then if we do not like what we see, let's change it. The sooner the better.

Not a Textbook

This is not intended primarily to be a textbook on Social Security or a treatise on the mathematics of pensions and insurance. I hope it doesn't sound like one. Accordingly, it does not have many footnotes and citations and it skips over some details that are not essential for a general understanding of Social Security.

This book is written for people who pay for and benefit from the Social Security program—people who want to understand how their Social Security program works. My sincere hope is that this book will help you gain the understanding of our Social Security program that will be necessary if you and the Congress and the Administration are to get together and cause the program to be changed so that it will meet our needs in a logical way and in accordance with our ability to pay for it.

If we do not gain a better understanding of our Social Security program and then either accept it or change it to satisfy our desires, the consequences are frightening.

Part Two
Basic Background
Information

For most of us, our knowledge of Social Security is based upon a hodgepodge of information we have gathered from radio, television, newspapers, magazines, employers, and friends. This is a difficult way to learn, especially when many of the fragments of information are misleading or even incorrect. It is no wonder that myths and misinformation abound.

Part Two is designed for the reader willing to discard all past information and misinformation received about Social Security and start with a clean slate. Chapters 2 through 7 present systematically the basic background information necessary to understand what Social Security is, how it works, and what it costs.

2
Social Security—
An Overview

Congress passed the Social Security Act in 1935 and it became effective on January 1, 1937. The original legislation has been amended many times since then and has become a complex maze of laws, rules, and regulations governing and influencing the lives of all Americans in one way or another. Some of these influences are obvious; others are not. Some of these influences are favorable; others may or may not be depending upon your viewpoint. This chapter gives a brief overview of some but not all of the many aspects of Social Security.

What Is Social Security?

Mention Social Security to a dozen people and they will conjure up a dozen different ideas—and for good reason. The *Social Security Handbook*[1] published by the government contains 530 pages of explanation of the Social Security Act and then refers the reader to thousands of additional pages of explanation contained in other volumes. In describing Social Security, this handbook makes a general statement,[2] which may be paraphrased fairly as follows:

The Social Security Act and related laws establish a number of programs that have the basic objectives of

13

providing for the material needs of individuals and families, protecting aged and disabled persons against the expenses of illnesses that could otherwise exhaust their savings, keeping families together, and giving children the opportunity to grow up in health and security. These programs include:

Retirement Insurance (frequently referred to as Old-Age Insurance)

Survivors Insurance

Disability Insurance

Medicare for the aged and the disabled:
Hospital Insurance
Supplementary Medical Insurance

Black Lung Benefits

Supplemental Security Income

Unemployment Insurance

Public Assistance and Welfare Services:
Aid to needy families with children
Medical assistance
Maternal and child-health services
Services for crippled children
Child welfare services

The federal government operates the first six programs listed above. The remaining programs are operated by the states with the federal government cooperating and contributing funds.

This book limits itself to a discussion of the first four programs listed above and refers to them collectively as Social Security. This is partly for simplicity but largely because these four programs are financed primarily by the Social Security payroll taxes paid by employees, employers, and self-employed persons, and thus are usually thought of by the public as Social Security. (The Supplementary Medical Insurance program, "Part B" of Medicare, is not financed by payroll taxes but rather by premiums paid by those electing to be covered and by general revenue.)

Who Participates in Social Security?

Who is covered by Social Security and is therefore eligible for Old-Age, Survivors, Disability, and Medicare benefits?

When Social Security took effect in 1937 it applied only to workers in industry and commerce and covered only about 60 percent of all working persons. Since then there has been a steady movement toward covering as many workers as possible under Social Security, and universal coverage has clearly been the ultimate goal. In the 1950s, coverage was extended to include most self-employed persons, most state and local government employees, household and farm employees, members of the armed forces, and members of the clergy. Approximately 90 percent of all jobs in the United States are now covered by Social Security. Chart 2.A illustrates the growth in coverage over the years.

The principal groups that are not now covered automatically by Social Security are as follows:

> Civilian employees of the federal government (military employees are covered by Social Security)
> Employees of state and local governments
> Employees of religious, charitable, and other nonprofit organizations
> Farm and domestic workers with irregular employment
> Low-income, self-employed persons

Chart 2.A

Workers in Covered and Noncovered Employment, 1940 and 1978

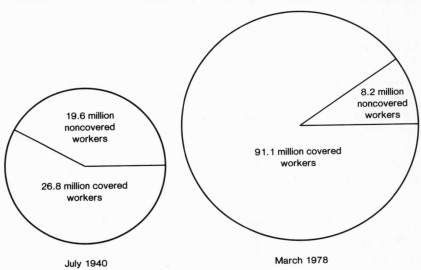

19.6 million noncovered workers

26.8 million covered workers

July 1940

8.2 million noncovered workers

91.1 million covered workers

March 1978

Chart 2.B illustrates the number of persons in these categories whose jobs are not covered by Social Security.[3] Considerable publicity has been given to the fact that most employees of the federal government are not covered by Social Security as a part of their government employment. Participation is optional for employees of state and local governments and for employees of nonprofit organizations. The fact that some employees of state and local governments have recently "opted out" of Social Security has given rise to considerable controversy. A typical reaction is, "If they can opt out, why can't I?" A few words of background on some of these employee groups may help explain the situation.

Federal Government Employees

In 1920 the civil service retirement system was established to provide retirement and other benefits to civilian employees of the federal government. It was not particularly unusual, therefore, when Social Security began operation on January 1, 1937,

Chart 2.B
**Principal Groups Not Covered by Social Security
as of March 1978 (in thousands)**

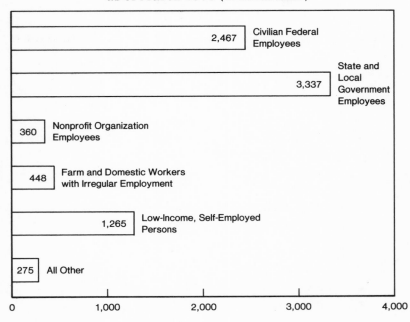

that federal government employees were excluded from it. On the other hand, it would have been logical to include federal government employees in Social Security and to adjust the benefits under the civil service retirement system accordingly. This is what most private employers did and still do; that is, they coordinate, or integrate, their private benefit systems with Social Security so that the two systems taken together provide the desired benefits.

Federal government employees have long been opposed to entering Social Security. One reason for this opposition is that the process of coordinating the two systems has not been explained adequately. Many federal employees believe, without justification, that if they entered Social Security their civil service retirement system would be abolished completely. Other employees believe, without justification, that they would receive full benefits—and pay the full employee costs—of both Social Security and the civil service retirement system. Still other employees believe that if they entered Social Security the assets of their civil service retirement system would be used to rescue an ailing Social Security. No one is considering such a consolidation of assets, however; and even if they were, it would be fruitless since the total assets of the civil service retirement system would be enough to provide only about 2 percent of the total Social Security benefits that will be paid in the next ten years.

There are other reasons that federal government employees have opposed entry into Social Security. The long-service career employees who qualify for benefits under both systems enjoy a distinct advantage that would be lost if they participated fully in Social Security, and paid taxes, throughout their career. Also, government-employee unions have vigorously opposed participation in Social Security—in part, probably, because they would then have influence over a smaller segment of the employee benefit area (if the civil service retirement system were reduced in order to coordinate with Social Security).

State and Local Government Employees

When Social Security was enacted in 1935 it was considered unconstitutional for the federal government to tax state governments. And since Social Security is financed from taxes paid by employees and employers, state and local government employees were not included.

In keeping with the steady movement to make Social Security coverage as universal as possible, legislation was enacted in 1950 and later to provide that employees of state and local governments could be covered under Social Security on a voluntary basis under certain conditions. For example, Social Security coverage was made available on a group voluntary basis through agreements between the Secretary of Health, Education, and Welfare and the individual states. After coverage of the employees of a state, or of a political subdivision of the state, has been in effect for at least five years, the state may give notice of its intention to terminate the coverage of such employees. The termination of coverage becomes effective on December 31 of the second full calendar year after such notice is given, unless the state withdraws the notice of termination within such period. Once the termination becomes effective, however, it is irrevocable and the same group cannot be covered again under Social Security. So, state and local employees can opt in; they can then opt out; but they cannot reenter Social Security after having gone through such a procedure.

Approximately 10 million state and local employees, about 75 percent of the total, are covered by Social Security under voluntary participation arrangements. Compared with these 10 million participants, the number of employees who have voluntarily terminated is very small. A total of about 130,000 employees have terminated during the program's entire history through June 1980. Most of these terminations have occurred within the last five years. There is still a relatively large number of pending terminations, hence this trend may continue for awhile longer. More detailed information on voluntary terminations is contained in Chapter 17.

In mid-1980 several states had never elected to enter Social Security: Colorado, Louisiana, Maine, Massachusetts, Nevada, and Ohio. Three of these states—Colorado, Maine, and Nevada—include teachers in their general state retirement systems; hence their teachers are not covered by Social Security. In ten states or jurisdictions with statewide teachers' systems, teachers are not covered by Social Security: Alaska,

California, Connecticut, Illinois, Kentucky, Louisiana, Massachusetts, Missouri, Ohio, and Puerto Rico.

The states that have not elected to enter Social Security maintain programs of retirement and other benefits for their employees that are more liberal than Social Security in some respects and less liberal in others. A strict comparison of benefits is difficult because of the basic differences between Social Security and most public employee systems. For various reasons, some states prefer to continue their own employee benefit programs and to remain outside of Social Security.

Alaska is the only state that has elected to cover its employees under Social Security and then terminated such coverage. The Alaska termination became effective December 31, 1979, and affected approximately 14,500 employees.

Employees of Nonprofit Organizations

Nonprofit organizations were not required to participate in Social Security when it was enacted, because of their tax-exempt status. Imposition of the employer Social Security tax on the organization would have violated this tax-exempt status.

Legislation has been enacted over the years to permit nonprofit organizations to be covered by Social Security on a voluntary basis. Today approximately 90 percent of the 4 million employees of nonprofit organizations have elected to be covered by Social Security.

Increased Possibility of Universal Coverage

As already indicated, during the entire history of the Social Security program the trend has been toward broader coverage. The increasing attention given in recent years to the question of Social Security coverage, how widespread it is and how widespread it "should be," was reflected in the Social Security Amendments of 1977. In these amendments, Congress directed the Secretary of Health, Education, and Welfare to undertake a study of the "feasibility and desirability" of covering federal employees, state and local government employees, and employees of nonprofit organizations under the Old-Age and Survivors Insurance, Disability Insurance, and Hospital Insurance programs on a mandatory basis. This study,[4] completed in March 1980, presented and discussed several options for achieving universal coverage but stopped short of recommending any specific option. Several other advisory groups and commissions are studying this question, and it is possible that their findings will result eventually in virtually universal coverage of the nation's work force by the Social Security program.

What Benefits Are Provided?

Because of the complexity of Social Security this chapter will give only an overview of the benefits provided. More detail is included in Chapter 3. The idea at this point is to explain how Social Security works in general, not to enable you to determine the benefits you would receive in a particular case. If you need specific information concerning your own situation, it is normally best to contact your local Social Security Administration office.

In a nutshell: *Social Security replaces a portion of the earnings that are lost as a result of a person's old age, disability, or death, and pays a portion of the expenses of illness of aged and disabled persons.*

The benefits that are provided under the Old-Age, Survivors, and Disability Insurance programs (usually referred to as OASDI) are as follows:

> Monthly benefits for workers who are retired or partially retired and are at least 62 years old, and monthly benefits for their eligible spouses and dependents
>
> Monthly benefits for disabled workers and their eligible spouses and dependents
>
> Monthly benefits for the eligible survivors of deceased workers
>
> A lump-sum death benefit payment for each worker

To be eligible to receive these benefits at the time of retirement, disability, or death, a person must satisfy several conditions that are different for each type of benefit. In addition, a person's spouse and dependents or survivors must satisfy a variety of requirements to be eligible for benefits. These requirements, which are somewhat complex, are described in more detail in Chapter 3.

As of June 30, 1979, approximately 35 million persons were receiving monthly Social Security benefit payments. That was more than one out of every seven persons since in mid-1979 there were approximately 231 million persons in the United States.[5] Total cash benefit payments in fiscal year 1979 amounted to $101 billion. Chart 2.C illustrates for fiscal year 1979 the numbers of OASDI beneficiaries and the amount of their benefits in each of the various categories.

The Medicare program has two parts, Hospital Insurance (HI) and Supplementary Medical Insurance (SMI). The Hospital Insurance program, which is compulsory for those covered by Social Security, provides benefits for persons aged 65 or older and persons receiving Social Security disability benefits for more than twenty-four months. The program helps pay for inpatient hospital care and for certain follow-up care after leaving the hospital.

The Supplementary Medical Insurance program, which is voluntary, is offered to almost all persons aged 65 and over. In addition, the program is offered to all disabled Social Security beneficiaries who have received disability benefits for more than twenty-four months (twenty-nine months for Railroad Retirement beneficiaries). The program helps pay for doctors' services, outpatient hospital services, and many other medical items and services not covered by the Hospital Insurance program.

During 1979, an average of 24.1 million persons aged 65 and over were covered under the Hospital Insurance program (that is, were eligible for hospital benefits in the event of illness). This represented 95 percent of all persons aged 65 and over in the United States and its territories. Another 2.9 million disabled persons under age 65 were covered by Hospital Insurance.

Approximately 23.8 million persons aged 65 and over were covered under the Supplementary Medical Insurance program in 1979. Again, this represented about 95 percent of all persons aged 65 and over in the United States and its territories. Another 2.7 million disabled persons under age 65 were covered by Supplementary Medical Insurance.

It is estimated that the total benefit payments in 1978 of $24.9 billion under the Hospital Insurance and Supplementary

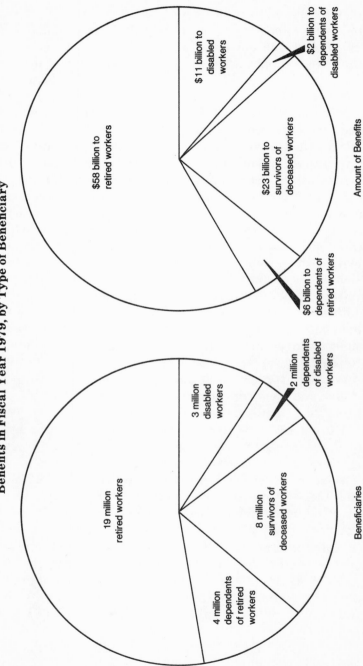

Chart 2.C

OASDI Beneficiaries as of June 30, 1979 and Amount of
Benefits in Fiscal Year 1979, by Type of Beneficiary

Medical Insurance programs represented approximately 45 percent of the total medical expenses of the persons participating in the two programs.[6]

Who Administers Social Security?

Social Security is administered by the Social Security Administration and the Health Care Financing Administration. For fiscal year 1979, these agencies of the Department of Health, Education, and Welfare accounted for roughly 60 percent of the total employees and 75 percent of the total expenditures of the Department.[7] Even more important, they accounted for approximately 27 percent of total government expenditures.[8]

The Social Security Administration (SSA) administers the Old-Age, Survivors, and Disability Insurance program, along with several other programs not included in our present discussion of Social Security; for example, the Supplemental Security Income program and Aid to Families with Dependent Children. The determination of eligibility for disability benefits is handled by state agencies under contract to the Social Security Administration.

The Health Care Financing Administration (HCFA) administers the Medicare program, both Hospital Insurance and Supplementary Medical Insurance. It also oversees Medicaid, a program providing hospital and medical expense benefits for the needy—not considered part of Social Security in our present discussion. Prior to the formation of HCFA in March 1977, Medicare was administered by the Social Security Administration and Medicaid was administered by the Social and Rehabilitation Service.

Social Security taxes are collected for the Social Security Administration and the Health Care Financing Administration by the Internal Revenue Service. The Department of the Treasury issues the benefit checks, at the direction of the Managing Trustee of the Social Security Trust Funds, on the basis of benefit certifications by the Social Security Administration and the Health Care Financing Administration.

The Social Security Administration had 1,325 district and branch offices in operation around the country in 1978, facilities normally shared with the Health Care Financing Administration. Most administrative contact with the public is handled by these district and branch offices which issue Social Security cards, process benefit claims, provide information about the program, and help resolve participants' problems. The local offices are supervised and assisted by ten regional offices. In addition, about thirty "teleservice centers" around the country provide assistance to participants by telephone, in order to give more prompt service and reduce the need for visits by the public to local offices.

The Social Security Administration's national headquarters, or central office as it is called, is located primarily in Baltimore, Maryland (with some offices in Washington, D.C.). The central office maintains the records of the millions of participants and oversees and directs the operation of the OASDI program and all its regional and local offices. The Health Care Financing Administration is also headquartered in Baltimore and Washington. To operate these offices and administer the Social Security program, there is a staff of some 80,000 people including about 20,000 in the central offices. This is not an unduly large administrative staff relative to the size and complexity of the program involved. Administrative expenses for the OASDI and Medicare programs combined were $2.5 billion in 1979, only 1.9 percent of total benefits paid during the year. With an appropriately increased budget, the Social Security Administration could provide better administrative service and do a more thorough job of explaining Social Security to the public, something that is certainly important at this critical time in the history of Social Security.

Conclusion

Any overview of Social Security reveals it to be almost overwhelming in size and complexity. Directly or indirectly, Social Security touches the lives of virtually every resident of the U.S., and it is startling to become more aware of its growing influence on our lives, individually and collectively as a nation. Social Security's significance to us and our children must not be underestimated if we are to retain any control over our lives.

3
Social Security Benefits

Social Security is simple in concept but complicated in actual operation. Essentially, Social Security replaces a portion of earned income that is lost as a result of a person's retirement, disability, or death; and it pays a portion of the hospital and medical expenses of aged and disabled persons. The complications arise in determining:

> when a person is eligible to *begin* receiving benefits;
>
> the amount of the benefits; and
>
> when a person is no longer eligible to *continue* receiving benefits.

To explain all this in an efficient way requires that a few definitions and explanations be given at the start. This will also make the subsequent commentary on benefits easier to follow. You should probably not expect to learn how to calculate your exact benefits and the precise conditions under which they will be payable. On the other hand, you should understand Social Security well enough to know when you and your family members may be eligible for benefits and the approximate amounts of such benefits. This will enable you to obtain maximum advantage from Social Security and your tax dollar.

Eligibility for Benefits to Begin

Monthly benefits can be payable to a wide variety of persons, or beneficiaries as they are sometimes called. Benefits can be paid to you as a worker, as well as to your spouse, children, grandchildren, and parents. They can even be payable to a divorced wife, a stepparent, a foster parent who adopted you before age 16, a stepchild, a legally adopted child, and an illegitimate child.

Various requirements must be met before benefits are payable to you or members of your family. An important underlying requirement for the payment of most benefits is that you have paid Social Security taxes for certain minimum periods called "quarters of coverage." During each year before 1978 a quarter of coverage was given for each calendar quarter in which you paid Social Security taxes on at least $50 of wages for employment covered under the law. In 1978 one quarter of coverage was credited (up to a total of four) for each $250 of wages on which you paid Social Security taxes. After 1978 this $250 amount is subject to an automatic increase each year to reflect increases in average wages of the nation's workers. For 1979 the amount was $260, for 1980 it was $290, and for 1981 it is $310. It will continue to rise in future years as average wages increase. For self-employed workers, quarters of coverage for 1978 and later are earned on the same basis as for employees. Prior to 1978, four quarters of coverage were earned for any year in which at least $400 of self-employment income was reported.

An individual has different levels of "insured status" depending upon the number of quarters of coverage that have been credited and the recency with which they have been earned. Different benefits require different levels of "insured status." There is a "currently insured" status, a "fully insured" status, and a "disability insured" status. All of this special terminology is the same as that used by the Social Security Administration.

Currently Insured Status

To be "currently insured" an individual must have at least six quarters of coverage in the thirteen-quarter period ending with the quarter in which death or entitlement to old-age or disability benefits occurs. This level of insured status is easily maintained by a steady worker in employment covered by Social Security.

Fully Insured Status

To be "fully insured" an individual usually must have at least one quarter of coverage for each year after 1950 (or, if later, the year of attainment of age 21) and before the year of death, disability, or attainment of age 62, whichever occurs first. A minimum of six and a maximum of forty quarters of coverage is required. Once fully insured status for retirement benefits is acquired, it continues throughout life and no further work in covered employment is needed. The attainment of this permanent fully insured status relates only to *eligibility* for benefits and not the *amount* of the benefits. The quarters of coverage do not have to be earned during the period used to define the required number of quarters. They can be earned also before or after that period.

Disability Insured Status

To be eligible for disability benefits, an individual must be both fully insured and:

> have earned at least twenty quarters of coverage during the forty-calendar-quarter period ending with the quarter in which disability begins; or

> if disability begins before age 31, have earned at least one half the quarters of coverage possible during the period after the attainment of age 21 and the quarter in which disability begins. (A minimum of six quarters of coverage earned during this period is also required.)

For an individual who meets the statutory definition of blindness, only the fully insured requirement need be met.

In addition to the insured status requirements, other conditions must be met before benefits will be payable to you or your dependents. These will be mentioned later when the various specific benefits are discussed.

Amount of Benefits

The amount of monthly cash benefits paid by Social Security is based principally upon the following factors:

> The average earnings upon which you have paid Social Security taxes, excluding earnings for certain years

and adjusted for changes over the years in the average
earnings of the nation's workers

The number and kind of your family members

Consumer Price Index changes that occur after you become
eligible for benefits

Furthermore, the amount of monthly cash benefits may be
reduced, or even terminated, as a result of earnings by you and
your family members after becoming eligible for benefits.

Medicare benefits, on the other hand, are the same for
everyone who is eligible for them and are not affected by
average earnings on which you have paid Social Security taxes,
or earnings after becoming eligible for benefits.

For the time being, let us concentrate on the amount of
monthly cash benefits initially payable to any given beneficiary,
ignoring subsequent upward adjustments because of changes in
the Consumer Price Index and downward adjustments because
of an individual's earned income.

The key factor in determining monthly cash benefits initially
payable is the Primary Insurance Amount. All monthly cash
benefits are based upon the Primary Insurance Amount. The
Primary Insurance Amount (PIA) is the monthly benefit
payable to a disabled worker or to a worker at the normal
retirement age of 65 before application of any delayed retirement credit. For those who attain age 62, become disabled, or
die in 1979 and later, the PIA is determined by a formula
applied to the individual's Average Indexed Monthly Earnings.
(Some individuals becoming eligible for benefits before 1984
may have their benefits calculated under an alternative procedure to permit a smoother transition to this new calculation
method.) Determination of the Average Indexed Monthly
Earnings is somewhat complicated; it is computed for retirement and disability benefits approximately as follows:

Only earnings on which Social Security taxes are paid are
used. Thus, earnings in excess of the maximum taxable
earnings in each year are not included. Table 6.2 in
Chapter 6 lists the maximum taxable earnings for each
year in the past. The amount has increased from
$3,000 prior to 1951 to $29,700 in 1981, and will
continue to increase in the future as average wages of
the nation's workers increase.

Only earnings after 1950 (or after the year a person reached age 21, if later), and up to and including the year before entitlement to old-age or disability benefits, are used (except as noted below).

Earnings in prior years are "indexed" by applying a ratio to the individual's earnings for each year. The ratio is the average earnings of all the nation's employees in the second year before the year of the individual's eligibility for benefits, divided by the average earnings of all the nation's employees in the year being indexed. For example, an individual with $3,600 of taxable earnings in 1951 who reached age 62 in 1979 would have these earnings indexed to become $12,577.34, thus adjusting the old earnings approximately to their equivalent value today.

The average of these indexed earnings is then computed, substituting years of actual earnings at age 61 and later if it increases the resulting average indexed earnings, and leaving out as many as five years of the lowest indexed earnings.

This is a rather complicated process intended to produce average earnings that are representative of the value of today's dollar and today's earnings. It is important to note that average earnings are based on virtually an entire working career; accordingly, years of no earnings or low earnings can result in reduced average earnings and thus in reduced benefits. People sometimes erroneously assume that if they are *fully insured* they are eligible for *maximum benefits*.

There is a limit on the total amount of benefits payable in any month to members of one family. This limit varies according to the level of the PIA; while difficult to calculate exactly, it is generally in the range of 150 to 188 percent of the PIA in retirement and survivor cases. In disability cases it can vary from 100 to 150 percent of the PIA. In January 1980, the family maximum benefit for an age 65 career maximum earner was $1,000.60. Benefits for family members other than the primary beneficiary are reduced proportionately to the extent necessary to stay within the family maximum.

In considering the amount of Social Security benefits payable, it is important to note that they are not subject to federal, state, or local income tax. Also important is the fact that after benefits commence, they are increased automatically to reflect increases in the Consumer Price Index. Generally speaking, benefit increases are made in June each year if an increase of at least 3 percent is indicated.

Eligibility for Benefits to Continue

Once benefits begin, their continuation hinges upon a variety of conditions being satisfied, depending upon the particular benefit. In every case benefits to an individual stop upon his or her death. A disability benefit normally terminates shortly after the disability ends (at age 65 it is converted to an old-age benefit). Benefits payable to children stop at age 18 (age 22 if a full-time student), but not if the child was disabled before age 22; children's benefits also stop if the child marries. Benefits to widows and widowers who are caring for young children terminate when the children reach 18 (unless they are disabled). Benefits payable to widows and widowers sometimes cease upon remarriage, but frequently do not.

Benefits usually stop or are reduced if the individual receiving the benefits has earnings in excess of specified amounts. This is because of the provision in the law usually referred to as the earnings test or earnings limitation. Only earned income can result in a loss of benefits; unearned income (such as investment income, rental income, pensions and retirement pay) is not taken into account. The amount of the earnings limitation is different for beneficiaries under age 65 than for those aged 65 or older. An individual aged 72 or older can have unlimited earned income and continue to receive full Social Security benefits. Beginning in 1982 this age will be lowered to 70.

An individual between the ages of 65 and 72 (age 70 in 1982 and later) can have earned income of $5,500 in 1981 without affecting the receipt of Social Security benefits; however, benefits will be reduced by $1 for every $2 of earned income in excess of $5,500. This earnings limitation will increase to $6,000 in 1982 and it will increase thereafter to keep up with increases in average earnings of all the nation's employees.

An individual who is under age 65 can have earned income of $4,080 in 1981 without affecting the receipt of Social Security benefits. Benefits will be reduced by $1 for every $2 of earned income in excess of $4,080. This earnings limitation increases each year to keep up with increases in average earnings of all the nation's employees.

In the case of a worker and dependents receiving Social Security benefits as a result of taxes paid by the worker, earnings of the worker in excess of the earnings limitation will reduce the benefits of both the worker and the dependents. On the other hand, earnings of a dependent in excess of the earnings limitation will reduce only the dependent's benefits.

This earnings limitation applies to earnings of dependent beneficiaries of a disabled worker but not to earnings of the disabled worker. Different criteria than this earnings limitation are used to determine continued eligibility for disability benefits.

Retirement Benefits

An individual must be "fully insured" to be eligible for retirement benefits under Social Security (sometimes referred to as old-age benefits since that terminology is used in the law). Monthly retirement benefits can begin as early as age 62 and are payable for life. The starting date depends upon the individual's election and the individual's earned income after the starting date selected.

For retirement at age 65, the benefit payable to a fully insured individual is equal to his Primary Insurance Amount. This amount is subject to a "regular" minimum benefit, and a "special" minimum benefit designed for individuals with low earnings but many years of employment. For an individual retiring at age 65 in January 1980, the retirement benefit ranges from the regular minimum of $133.90 to a maximum of $572.00 per month. The higher the worker's average earnings, the higher the benefit. The monthly benefit for an individual whose career earnings had always been the average for persons covered by Social Security would be approximately $450.00. After the retirement benefit begins, it increases with the benefit escalator provisions of the law.

If retirement is delayed beyond age 65 or if benefits are withheld under the earnings test, the benefit otherwise determined at actual retirement date is increased for each month that retirement is delayed. For individuals born in 1917 or later, the amount of the increase is ¼ of 1 percent for each month benefits are not received between ages 65 and 70. For individuals born before 1917, the amount of the increase is $\frac{1}{12}$ of 1 percent for each month that benefits are not received between ages 65 and 72. The increase applies to old-age benefits and widow's and widower's benefits only, and not to benefits to other family members.

Retirement may be elected as early as age 62 with the Primary Insurance Amount reduced by ⅝ of 1 percent for each month that retirement precedes age 65.

Benefits are subject to reduction or complete withholding between ages 62 and 72 if the individual's earned income exceeds the earnings limitation mentioned previously. In 1982 and later this reduction in benefits will be applicable only through age 70.

Disability Benefits

An individual must be "disability insured" to be eligible for disability benefits under Social Security. Disability generally means the inability to engage in any substantial gainful activity by reason of any medically determinable physical or mental impairment that can be expected to result in death or has lasted, or can be expected to last, for a continuous period of not less than twelve months; or after age 55, blindness which prohibits an individual from engaging in substantial gainful activity requiring skills or abilities comparable to those of any gainful activity in which he previously engaged with some regularity over a substantial period of time.

The disability benefit is payable following a waiting period of five consecutive calendar months throughout which the individual has been disabled. The disability benefit is equal to the Primary Insurance Amount, computed as though the individual had attained age 62 in the first month of his waiting period. Accordingly, the amount of the disability benefit is the same as the age-65 retirement benefit, if the average earnings on which benefits are based are the same. Since average earnings vary with the age at disability, however, so does the amount of the disability benefit. For an individual becoming disabled in July 1979 and thus eligible for benefits in January 1980, the minimum benefit is $122.00 per month and the maximum benefit is $552.40 per month. The disability benefit increases with the benefit escalator provisions in the law.

If a disabled individual is under age 62, the total disability benefits paid to him and his dependents may be reduced if he is receiving workers' compensation benefits. Social Security disability benefits plus workers' compensation benefits cannot exceed 80 percent of "average current earnings" prior to disability. Average current earnings for this purpose means actual earnings, not merely Social Security-taxed amounts, and is usually defined as the individual's best year in the period consisting of the calendar year in which disability started and the five years immediately preceding that year. If applicable state law provides that workers' compensation benefits are reduced by Social Security disability benefits, there will be no reduction in Social Security disability benefits.

An individual's disability benefits end with the month preceding the earliest of (a) the month in which he dies, (b) the month in which he attains age 65, and (c) the third month following the month in which disability ceases. The retirement benefit at age 65 for an individual entitled to a disability benefit until then generally will be equal to the Primary Insurance Amount on which the disability benefit is based.

An individual who applies for disability benefits, whether he receives monthly benefits or not, is considered for rehabilitation services by his state vocational rehabilitation agency. These services include counseling, teaching of new employment skills, training in the use of prostheses, and job placement. Benefits may be denied for any month in which the worker refuses to accept such rehabilitation services.

The earnings limitation that applies to retirement benefits does not apply to the payment of disability benefits. Instead, special limitations are used which are intended to measure the continuation of disability on an all-or-none basis.

Wife's or Husband's Benefits

At age 65 a wife or husband will receive 50 percent of the spouse's Primary Insurance Amount, a benefit which is payable, of course, only if the spouse was fully insured or disability insured and is receiving benefits. Payments may commence before age 65 (as early as age 62), but in that event will be reduced by $^{25}/_{36}$ of 1 percent for each month in the reduction period. This same benefit is payable to a divorced wife with at least ten years of marriage. Payments will cease with the month before the month in which (a) either spouse dies, (b) they are divorced (except if the duration of the marriage was at least ten years), or (c) the primary insured individual is no longer entitled to disability benefits and is not entitled to retirement benefits.

A wife or husband under age 65 may also be eligible for spouse's benefits if she or he is caring for a child of the worker entitled to a child's benefit, provided the child is not receiving his benefits solely because he is a student. The spouse's benefit in this case is 50 percent of the worker's Primary Insurance Amount. Benefit payments will cease with the month before the month in which (a) either spouse dies, (b) the primary insured individual is no longer entitled to disability benefits and is not entitled to retirement benefits, or (c) there is no longer a child entitled to benefits. If benefit payments cease as a result of the death of the worker, the surviving spouse may be entitled to widow's or widower's benefits, or mother's or father's benefits as described below.

Widow's or Widower's Benefits

At or after age 65 a widow or widower will receive 100 percent of the Primary Insurance Amount of the deceased spouse, provided that such spouse was fully insured and had not received a reduced old-age benefit before death. If the deceased spouse was receiving a reduced old-age benefit at the time of death, the widow's or widower's benefit may not exceed the greater of (a) the amount of the reduced old-age benefit of the spouse, and (b) 82½ percent of the spouse's Primary Insurance Amount. Payments may commence before age 65 (as early as age 60) but in that event will be reduced by $^{19}/_{40}$ of 1 percent for each month in the reduction period. Severely disabled widows or widowers are entitled to a percentage of the spouse's Primary Insurance Amount at or over age 50 (50 percent at age 50, grading up to 71½ percent at age 60 and graded further to 100 percent at age 65). The disability must have occurred within seven years after the death of the spouse (or, if later, seven years after the last eligible child attains age 18 or ceases to be disabled). This same benefit is payable to a surviving divorced wife with at least ten years of marriage. These benefits cease with the month before the month in which the surviving spouse dies or remarries (prior to age 60). Under certain circumstances a widow's remarriage prior to age 60 will not cause benefits to terminate.

Child's Benefits

Every child of an individual entitled to old-age or disability insurance benefits, or of an individual who dies while fully or currently insured, is entitled to a monthly benefit equal to 50 percent of the individual's Primary Insurance Amount if the individual is living, or 75 percent of his Primary Insurance Amount if he is deceased.

Payments cease with the month preceding the earliest of (a) the month in which such child dies or marries, (b) the month in which such child attains the age of 18 and is neither disabled nor a full-time student, (c) the earlier of a month during no part of which he was a full-time student or the month in which he reaches age 22 (under certain circumstances benefits may continue through the current semester in which he is enrolled), and (d) if the child's entitlement was based solely on his being disabled, the third month following the month in which he ceases to be disabled.

A grandchild can qualify as a "child" of a grandparent if both parents are disabled or dead and if the grandchild is living with and being supported by the grandparent.

Mother's or Father's Benefits

A mother's or father's benefit is payable to the surviving spouse of an individual who dies while fully or currently insured, provided the surviving spouse (a) is not remarried, (b) is not entitled to a widow's or widower's benefit, and (c) at the time of filing an application is caring for a child of the deceased spouse entitled to a child's benefit, provided the child is not receiving his benefit solely because he is a student. This same benefit is payable to a divorced wife (and, as a result of court decisions, to a divorced husband) even though the marriage did not endure ten years, provided she or he has not remarried. The mother's or father's benefit is equal to 75 percent of the Primary Insurance Amount of the deceased individual. Benefit payments will cease with the month before the recipient remarries, dies, becomes entitled to a widow's or widower's benefit, or has no child of the deceased individual entitled to a child's benefit.

Parent's Benefits

A parent of an individual who dies while fully insured is entitled to monthly benefits if such parent (a) has attained age 62, (b) was receiving at least one half of his support from such individual, (c) has not married since the individual's death, and (d) has filed an application for parent's benefits. Generally, the parent's benefit is equal to 82½ percent of the Primary Insurance Amount of such deceased individual. For any month for which more than one parent is entitled to parent's benefits, the benefit for each parent is equal to 75 percent of the Primary Insurance Amount. The parent's benefits cease upon death or, in certain circumstances, remarriage.

Maximum Limit on Family Benefits

The law limits the total of monthly benefits payable to a family entitled to benefits on the basis of wages of an insured individual. In retirement and survivor cases this maximum is about 175 percent of the individual's Primary Insurance Amount, except that for low-wage earners the percentage varies between 150 and 188 percent. In disability cases the percentage varies from 100 percent at very low wage levels to 150 percent at higher wage levels.

Generally, when benefits are subject to reduction because they exceed the limits on maximum family benefits, each monthly benefit except the old-age or disability benefit is decreased proportionately.

Lump Sum Death Payments

If an individual dies while fully or currently insured, an amount equal to $255 is normally paid to help meet the cost of burial expenses. Application for the payment must generally be filed within two years after the death of the insured individual.

Nonduplication of Benefits

An individual entitled to benefits both on his own earnings record and as a dependent or survivor of another worker may receive only the larger of the two benefits.

Medicare Benefits

The Medicare program consists of Hospital Insurance (HI) and Supplementary Medical Insurance (SMI), frequently referred to as Part A and Part B, respectively. Hospital Insurance provides partial protection against the cost of inpatient hospital services as well as a number of other services such as those provided by a skilled nursing facility or a home health agency. Supplementary Medical Insurance helps pay for the cost of physician services plus certain other expenses such as outpatient hospital care and home health agency visits. Not all medical services are covered by Medicare, the major exceptions being routine care, outpatient drugs, eyeglasses, and dental care.

HI benefits are payable automatically once you reach age 65 if you are entitled to a Social Security benefit as a retired worker, spouse, widow(er), or other beneficiary. HI benefits are available even if your monthly cash benefit is withheld completely because of earnings in excess of the earnings limitation. If you are not receiving monthly cash benefits at age 65, however, you may have to apply specifically for HI benefits.

The SMI program is voluntary and requires payments of $9.60 per month after July 1, 1980. (These premiums are subject to increase in the future as the cost of medical care increases.) If you are receiving a Social Security monthly benefit, the SMI premium will be deducted automatically from your benefit unless you specifically elect *not* to participate in the SMI program.

If you have been receiving Social Security benefits as a disabled beneficiary for at least twenty-four months (or twenty-nine months under the Railroad Retirement system), you are eligible for Medicare benefits, even if you are under age 65. Medicare benefits are also available if you (or one of your dependents) have chronic kidney disease requiring dialysis or kidney transplant.

Under the HI program, the cost of a hospital stay is reimbursed after certain deductible and coinsurance requirements are met. Hospital services for up to ninety days in a "spell of illness" are covered; furthermore, you have a "lifetime reserve" of an additional sixty days that can be drawn on if you stay in a hospital for more than a total of ninety days in one spell of illness. (A "spell of illness" ends once you have remained out of the hospital or skilled nursing facility for sixty days.) The hospital is usually reimbursed directly for the cost of your care over and above the amount you are required to pay. You must pay the first $180 of expenses (the "HI deductible" for 1980, subject to future increases) and you must pay $45 per day if your hospital stay lasts longer than sixty days and $90 per day if you use any of your "lifetime reserve" days. These "coinsurance" amounts of $45 and $90 are also subject to increase in future years.

If you have been hospitalized for at least three days and then enter a skilled nursing facility for follow-up care within two weeks after leaving the hospital, the services provided by the facility will be covered in part by the HI program for up to 100 days in a spell of illness. For days 21 through 100 you must pay a daily coinsurance amount of $22.50 (subject to future increase). In the first year after hospitalization, up to 100 home health agency visits are provided under HI.

The SMI program helps pay for the costs of physician services, outpatient services by hospitals and clinics, and home health agency visits. Reimbursement is on the basis of "reasonable charges" for such services, that is, maximum amounts that Medicare can, according to the law, pay for services covered under SMI. You pay the first $60 of reasonable charges each calendar year (a deductible that is *not* subject to automatic increase) and coinsurance of 20 percent of reasonable charges in excess of the deductible. You also pay all amounts in excess of Medicare's reasonable charges. In some cases the physician or other person or organization who provides covered services may agree to bill Medicare directly and accept as payment in full the amounts determined to be reasonable charges, in which event there will be no excess charges. The deductible is on a calendar year basis, and expenses incurred in the last quarter of a year can be carried over and applied toward meeting the deductible in the following year if the deductible was not met in the first year.[1]

Conclusion

This relatively brief description makes it obvious that Social Security is so complicated that it is not possible to explain in detail in just a few pages all the benefits and all the conditions surrounding their payment. It is possible, however, to give a general idea of the type of benefits payable, how they are determined, and who is eligible to receive them. With this information you should be able to work more effectively with your local Social Security office in making sure that you get maximum advantage from the program and receive all the benefits to which you are entitled. Getting the most possible value from Social Security is discussed further in later chapters, particularly Chapter 21.

4
How Much Do Social Security Benefits Cost?

There are several ways to state the money cost of Social Security. For the purpose of this chapter let us use a simple definition: The cost of the Social Security program in any given year is the amount paid in benefits and administrative expenses for that year—a simple but valid definition.

For many years after a social insurance program is adopted, costs can be expected to rise. This is true for several reasons. During the first year of a new program very few retired persons receive benefits (persons who are already past the retirement age when a program is adopted are not usually eligible for benefits). During the second year of a program there are a few more retired persons receiving benefits, the third year a few more, and so on. Eventually the retired persons begin to die, but there is still a net increase in the number of retired persons receiving benefits for many years after a new program is adopted. The same is true of benefits paid to survivors of deceased workers: the number of survivors receiving benefits increases steadily for many years after a program is adopted.

Costs also increase as new benefits are added. For example, disability benefits were added to the Social Security program in 1956. The predictable result was a steady increase in the number of disabled persons receiving benefits for many years to

Table 4.1

Social Security Beneficiaries at End of Selected Calendar Years

| | Number of Persons (in thousands) at End of Year Who Were | | | |
| | Receiving. . . | | Eligible for Benefits under. . . | |
Calendar Year	Old-Age and Survivors Insurance Benefits	Disability Insurance Benefits[a]	Hospital Insurance Program[b]	Supplementary Medical Insurance Program[b]
(1)	(2)	(3)	(4)	(5)
1940	222	—	—	—
1950	3,477	—	—	—
1960	14,157	687	—	—
1970	23,564	2,665	20,361	19,584
1979	30,348	4,777	26,800	26,700

[a]The Disability Insurance program was enacted in 1956 and began operation in 1957.
[b]The Medicare program was enacted in 1965 and began operation in 1966. Figures represent the average number eligible for benefits in the year shown.

come. Medicare benefits, paying part of the hospital and other medical expenses of retired persons, were added in 1965. As a result, the number of persons receiving Medicare benefits should increase along with the increase in the number of persons receiving retirement benefits.

Social Security costs can be expected to increase for other reasons, such as an increased number of persons covered by the program and increased benefits (as a result of inflation as well as benefit liberalizations). Accordingly, it is predictable and not at all unusual for the total cost of a new social insurance program to increase steadily for many years after it is adopted.

How does this theory hold up in light of past experience? Table 4.1 shows the number of persons who were receiving various types of Social Security benefits at the end of selected calendar years. As was to be expected, the number of beneficiaries has increased steadily since Social Security was enacted. The total number of beneficiaries is not meaningful and is not shown since some persons receive more than one type of benefit (for example, both Old-Age and Medicare benefits).

Just as an increase in the number of beneficiaries was to be expected, so was an increase in the amount of benefits paid. Table 4.2 shows the amounts that were paid in benefits and

Table 4.2
**Amount of Benefits and Administrative Expenses Paid
during Calendar Year
(in millions of dollars)**

Calendar Year	Old-Age and Survivors Insurance Program	Disability Insurance Program[a]	Hospital Insurance Program[b]	Supplementary Medical Insurance Program[b]	Total
(1)	(2)	(3)	(4)	(5)	(6)
1940	$ 62	—	—	—	$ 62
1950	1,022	—	—	—	1,022
1960	11,198	$ 600	—	—	11,798
1970	29,848	3,259	$ 5,281	$2,212	40,600
1979	93,133	14,186	21,073	9,265	137,657

[a]The Disability Insurance program was enacted in 1956 and began operation in 1957.
[b]The Medicare program was enacted in 1965 and began operation in 1966.

administrative expenses for the four separate parts of the Social Security program during selected calendar years. There has been a spectacular increase in costs since Social Security began: from $62 million in 1940 to $137,657 million in 1979. These figures are almost meaningless, however, taken by themselves. It is more appropriate to view them in relation to the size of the U.S. population, or the Gross National Product (the total amount of goods and services produced by the population), or some other measure of the population affected by Social Security.

As we will see in a later chapter, our Social Security program is financed primarily by taxes based upon the earnings of the active working population that participates in Social Security. Therefore, it is convenient and meaningful to compare the cost of Social Security with the total earnings of persons covered by Social Security, excluding that portion of earnings exempt from the Social Security tax.

This procedure may be illustrated with the following statistics for calendar year 1978. Approximately 110 million persons worked in employment that was covered by Social Security. Their total earnings in such employment were about $1,091 billion. But the portion of an individual's earnings in excess of $17,700 per year did not count for Social Security purposes;

Table 4.3

Amount of Benefits and Administrative Expenses as a Percentage of Effective Taxable Payroll[a] during Past Calendar Years

Calendar Year	Old-Age and Survivors Insurance Program	Disability Insurance Program[b]	Hospital Insurance Program[c]	Total for OASDHI	Supplementary Medical Insurance Program[c]	Total for OASDHI & SMI
(1)	(2)	(3)	(4)	(5)	(6)	(7)
1940	0.19%	—	—	0.19%	—	0.19%
1945	0.48	—	—	0.48	—	0.48
1950	1.17	—	—	1.17	—	1.17
1955	3.34	—	—	3.34	—	3.34
1960	5.59	0.30%	—	5.89	—	5.89
1965	7.23	0.70	—	7.93	—	7.93
1970	7.32	0.81	1.21%	9.33[d]	0.51%	9.84
1975	9.29	1.36	1.69	12.32[d]	0.69	13.01
1979	8.95	1.36	2.00	12.31	0.88	13.19

[a]"Effective taxable payroll" consists of the total earnings subject to Social Security taxes, after adjustment to reflect the lower contribution rates on self-employment income, tips, and multiple-employer "excess wages." This adjustment is made to facilitate both the calculation of contributions (which is thereby the product of the tax rate and the payroll) and the comparison of expenditure percentages with tax rates. This effective taxable payroll is slightly different for OASDI and HI because of the tax treatment of self-employed persons; however, it does not materially affect the comparisons.

[b]The Disability Insurance program was enacted in 1956 and began operation in 1957.

[c]The Medicare program (both SMI and HI) was enacted in 1965 and began operation in 1966. Although the SMI program is not financed by payroll taxes, its cost is shown for comparative purposes as a percentage of payroll that is taxable for HI purposes. Participation in SMI is optional and is financed by premiums paid by the enrollees, and by general revenue.

[d]The total is not the exact sum of the preceding columns because of "rounding."

that is, it did not count for computing benefits and it was not subjected to tax. Only about 84 percent of total earnings, or $913 billion, was subjected to Social Security tax. Total expenditures in 1978 for benefits and administrative expenses amounted to about $96 billion under the Old-Age, Survivors, and Disability insurance programs. This was some 11 percent of the total taxable payroll of $913 billion.

Table 4.3 shows the cost as a percentage of taxable payroll for the four separate parts of the Social Security program during selected calendar years in the past. It is important to note that the Supplementary Medical Insurance program is not financed by a payroll tax; nevertheless, this method of expressing costs is used in order to have a convenient method of comparing the cost of this program and its growth with the other parts of the Social Security program. In reviewing Table 4.3 it may be useful to note that the percentage of the total earnings subject to tax has not always been 84 percent. Table 4.4 indicates what these percentages have been for selected years in the past as well as what they are projected to be in the future. It should also be noted that in 1978 the total amount of covered earnings of persons participating in Social Security represented about three-fourths of the total earnings of all workers in the United States.

A review of Tables 4.2 and 4.3 substantiates the obvious. The cost of Social Security has grown by leaps and bounds not only in dollar amounts but also in relation to the earnings of those who are covered by Social Security.

How long will the cost of Social Security continue to rise? As a matter of fact, barring major legislative changes, costs will continue to rise until the population of active workers and

Table 4.4

Percentage of Total Earnings in Covered Employment That Is Subjected to Social Security Payroll Tax

Calendar Year	Percentage
(1)	(2)
1940	92
1945	88
1950	80
1955	80
1960	78
1965	71
1970	78
1975	84
1978	84
1979	88
1980	89[a]
1981 and later	90[a]

[a]Estimated.

beneficiaries (retired workers, disabled workers, surviving spouses, etc.) reaches a mature stage—that is, at least seventy-five to one hundred years after the program is adopted. Another way to think about it: the program and the population covered by the program reach a mature stage when the program has existed unchanged for the entire adult lifetime of every person who is covered by the program, and when the characteristics of the population (birth rates, death rates, retirement ages, etc.) have remained unchanged for the entire lifetime of the existing population. A further requirement for the maturity of the program is that there have been no large fluctuations in the economic experience (wage increases, Consumer Price Index changes, unemployment, etc.) during the working lifetime of every person who is covered by the program.

These conditions make it seem as if our Social Security program will never mature, and it probably will not; but for all practical purposes we can assume that it will mature approximately seventy-five years from now. In the year 2050 most of the active workers and the retired workers and other beneficiaries will have participated in the program throughout their entire working lifetime. Of course, we have no assurance that population characteristics, economic conditions, and the program itself will remain stable throughout this period, but if they should do so, then we could expect program costs to level off around the middle of the next century.

It is possible to obtain a more specific idea of future Social Security costs. Every year the Board of Trustees of the Social Security program issues reports based on studies made by the actuaries of the Social Security Administration and the Health Care Financing Administration. These reports include projected future costs of the program for as long as seventy-five years in the future. The projected costs, based on the 1979 Trustees Reports and on a limited number of unpublished studies, are summarized in Table 4.5. Total expenditures for benefits and administration are projected to increase from about 13 percent of taxable payroll in 1979 to approximately 17 percent by the year 2000 and to 26 percent by the year 2025, remaining approximately level thereafter.

Do these figures surprise you? Do you believe them? It is

Table 4.5

Projected Expenditures for Benefits and Administration as a Percentage of Effective Taxable Payroll[a] during Future Calendar Years

Calendar Year	Old-Age and Survivors Insurance Program	Disability Insurance Program	Hospital Insurance Program	Total for OASDHI	Supplementary Medical Insurance Program[b]	Total for OASDHI & SMI
(1)	(2)	(3)	(4)	(5)	(6)	(7)
1980	9.16%	1.40%	2.12%	12.68%	0.95%	13.63%
1985	9.12	1.38	2.73	13.23	1.18	14.41
1990	9.27	1.42	3.51	14.20	1.39	15.59
1995	9.13	1.54	4.27	14.94	1.57	16.51
2000	8.90	1.74	4.92	15.56	1.60	17.16
2025	13.49	2.18	7.52	23.19	2.35	25.54
2050	14.02	2.13	8.20	24.35	2.43	26.78

[a]"Effective taxable payroll" consists of the total earnings subject to Social Security taxes, after adjustment to reflect the lower contribution rates on self-employment income, tips, and multiple-employer "excess wages." This adjustment is made to facilitate both the calculation of contributions (which is thereby the product of the tax rate and the payroll) and the comparison of expenditure percentages with tax rates. This effective taxable payroll is slightly different for OASDI and HI because of the tax treatment of self-employed persons; however, it does not materially affect the comparisons.

[b]Although the SMI program is not financed by payroll taxes, its cost is shown for comparative purposes as a percentage of payroll that is taxable for HI purposes. Participation in SMI is optional and is financed by premiums paid by the enrollees, and by general revenue.

difficult *not* to believe the figures that are shown in Table 4.3 for the forty years from 1940 through 1979, because this is past history. What about the future—is it possible for the total cost of the Social Security program to be as high as 25 percent to 30 percent of taxable payroll? Yes, it is not only possible, it is quite likely if there are no significant changes in the present program.

These figures are no surprise to an actuary who is familiar with the Social Security program. It is no surprise that they increased rapidly in the past and it is no surprise that they are expected to increase in the future. It may be of interest to note that the early actuarial studies in 1938 indicated that the cost of retirement benefits under Social Security would rise steadily from 0.2 percent of taxable payroll in 1940 to 9.35 percent of taxable payroll by 1980.[1] These figures are quoted not to prove the accuracy of long-range projections, but rather to illustrate that from the very start of Social Security, actuaries have been providing information about the trend and level of future costs.

What Is an Actuary?

A short digression about actuaries may be in order. What is an actuary? I have heard it said that somewhere in the Congressional Record the statement is made that an actuary is a person who is "always taking the pessimistic view by looking many years into the future." It is true that the actuary's job is to look into the future; however, whether this is a pessimistic exercise is in the eye of the beholder. If you like the result that is projected, you would probably consider it optimistic; if you don't like the result, you would probably consider it pessimistic.

The most widely accepted standard of professional qualification in the United States for actuaries who work with life insurance, health insurance, pensions, and social insurance is membership in the Society of Actuaries. There are other actuarial organizations designed to serve the specialized needs of their membership: American Academy of Actuaries, Conference of Actuaries in Public Practice, Casualty Actuarial Society, and American Society of Pension Actuaries.

The Society of Actuaries is a professional organization of actuaries whose purpose is to advance the knowledge of actuarial science and to maintain high standards of competence within the actuarial profession. At the end of 1979, there were 6,997 members of the Society of Actuaries, of whom 3,955 were Fellows (the ultimate membership designation). In mid-1980, the Social Security Administration employed eighteen members of the Society of Actuaries and the Health Care Financing Administration employed thirteen members.

In its publication describing the actuarial profession, the Society of Actuaries states:

> An actuary is an executive professionally trained in the science of mathematical probabilities. He uses mathematical skills to define, analyze, and solve

complex business and social problems. He designs insurance and pension programs which meet the public's needs and desires, and which are financially sound. He forecasts probabilities and he commits his company or his client to long-range financial obligations for a generation or more.

One of the principal jobs of the actuaries of the Social Security Administration and the Health Care Financing Administration is to make long-range forecasts of the cost of the present Social Security program, as well as any proposed changes, and thus provide the information that will enable the program to be financed on a sound basis both now and in the future.

Long-Range Forecasts

In making long-range forecasts of the amounts that will be paid out in benefits under the Social Security program, actuaries must make assumptions regarding a host of factors, including:

mortality
disability
immigration and emigration
birth rates
wages and salaries
Consumer Price Index changes
unemployment rates
age at retirement
participation in work force by males and by females
marriage rates

For a given set of assumptions, projections of future costs can be made with a reasonably high degree of accuracy. But it is obvious that no one can accurately select these assumptions, particularly those concerning wages, the Consumer Price Index, and birth rates, all of which are important determinants of future costs. By expressing future costs as a percentage of future taxable payroll, rather than in dollar amounts, the predictability of future costs is greatly improved. Nevertheless, the overall level of certainty of long-range cost projections for a program like Social Security is still less than we might hope for.

The trustees of Social Security, as well as the government actuaries, recognize that it is impossible to predict the future accurately. They also recognize, however, that it is essential to adopt one or more sets of assumptions about the possible future social and economic environment and then to project future income and outgo under Social Security to determine whether or not it would be financially sound under those conditions.

In recent years the trustees have employed three alternative sets of assumptions about the future, usually labeled optimistic, pessimistic, and intermediate. Projections of future expenditures under the optimistic and pessimistic assumptions indicate a broad range within which it might reasonably be expected that expenditures will fall during the coming years. Projected expenditures based upon an intermediate set of assumptions are normally used for planning purposes since it is too cumbersome to deal in every instance with a range of future costs. The projected expenditures, as well as the projected income, shown throughout this book are based upon the intermediate assumptions used in the 1979 Trustees Reports, unless indicated otherwise.[2] The Appendix contains a summary of the more important of these assumptions.

Table 4.6 and Chart 4.A illustrate the range of projected expenditures for Social Security under the optimistic, pessimistic, and intermediate sets of assumptions. Expenditures include both benefits and administrative costs for all elements of the Social Security program that are under consideration here: Old-Age, Survivors, and Disability Insurance and Medicare (Hospital Insurance and Supplementary Medical Insurance). While it may be reasonable to assume that actual experience will fall within the range defined by these alternative projections, particularly during the first twenty-five years of the projection, there can be no assurance that this will be the case because of the high degree of uncertainty in the selection of assumptions for long-range forecasting.

Accordingly, the future costs shown in Table 4.6, particularly the costs after the turn of the century, should not be viewed as absolute amounts but rather as trends based upon assumptions

Table 4.6

Projected Expenditures for Benefits and Administration of the Social Security Program[a] under Alternative Demographic and Economic Assumptions,[b] Expressed as a Percentage of Effective Taxable Payroll[c]

Calendar Year	Optimistic Assumptions	Intermediate Assumptions	Pessimistic Assumptions
(1)	(2)	(3)	(4)
1980	13.54%	13.63%	13.95%
1985	13.75	14.41	15.03
1990	14.38	15.59	17.09
1995	14.57	16.51	18.89
2000	14.61	17.16	20.54
2025	19.73	25.54	35.95
2050	18.31	26.78	47.50

[a]Amounts shown include expenditures for OASDI, HI, and SMI combined.
[b]See text and Appendix for discussion of alternative sets of assumptions.
[c]"Effective taxable payroll" consists of the total earnings subject to Social Security taxes, after adjustment to reflect the lower contribution rates on self-employment income, tips, and multiple-employer "excess wages." This adjustment is made to facilitate both the calculation of contributions (which is thereby the product of the tax rate and the payroll) and the comparison of expenditure percentages with tax rates. This effective taxable payroll is slightly different for OASDI and HI because of the tax treatment of self-employed persons; however, it does not materially affect the comparisons. Although the SMI program is not financed by payroll taxes, its cost is shown for comparative purposes as a percentage of payroll that is taxable for HI purposes. Participation in SMI is optional and is financed by premiums paid by the enrollees, and by general revenue.

that seem reasonable to us at the present time. By updating the cost projections on a regular basis and by revising the assumptions in the light of emerging trends, actuaries can provide extremely important information for making sound future financial plans for the Social Security program. We should not ignore these future cost estimates just because they will affect *future* generations and not us, or just because we know that actual future costs will not be exactly the same as projected future costs.

As Table 4.6 and Chart 4.A indicate, under all three sets of assumptions, expenditures are projected to rise slowly until the turn of the century and to grow much more rapidly thereafter. The relatively small increase in costs between now and about

Chart 4.A

Projected Expenditures for Benefits and Administration of the Social Security Program[a] under Alternative Demographic and Economic Assumptions,[b] Expressed as a Percentage of Effective Taxable Payroll[c]

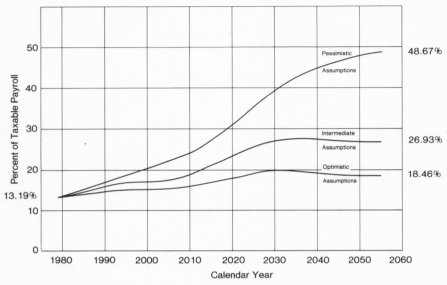

[a]Amounts shown include expenditures for OASDI, HI, and SMI combined.

[b]See text and Appendix for discussion of alternative sets of assumptions.

[c]"Effective taxable payroll" consists of total earnings subject to Social Security taxes, after adjustment to reflect the lower contribution rates on self-employment income, tips, and multiple-employer "excess wages." This adjustment is made to facilitate both the calculation of contributions (which is thereby the product of the tax rate and the payroll) and the comparison of expenditure percentages with tax rates. This effective taxable payroll is slightly different for OASDI and HI because of the tax treatment of self-employed persons; however, it does not materially affect the comparisons. Although the SMI program is not financed by payroll taxes, its cost is shown for comparative purposes as a percentage of payroll that is taxable for HI purposes. Participation in SMI is optional and is financed by premiums paid by the enrollees, and by general revenue.

the year 2010 is attributable primarily to the Hospital Insurance and Supplementary Medical Insurance programs[3] and, to a lesser extent, to the Disability Insurance program.

The much larger increases during the twenty-year period following the year 2010 are attributable primarily to the large number of persons then attaining age 65 (from among the children born during the post-World War II "baby boom" period from 1946 to the mid-1960s). The birth rate among these baby boom generations has been and is expected to continue to be lower than that of their parents, resulting in an eventual increase in the size of the older benefit-collecting population relative to the younger tax-paying population. Chart 4.B compares the size of these two segments of the population at three points in time: 1950, 1979, and 2025. The figures for 2025 are estimates based upon the intermediate set of birth rate and mortality assumptions.

As indicated in Table 4.6, the costs under the intermediate assumptions are projected to rise rapidly after the turn of the century to about 26 percent of taxable payroll before leveling off some fifty years from now. This is twice the current expenditures of about 13 percent of taxable payroll. Under the more optimistic assumptions, costs would still rise substantially above current levels but to an ultimate level of only about 18 to 20 percent of taxable payroll. Under the more pessimistic assumptions, projected expenditures would rise to about 36 percent of taxable payroll by the year 2025 and would continue increasing to some 48 percent by the year 2050. We are probably deluding ourselves by relying unduly on "optimistic-intermediate" assumptions rather than truly intermediate assumptions and by failing to emphasize that future costs can be predicted only within a broad range. Although it is a matter of judgment, I believe that future Social Security costs are much more likely to be higher than lower than the intermediate cost projections.

The so-called pessimistic assumptions selected by the Board of Trustees do not represent the most pessimistic view that it would be reasonable to take in determining whether Social Security will be viable in the future. For example, it can be argued that improvements in life expectancy will continue at a faster rate than has been assumed; or it is possible that average wages will not increase much, if any, faster than the cost of living, reflecting a marked slowdown in the steady improvement in the standard of living to which we have become accustomed—and which has been assumed for the future. Either of these events would result in much higher future Social Security costs (expressed as a percentage of taxable payroll).

Furthermore, none of the customary projections takes into account a variety of significant events that are conceivable, but

Chart 4.B

Past, Present, and Projected Retired Workers and Other
Social Security Beneficiaries, and Covered Workers

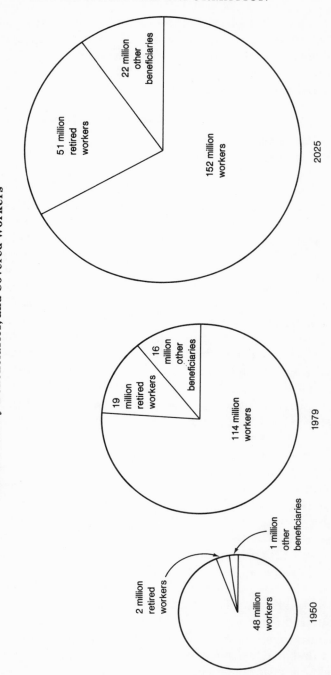

that would not ordinarily be expected. Unfortunately, there is no obvious way to prepare in advance to cope with some of these events. A significant improvement in health at the older ages is one of the easiest to comprehend of such possible events. People who were aged 60 in 1980 could expect to live another twenty years, on average, or until about age 80. It should be emphasized that 80 is the average age; some persons will live to age 100, others will die soon after age 60. About 90 percent of persons aged 60 in 1980 will die before reaching age 93. Fifty years ago in 1930, persons aged 60 could expect to live to age 75, on average. Fifty years from now in the year 2030, the projections assume that persons who are then aged 60 can expect to live to age 83, on average (according to the intermediate set of assumptions). It is entirely possible, however, that the average life span for persons aged 60 could be somewhat higher in the future, say 85 or 90; and with major breakthroughs in health care or improved understanding of the aging process, it could even be 95 or 100. Even if there are no remarkable increases in our average life span, we can expect generally improved health during our old age. Some analysts predict that life-extending techniques will become so developed in the twenty-first century that we may live well beyond 100 years, perhaps for 200 years or more! Major improvements in the health of the elderly or significant increases in life span would make our present Social Security system totally inappropriate.

Another example of a possible event that is difficult to comprehend, much less assess the impact of, is cataclysmic change in the earth resulting from volcanic eruptions, earthquakes, or polar shifts. These would lift large areas of land, submerge others in the sea, change underwater currents and tides, revise weather patterns, and generally transform the nation's coastal areas and mountain regions. Such changes would undoubtedly have a dramatic effect on human life, not only the size of the population initially surviving these disasters but also the population's ability for continued survival.

A still different type of development that is almost impossible to understand or predict the consequences of is the social evolution going on in this country and throughout the world. If this evolution should turn into a revolution, we could easily find our present Social Security system as well as most other institutions to be completely obsolete and all of our projections about future costs to have been of no avail.

None of this is to say that we should ignore the future because it is not predictable with certainty or because it may be calamitous. We must make every effort to design our institutions, including Social Security, so that they:

appear to be appropriate in a future environment that we can postulate and comprehend; and

are adaptable to non-calamitous future change.

Long-term projections such as those presented in this chapter provide information that is vital to our long-range planning and to our assessment of whether the present Social Security program is appropriate for the future. The projections indicate that future costs will continue to rise in the future no matter what assumptions are employed; it is just a question of how much they will rise. It is clearly inappropriate, therefore, to rely upon some undefined good fortune to enable us to continue our present Social Security program without paying substantially higher costs. Unfortunately these long-term projections and their significance do not appear to be widely known and understood by the public or the Congress or the Administration. Continued failure to heed these indications of the future could prove disastrous.

5
How Is the Money Obtained to Pay for Social Security Benefits?

In the last chapter we saw how the cost of any social insurance program can be expected to rise steadily as it matures. And we saw, in particular, how the cost of our Social Security program has grown in the past and how it is likely to grow in the future.

The question we turn to now is how we obtain the money necessary to pay these costs in order to fulfill the promise of the Social Security program to pay the various benefits outlined in Chapter 3. Obviously, we must levy some kind of tax against some segment of the population.

Sources of Federal Government Income

There are numerous ways taxes can be assessed. Chart 5.A illustrates the major sources of income to the federal government in fiscal year 1979 to operate all our government programs (not just Social Security).

Federal Income Tax

The federal income tax is the tax we are most familiar with. It is paid by most individuals and businesses. In fiscal year 1979

Chart 5.A
Federal Government Income by Source, Fiscal Year 1979

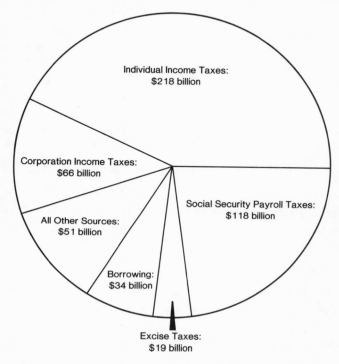

Fiscal Year 1979 Total: $506 billion

the federal government received $218 billion in personal income taxes paid by individuals, and $66 billion in income taxes paid by corporations. This was 56 percent of all income received by the government.

Miscellaneous Taxes

A variety of special taxes of one kind or another are collected by the federal government: excise taxes (on alcohol, tobacco, gasoline, and entertainment, for example), gift taxes, estate taxes, licensing fees, customs taxes, and so on. In fiscal year 1979, the total of these miscellaneous taxes amounted to $70 billion, or 14 percent of all income received by the government.

Borrowing

The money to pay for federal programs does not necessarily have to be collected immediately in the form of taxes. Any excess of appropriations for expenditures over tax income constitutes a "budget deficit" and is made up by borrowing additional money from the general public. This borrowing is carried out by the sale of U.S. government securities, with the repayment of principal and interest to be made from future income (from taxes or further borrowing). In fiscal year 1979, an additional $34 billion was borrowed. This represented about 7 percent of total federal government income.

General Revenue

The total of the federal income taxes, the miscellaneous taxes mentioned above (excluding amounts specified by law for a particular purpose, such as the Highway Trust Fund), and newly borrowed amounts is sometimes called "general revenue." General revenue is available to the government to spend for general purposes; that is, there is not usually a direct connection between the source of the tax and how it is spent. Last year, general revenue was spent for national security, interest on the public debt, veterans' services and benefits, welfare (Supplemental Security Income, Medicaid, Food Stamps, Aid to Families with Dependent Children, etc.), operating the federal government, and other purposes. Approximately 70 percent of total income to the federal government in fiscal year 1979 (including the amounts borrowed from the public to finance the budget deficit) represented "unallocated" income or general revenue.

General revenue is used to pay for a relatively small part of the total Social Security program. In 1979 about 6 percent of the total expenditures for Social Security ($8.2 billion out of total expenditures of $137.7 billion) was accounted for by general revenue.

General revenue is used to pay a relatively large portion of the cost of the Supplementary Medical Insurance part of the Medicare program. In 1979 approximately 70 percent of expenditures for Supplementary Medical Insurance was accounted for by general revenue; the other 30 percent came from contributions, or "premiums," paid by those who elected to have this benefit. General revenue is also used in cases where special benefits are granted a person even though he has not paid the normal Social Security taxes to be eligible for such benefits. If Supplementary Medical Insurance is excluded, only about 1 percent of the cost of Social Security is financed by general revenue.

Payroll Tax

Sometimes special taxes are assessed based on a worker's gross earnings without any exemptions or deductions. They are referred to as payroll taxes and are usually earmarked for special purposes.

This is the way the money is raised to pay for most (94 percent) of the cost of the present Social Security program. In 1980 an employee paid taxes of 6.13 percent of his earnings; his employer also paid taxes equal to 6.13 percent of the employee's earnings (but this amount was not deducted from the employee's earnings); and a self-employed person paid taxes of 8.1 percent of his earnings. In each case, no tax was payable on earnings in excess of $25,900 in 1980. Payroll taxes such as these, which are collected by the Internal Revenue Service, and the relatively small amounts of general revenue referred to earlier are placed in special trust funds that are invested in U.S. government securities until they are used to pay Social Security benefits. These taxes can be used only to pay Social Security

Table 5.1
Social Security Taxes Payable in 1980 with Respect to Selected Individuals

If Your Earnings in 1980 Were	Your Social Security Taxes Were			If You Are Self-Employed Your Social Security Taxes Were
	Paid by Employee	Paid by Employer	Total	
(1)	(2)	(3)	(4)	(5)
$ 6,000	$ 367.80	$ 367.80	$ 735.60	$ 486.00
12,000	735.60	735.60	1,471.20	972.00
25,900 or more	1,587.67	1,587.67	3,175.34	2,097.90

benefits (and related administrative expenses) and cannot be used for any other purposes. Table 5.1 shows the Social Security taxes payable in 1980 by several individual workers and their employers, as well as by self-employed persons.

Why Do We Pay for Social Security the Way We Do?

When Social Security was adopted, only about 60 percent of the working population was eligible for its benefits. There was apparent justification, therefore, in assessing a payroll tax on the segment of the population eligible for its direct benefits rather than using general revenue paid by a broader segment of the population. The use of a payroll tax was also consistent with the notion that there was a strong relationship between taxes and benefits for an individual under the Social Security program. Now, even more than when Social Security was enacted, this logic is more apparent than real. More than 90 percent of the working population is currently covered by Social Security. Furthermore, the relationship between taxes and benefits for an individual is so tenuous as to be virtually nonexistent.

There is no particular reason an employee and his employer should share equally the cost of Social Security; that is, there is no reason the worker and his employer should pay the same amount in Social Security payroll taxes—except that it happens to be the law. Also, there is no particular reason the tax rate should be the same for all levels of earnings. The Social Security tax rate could be variable rather than constant. It could increase or decrease as the level of earnings increases. In fact, Social Security could be financed by general revenue or some form of tax other than the present payroll tax.

If there is no particular theoretical reason why we should pay for most of our Social Security benefits with a tax that is a constant percentage of payroll and that is paid in equal amounts by an employee and his employer, why do we do it this way? Why do we use a payroll tax instead of general revenue? Many justifications can be given and many theoretical arguments can be constructed; but in fact, the reasons seem to be rather arbitrary.

It may be interesting to note the recollections of a member of the staff of President Roosevelt's Committee on Economic

Security which made the recommendations in 1934–35 leading to the adoption of the Social Security Act on August 14, 1935:

> From the first, we assumed that contributions to old age insurance should be "in equal shares by employer and insured employee" as stated in the September 13th draft. A "fifty-fifty" ratio seemed to us to be justified by an "esthetic" logic difficult to controvert. I remember proposing this ratio to William Green, then president of the American Federation of Labor, as we were going to the White House for the President's reception on November 14th. He agreed that labor should go along with an equal sharing of the cost of old age insurance. . . . There never was any objection from the labor movement against equal contributions to old age insurance.[1]

> Departing from European tradition, we proposed the use of a uniform percentage of wages in determining the amount of contribution rather than a flat dollar amount or a series of amounts by wage classes.[2]

The above memoirs are not quoted to suggest that the decisions made in 1934–35 were anything less than well thought out and sound. Undoubtedly there were other considerations than those reflected in the memoirs. One of those considerations is suggested by an observation made by President Franklin D. Roosevelt in responding to a visitor who complained about the economic effect of the tax:

> I guess you're right on the economics, but those taxes were never a problem of economics. They are politics all the way through. We put those payroll contributions there so as to give the contributors a legal, moral, and political right to collect their pensions. . . . With those taxes in there, no damn politician can ever scrap my social security program.[3]

How High Will Future Tax Rates Be?

As indicated in Chapter 4, projections have been made of the future cost of Social Security. If the benefits are not changed and if Social Security continues to be financed the way it is now, future tax rates are projected to be approximately as indicated in Table 5.2 for the Old-Age, Survivors, and Disability Insurance and the Hospital Insurance portion of the Medicare program (i.e., the part of Social Security that is currently financed by the payroll tax). It should be noted that the rates shown represent the tax rates required to finance Social Security adequately (based on the intermediate assumptions in the 1979 Trustees Reports) and are not always equal to the actual tax rates scheduled in present law.

The tax rates in Table 5.2 from 1980 through 1990 are the tax rates scheduled in present law. It is possible that these tax rates will be barely sufficient in the aggregate; however, if each segment of Social Security is to be financed adequately, some reallocation of taxes will be necessary. In October 1980, a law was enacted providing for a reallocation of taxes in 1980 and

Table 5.2

Projected Tax Rates Necessary to Finance Present Social Security Program[a]

| Calendar Year | Tax Rates for Employed Persons | | | Tax Rates for Self-Employed Persons |
	Paid by Employee	Paid by Employer	Total	
(1)	(2)	(3)	(4)	(5)
1980	6.13%	6.13%	12.26%	8.10%
1981	6.65	6.65	13.30	9.30
1982–84	6.70	6.70	13.40	9.35
1985	7.05	7.05	14.10	9.90
1986–89	7.15	7.15	14.30	10.00
1990	7.65	7.65	15.30	10.75
2000	7.80	7.80	15.60	10.75
2010	8.60	8.60	17.20	11.50
2020	10.55	10.55	21.10	14.10
2030	12.30	12.30	24.60	16.40
2040	12.35	12.35	24.70	16.40
2050	12.20	12.20	24.40	16.20

[a]Figures from 1980 through 1990 are the tax rates scheduled in present law. The figures for the year 2000 and later represent the tax rates necessary, based on the intermediate assumptions in the 1979 Trustees Reports, to finance benefits and administrative expenses assuming no change is made in present law. This does not include the taxes necessary to support the Supplementary Medical Insurance program, which is not financed by payroll taxes.

1981 (an increase in OASI taxes and a corresponding decrease in DI taxes). Further tax reallocation or interfund borrowing will probably be necessary in 1982 and later; also, it appears likely that additional taxes in the aggregate will be necessary beginning in the mid-1980s.

The tax rates in present law are scheduled to rise between now and 1990 to the amounts shown in Table 5.2 for the year 1990 and then remain at that level in the future. If benefits are to be paid after 1990, however, the payroll tax rates must continue rising as indicated in the table from the year 2000 to 2050. The "financial deficits" for the next century (the difference between the tax rates that are scheduled in law and the tax rates that will be required to pay benefits) are given remarkably little attention. Yet just as costs have risen in the past, they will rise in the future. Ignoring the projected high future costs will not change them. These deficits are explored in more detail in Chapter 7.

The tax rate is applied to a worker's earnings subject to an upper limit called the "maximum contribution and benefit base." For 1980 the maximum was $25,900; thus the portion of an individual's earnings in excess of $25,900 in 1980 does not count for computing benefits and was not subjected to tax. This maximum is scheduled to be $29,700 in 1981 and to increase thereafter at the same rate as the average wages and salaries of the nation's workers increase. Consequently, although the dollar amount of the maximum taxable wage base will increase in the future, it will remain approximately constant relative to its 1981 level.

The Supplementary Medical Insurance portion of Medicare is an optional program available to most persons aged 65 and over and to certain disabled persons. About 95 percent of those eligible for this program have elected to participate. The cost of SMI benefits is not financed by payroll taxes as is the rest of Social Security. The cost of SMI benefits was met originally by premiums paid by the participants and approximately matching payments from general revenue; at the present time, however, about 70 percent of the total cost is being paid from general revenue because premiums have been prevented by law from rising as rapidly as total costs have risen. The percentage of the total cost paid by general revenue can be expected to

Table 5.3

Projected Supplementary Medical Insurance Expenditures and Proportion Financed by General Revenue

Calendar Year	Supplementary Medical Insurance Expenditures in Dollars (in billions)	Supplementary Medical Insurance Expenditures as a Percentage of Hospital Insurance Taxable Payroll[a]	Percentage of Total Financed by General Revenue
(1)	(2)	(3)	(4)
1980	$10.6	0.95%	71%
1990	34.2	1.39	82
2000	b	1.60	90
2010	b	1.70	92
2020	b	2.11	93
2030	b	2.50	94
2040	b	2.48	95
2050	b	2.43	96

[a]Although the SMI program is not financed by payroll taxes, its cost is shown for comparative purposes as a percentage of payroll that is taxable for HI purposes.
[b]Dollar amounts are not shown in the distant future since they tend to lose their meaning except when related to an index such as taxable payroll.

increase in the future, probably to as much as 90 percent by the year 2000 and 96 percent by the middle of the twenty-first century.

The SMI Trustees Report normally shows projected expenditures only for a three-year period; however, the same demographic changes in the population that will cause the projected OASDI and HI program costs to accelerate rapidly after the turn of the century will also cause the SMI program costs to increase rapidly. Table 5.3 illustrates the projected expenditures under the SMI program for the next seventy-five years. Although the SMI program is not financed by payroll taxes, its cost for comparative purposes has been computed as a percentage of the payroll that is taxable for Social Security purposes. On this basis, as shown in column (3) of Table 5.3, the expenditures under the SMI program are projected to increase from the equivalent of 0.95 percent of taxable payroll in 1980 to 2.50 percent in the year 2030. Within ten years (by 1990) the cost of Supplementary Medical Insurance will equal the present cost (in 1980) of the Disability Insurance program. Congress is very concerned about the costliness of the Disability Insurance program (witness the recently enacted Social Security Disability Amendments of 1980) and numerous groups are studying ways to reduce the cost. On the other hand, no one seems to be aware of, much less concerned about, the cost of SMI.

General Revenue versus Payroll Tax Financing

As indicated previously, approximately 99 percent of the cost of the Old-Age, Survivors, and Disability Insurance and Hospital Insurance programs is financed by payroll taxes; the other 1 percent is financed by general revenue. With respect to the Supplementary Medical Insurance program, approximately 30 percent is financed by premiums paid by the participants and the remaining 70 percent is financed by general revenue.

There is an ongoing debate about whether these financing methods are proper and whether we should rely more on general revenue and less on payroll taxes. It is not the purpose of this section to discuss the relative advantages of general revenue and payroll tax financing or other forms of taxation. A few general statements, however, may be helpful in establishing a perspective on financing.

It is important to note that if more general revenue and less payroll tax were used it would not change the total cost of Social Security or the total amount of taxes collected—it would simply change the way the tax is spread among the taxpayers, and some people would pay more and some would pay less than they do now.

To the extent that payroll taxes are used to finance Social Security, the taxes are paid by the same groups of persons who receive benefits. That is not to say that each person receives the exact benefits that can be "purchased" by his taxes. The relationship between the value of taxes paid and benefits received is discussed in Chapter 11.

To the extent that general revenue is used to finance Social Security, the taxes are paid by the entire population without regard to whether they participate in Social Security. Consider, for example, an employee of the federal government who never works in employment covered by Social Security. Such a person will never pay Social Security taxes and will never be eligible for

Social Security benefits (unless he enrolls in the SMI program at age 65). Nevertheless, the federal income taxes he pays contribute to general revenue which is used to pay for 6 percent of total Social Security benefits.

One of the most important drawbacks of general revenue financing as currently practiced is that it seems to facilitate ignoring the future. The Supplementary Medical Insurance program provides a good example. The government does not make long-range plans to finance the Supplementary Medical Insurance program. Provision is made only two years in advance. There seems to be a feeling that since the program is financed primarily by general revenue there is no need to be aware of the future cost or to make any advance plans to finance future benefits. The theory is apparently that "We can always increase general taxes enough to pay for SMI, so why worry about it." This viewpoint is clearly inappropriate in a program like Social Security, under which it is entirely possible to promise more in future benefits than the nation will be able and willing to pay for when they fall due.

Conclusion

In summary, Social Security benefits must be financed by taxes of one kind or another. The particular tax that is selected is important because of the way in which it spreads the burden among the various segments of the population. It is important psychologically because the taxpayer may be more willing to pay one form of tax than another. Finally, it is important because of the degree of fiscal responsibility it encourages—or discourages—among the Congress and other policymakers, as well as the taxpayers.

6

When Do We Pay for Social Security Benefits?

In Chapter 4 we saw how expenditures for benefits and administration under a social insurance program can be expected to grow steadily until the program matures—that is, for at least fifty to seventy-five years after it begins. In particular, we saw how expenditures under our Social Security program have grown in the past and how they are likely to grow in the future. For convenient reference this pattern of expenditures is shown in Table 6.1 for the Old-Age, Survivors, Disability, and Hospital Insurance parts of the Social Security program (i.e., everything except Supplementary Medical Insurance, which is optional and is financed principally by general revenue). The dollar amounts in column (2) are shown only through 1990 since the figures in the later years tend to lose their meaning except when related to an index such as taxable payroll. The projected future costs are based upon the "intermediate" set of assumptions as discussed in Chapter 4, and actual future costs may be higher or lower than those indicated in Table 6.1.

In Chapter 5 we discussed the various kinds of taxes that could be collected to pay for these benefits and saw that traditionally a payroll tax, shared equally by the worker and his employer, has been used as the principal means of financing our Social Security program.

Table 6.1

Expenditures for Benefits and Administration under the Old-Age, Survivors, Disability, and Hospital Insurance Program for Selected Years

| | Expenditures Expressed as a... | |
Calendar Year	Dollar Amount (in millions)	Percentage of Taxable Payroll[a]
(1)	(2)	(3)
1940	$ 62	0.19%
1945	304	0.48
1950	1,022	1.17
1955	5,079	3.34
1960	11,798	5.89
1965	19,187	7.93
1970	38,388	9.33
1975	80,765	12.32
1980	146,330[b]	12.68[b]
1985	235,967[b]	13.23[b]
1990	352,928[b]	14.21[b]
1995	c	14.94[b]
2000	c	15.57[b]
2025	c	23.19[b]
2050	c	24.35[b]

[a]Taxable payroll is adjusted to take into account the lower tax rates on self-employment income, tips, and multiple-employer "excess wages" as compared to the combined employer-employee rate. Taxable payroll is slightly different for OASDI and HI because of the tax treatment of self-employed persons; however, it does not materially affect the results.
[b]Estimated.
[c]Dollar amounts are not shown in the distant future since they tend to lose their meaning except when related to an index such as taxable payroll.

In this chapter we will discuss the question of how the amount of payroll tax to be paid by a worker and his employer at any given time is determined. In 1940 a worker paid taxes of 1 percent of the first $3,000 of his earnings, a maximum of $30.00; in 1980 a worker paid 6.13 percent of the first $25,900 of his earnings, a maximum of $1,587.67. How was it decided that the tax rate would be 1 percent in 1940 and 6.13 percent in 1980? How was it decided that a worker would pay tax on $3,000 of earnings in 1940 and $25,900 of earnings in 1980? What will these amounts be in the future?

Current-Cost Financing Method

There are a variety of "financing methods" available to pay for a social insurance program just as there are a variety of financing methods available to pay for automobiles, houses, life insurance policies, and almost everything else we buy.

The most obvious financing method for a social insurance program is what is sometimes called the pay-as-you-go method, or the "current-cost method." Under this method, just enough taxes are collected each year to pay the benefits and administrative expenses which fall due that year—the "current costs." Since it is difficult to estimate the exact amount of expenditures for a given year, it is usual to plan to collect slightly more in taxes than is likely to be needed. This excess amount of taxes is set aside in a reserve fund, or a "trust fund," to be used in years when benefit payments are higher than expected or tax collections are lower than expected or a combination of both. Under current-cost financing the trust fund never becomes very large since it serves merely as a contingency fund.

What is the pattern of tax collections that can be expected under a current-cost financing method? Basically, it is about the same as the pattern of program expenditures illustrated in column (2) of Table 6.1. The current cost of benefits and administration started very low at $62 million in 1940 and rose steadily to an estimated $146,330 million by 1980. Column (3) of Table 6.1 expresses these costs as a percentage of taxable payroll and permits a more meaningful comparison from year to year.

A few words of review about the "taxable payroll" may be of help in interpreting the figures in Table 6.1. The taxable payroll in a given year is the total earnings subject to Social Security tax for persons who pay Social Security taxes during that year, but it does not include earnings for any individual in excess of the "maximum contribution and benefit base," sometimes loosely referred to as the "maximum taxable earnings base." In 1980, for example, this maximum was $25,900; thus the taxable payroll was the total earnings subject to Social Security tax for all persons who paid Social Security taxes in 1980, but it did not include earnings in excess of $25,900 for any individual. Reference was made to "earnings subject to Social Security tax" to

Table 6.2
History of Increases in the Maximum Taxable Earnings Base

Calendar Year	Maximum Taxable Earnings Base
(1)	(2)
1937–50	$ 3,000
1951–54	3,600
1955–58	4,200
1959–65	4,800
1966–67	6,600
1968–71	7,800
1972	9,000
1973	10,800
1974	13,200
1975	14,100
1976	15,300
1977	16,500
1978	17,700
1979	22,900
1980	25,900
1981	29,700

recognize that some earnings are not taxable: earnings in jobs not covered by Social Security and investment earnings, for example.

From 1937 to 1950 the maximum earnings subject to Social Security tax was $3,000. It is estimated that 97 percent of the persons covered by Social Security earned less than $3,000 in 1937, and 71 percent earned less than $3,000 in 1950. Table 6.2 illustrates how this maximum taxable earnings base has increased from time to time. Under present law, the maximum taxable earnings base will increase automatically after 1981 to keep up with increases in the average wages and salaries of American workers.

In 1980 an estimated 92 percent of those covered by Social Security earned less than the maximum earnings base and thus had all of their earnings taxed under the Social Security program. It is estimated that this percentage will be 93 percent in 1981, and that it will remain at about that level unless the law is amended to provide otherwise. It is estimated that 90 percent of total earnings in covered employment in 1981 and later will be subjected to Social Security tax.

Table 6.3 shows the total amount of taxes needed to meet the current costs compared with the actual tax rates used in the past under our Social Security program. The table covers the Old-Age, Survivors, Disability, and Hospital Insurance parts of the Social Security program; the Supplementary Medical Insur-

Table 6.3

Comparison of Current Costs and Tax Rates, and Trust Fund Levels, under the Old-Age, Survivors, Disability, and Hospital Insurance Program for Selected Years

Calendar Year	Current Costs: Expenditures as Percentage of Taxable Payroll[a]	Actual Tax Rate[b] as Percentage of Taxable Payroll	Amount in Trust Funds at Beginning of Year	
			Dollar Amount (in millions)	Multiple of Expenditures during Year
(1)	(2)	(3)	(4)	(5)
1937	c	2.00%	$ 0	—
1940	0.2%	2.00	1,724	27.81
1945	0.5	2.00	6,005	19.75
1950	1.2	3.00	11,816	11.56
1955	3.3	4.00	20,576	4.05
1960	5.9	6.00	21,966	1.86
1965	7.9	7.25	21,172	1.10
1970	9.3	9.60	36,687	.96
1971	10.6	10.40	41,270	.93
1972	10.4	10.40	43,468	.87
1973	11.0	11.70	45,710	.76
1974	11.2	11.70	50,881	.73
1975	12.3	11.70	55,005	.68
1976	12.7	11.70	54,859	.60
1977	12.9	11.70	51,738	.50
1978	12.8	12.10	46,303	.41
1979	12.3	12.26	43,223	.34

[a]Taxable payroll is adjusted to take into account the lower tax rates on self-employment income, tips, and multiple-employer "excess wages" as compared to the combined employer-employee rate. Taxable payroll is slightly different for OASDI and HI because of the tax treatment of self-employed persons; however, it does not materially affect the results.

[b]Combined tax rate paid by employee and employer.

[c]During 1937–39 no benefit payments were made except a return of employee taxes in the event of death.

ance program is discussed later. Although tax collections began in 1937, no benefits were paid from 1937 through 1939 except a return of the workers' taxes in the event of death. The tax rates indicated in column (3) are the combined worker and employer tax rates. For example, in 1937 the workers' tax rate was 1 percent and the employers' tax rate was 1 percent, or a combined tax rate of 2 percent.

Self-employed persons first became covered in 1951 and pay taxes in amounts larger than the workers' tax and smaller than the combined worker and employer tax. For convenience of presentation, the figures in Table 6.3 have taken these different tax rates into account by expressing the current costs in column (2) as a percentage of a "hypothetical taxable payroll." This payroll was constructed so that the application of the worker and employer tax rates to such payroll would yield the same total taxes as would the application of the actual different tax rates to the actual taxable payroll in each category of employment. This procedure also adjusts for other minor deviations in the financing.

A study of the figures in Table 6.3 indicates that during its first twenty years of operation Social Security collected considerably more in taxes than it paid out in benefits but that during the past twenty years or so the taxes have been approximately equal to the current expenditures. The years since 1974 have been an important exception, and expenditures for benefits and administration have exceeded tax collections, thus requiring previously accumulated funds to pay a portion of the benefits. During the next few years, provision has been made for increased taxes that will approximate projected expenditures, although there still may be some deficits unless further tax increases are made.

The Supplementary Medical Insurance program has always been financed on a current-cost basis, so far as is practical. Participants pay premiums specified by law, and Congress appropriates whatever amount of general revenue is necessary to pay the balance of the cost each year. Of course, this is done on an estimated basis and income and outgo do not always come out even; therefore, a small trust fund balance is maintained. Also, provision is made for medical expense claims that begin in one year but carry over into the next year.

For all practical purposes, therefore, Social Security is financed on a current-cost basis; and the trust funds are intended to reflect all financial transactions and to serve as contingency funds in absorbing temporary differences between income and expenditures. The trust funds are adequate to pay only about 2 percent of the benefits during the next ten years and thus play a relatively minor role in ensuring the payment of future benefits; it is the ongoing collection of Social Security taxes that is the most important factor in providing benefits under the program.

Although the trust funds are relatively small, some background information on how they are invested may be useful in understanding certain aspects of the financing questions to be discussed later. The portion of each trust fund that, in the judgment of the Secretary of the Treasury (the Managing Trustee of the trust funds), is not required to meet current expenditures for benefits and administration is invested on a daily basis in one of the following types of security:

> Interest-bearing obligations of the U.S. government, including special public-debt obligations utilized only by the trust funds
>
> Obligations guaranteed as to both principal and interest by the United States
>
> Certain federally sponsored agency obligations designated as lawful investments for fiduciary and trust funds under the control and authority of the United States or any officer of the United States

The trust funds earned interest amounting to $3.5 billion during fiscal year 1979, equivalent to an effective annual rate of about 7.6 percent on the total assets of the trust funds.

Alternatives to Current-Cost Financing

There are alternatives to the current-cost financing method. Instead of collecting just enough in taxes each year to pay the benefits for the year, we could collect more in taxes than needed to pay current benefits and place the excess contributions in a reserve fund or a trust fund. The higher the taxes, the larger the trust fund. This procedure is usually termed "advance funding." There are different levels at which advance funding can take place, depending upon the theory being followed as well as certain practicalities. Columns (4) and (5) of Table 6.3 indicate the extent to which Social Security was advance funded during its early history.

Why would we want to collect more in taxes than we need to pay current benefits? Why would we want to accumulate sizable trust funds? There are advantages and disadvantages to both the current-cost and the advance-funding methods, some of which are obvious but many of which are not.

Current-cost financing is easy to understand. Simply collect enough taxes each year to pay the benefits falling due that year. Most governmental programs are financed in this way. The taxes are low in the early years of the program and increase gradually as the public "gets used to paying the taxes." There is no sizable fund to invest, thus numerous investment problems are avoided. If a large fund were to exist, the public might misunderstand the purpose of the fund and believe that benefits could be expanded more than was in fact economically sound.

On the other hand, current-cost financing may mislead the public. The public may think the low cost in the early years will continue indefinitely and thus may demand or be enticed into accepting a Social Security program that is more generous than will be affordable at some time in the future. Steadily increasing tax rates which are an integral part of the current-cost method may not be desirable. The public may prefer to have tax rates that are more predictable and that remain the same for several years at a time.

If the Social Security program were a private system, under normal circumstances it would be considered desirable to collect more income than is necessary for current benefit payments and to accumulate a substantial fund. This is in fact the normal procedure for a private employee benefit system for reasons which include the following:

> *Security of benefits.* The existence of a large fund gives the employees some assurance that if the system terminates and no future income to the system is available, the benefits accrued to date can in fact be paid, at least to the extent the accumulated fund is adequate. (The Employee Retirement Income Security Act of 1974 requires

that most private pension plans accumulate a fund in order to give employees this added security.)

Reduction of future contributions. The amount of investment earnings on the trust fund can be used to pay a portion of future benefits and thus permit a reduction in the amount of future contributions otherwise required to finance the benefits.

Allocation of costs to period during which they are incurred. Even though benefits may not be paid until some future date, the cost of these benefits can be considered as having been incurred gradually over an employee's working lifetime as he earns the benefits. The recognition of this principle through payment of sufficient contributions to fund the benefit obligations as they accrue will generally lead to the accumulation of a substantial fund.

Although these are valid reasons for the advance funding of a private pension system, they are less valid for national compulsory social insurance—such as the Social Security program—covering substantially the entire population.

With respect to security of benefits, it is usually assumed that the Social Security program will continue indefinitely and that the taxing power of the federal government is adequate assurance that the benefits will be provided. This is probably a justifiable assumption provided that the Social Security benefits, together with all the other benefits and services supplied through the government, that have been promised for the future are not unreasonable.

With respect to reduction of future contributions, the accumulation of a fund for Social Security would have a paradoxical effect. Higher Social Security taxes would be required from today's generation of taxpayers, but tomorrow's generations of taxpayers, considered as a whole, would pay the same total amount of taxes to support Social Security—Social Security and general—as if there were no fund. This is true because Social Security trust funds are invested in government securities, the interest on which is paid from general revenue; therefore, the accumulation of a fund would result in lower future Social Security taxes but higher future general taxes. In other words, the total future cost of Social Security would be the same but would be distributed differently within each generation and would be paid not only by persons who pay Social Security taxes but also by those who do not pay such taxes. On the other hand, the accumulation of a trust fund that is invested in government securities could serve to reduce the amount of government securities issued to other parties to finance government activities. Accordingly, the total outstanding government securities, including those issued to the trust fund, could be the same before and after the accumulation of a trust fund. In this event, total general revenue paid in the future to the government for all purposes would be unaffected by the accumulation of a trust fund, Social Security payroll taxes would eventually be lower, and the nation's total tax burden would be reduced.

With respect to the appropriate allocation of costs to the periods during which they are incurred, an argument can be made (under a national social insurance system as well as under a private pension system) for recognizing that a liability is accruing during a person's active working lifetime, even though the benefits and the costs thereof may not be paid until a later date. Recognition of this liability does not necessarily take the form of accumulating a fund that is related to the value of the benefits being accrued.

An argument is being made in some quarters these days for advance funding of the Social Security program for a reason that does not apply to an individual private pension plan. It goes something like this: Since a large part of a person's retirement needs are met by the Social Security program, his private saving for retirement is reduced; the result is that the nation's capital accumulation needs are partially unmet; to offset this reduced saving by the individual, the Social Security program should collect more in taxes than is needed for current benefits payments and thus accumulate a sizable trust fund; the assets of the trust fund would be invested in government securities; thus the amount of government securities held privately would be reduced and more private savings would be freed for use in developing the economy. Elaboration of this argument will not be made here. It should be noted, however, that this argument for funding is a controversial one, and it is difficult for various experts to reach agreement on the extent, if any, to which the Social Security program has resulted in a reduction in private saving.

With respect to the general question of funding, whatever the rationale, it is important to note the difficulty of assessing the effect on the economy, particularly over the longer term, of collecting higher taxes from today's generation of taxpayers and the same or lower taxes from tomorrow's generations. The effect would depend in part upon how the government utilized the additional funds placed at its disposal as well as the ways in which private saving would in fact be affected. These matters are extremely difficult to evaluate retrospectively; they are even more difficult to evaluate in advance.

In assessing the financial stability of Social Security, much more is involved than the question of whether to use current-cost or advance-funding methods. The most important test of financial soundness for Social Security is whether the future income (taxes and interest on the trust funds) can reasonably be expected to equal future benefits and administrative expenses.

This condition does not prevail uniformly for the various segments of the Social Security program. Under the Old-Age, Survivors, and Disability Insurance program, projected future income is approximately equal to future outgo for the next fifty years, on the average, according to the intermediate assumptions described in the Appendix; however, more recent projections indicate that relatively small deficits (less than 1 percent of taxable payroll) may be expected throughout the 1980s. On the other hand, substantial deficits are expected during the second quarter of the next century as the children of the post-World War II baby boom reach retirement age. Under the Hospital Insurance program, deficits are projected to begin to occur within ten years and to continue in rapidly increasing amounts each year thereafter. Under the Supplementary Medical Insurance program, there are no earmarked taxes scheduled beyond the next three years; hence it is difficult to define the deficit. Nonetheless, substantial increases in expenditures are projected for the next fifty years or so.

The matter of future financial deficits in the Social Security program is extremely important and is discussed in more detail in Chapter 7.

7
Trillion Dollar "Actuarial Deficits" and "Accrued Liabilities"

Actuarial Deficits

As discussed in Chapter 6, Social Security operates on a pay-as-you-go financing basis, sometimes called a current-cost basis. The trust funds are not large, relative to expenditures, and serve only as contingency funds, not as guaranty funds. The financial stability of Social Security depends, therefore, upon the ability and willingness of the nation's workers and employers to continue to pay the taxes necessary to support the benefit payments. Accordingly, it is essential that we constantly monitor estimated future income and expenditures to determine whether they are still in "actuarial balance" and whether our Social Security program is still viable. When projected future income and expenditures are not in balance, an "actuarial deficit" or an "actuarial surplus" exists—depending upon whether projected expenditures are greater than income, or vice versa. Actuarial projections made during the past several years, including the most recent projections, indicate that Social Security has a significant actuarial deficit. This deficit is discussed in the following sections for each of the major portions of the Social Security program.

OASDI Deficit

In determining the actuarial balance of the Old-Age, Survivors, and Disability Insurance program, projections have been made customarily during a seventy-five-year future period. This covers the remaining lifetime of most current participants in Social Security.

Chart 7.A shows graphically the projected expenditures and tax income under the OASDI program based upon the 1979 Annual Report of the Board of Trustees.[1] Expenditures are shown based upon the "intermediate" assumptions contained in this report and would, of course, have been lower or higher if the "optimistic" or "pessimistic" assumptions had been depicted. Table 7.1 gives the corresponding numerical comparison of the projected expenditures and tax income, and the resulting differences, over various periods. For convenience of presentation, both the chart and the table ignore the trust fund balances since they play a relatively small role in the financing of a current-cost system.[2]

As indicated in Chart 7.A, tax income rises in steps in accordance with increases scheduled under the law. The expenditures rise in dollar amounts but generally decline as a percentage of taxable payroll from 1978 to 1981. This is because of the gradual expansion of the taxable payroll during that period from 84 percent of total payroll in covered employment to 90 percent. Expenditures then remain relatively level for the next twenty-five years, reflecting the combined effect of a projected rise in Disability Insurance expenditures and an expected temporary decline in Old-Age Insurance expenditures as small birth cohorts of the Depression years reach retirement age. Expenditures start rising rapidly early in the twenty-first century as the children of the post-World War II "baby boom" begin reaching retirement age. Around the year 2035 after all the children of this baby boom period (which ended in the 1960s) have reached retirement age, expenditures decline slightly and then level off.

Under the intermediate assumptions, OASDI tax income is

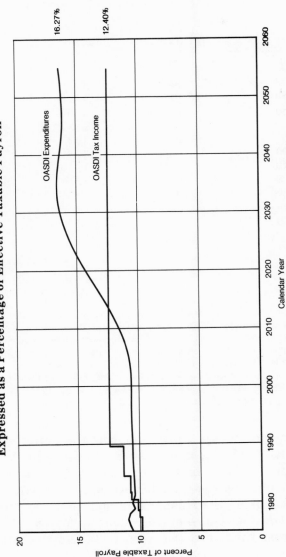

Chart 7.A

Projected Expenditures and Legislated Tax Income for Old-Age, Survivors, and Disability Insurance Program[a] Expressed as a Percentage of Effective Taxable Payroll[b]

16.27%

12.40%

OASDI Expenditures

OASDI Tax Income

Percent of Taxable Payroll

Calendar Year

[a]Projected under intermediate set of demographic and economic assumptions in 1979 Trustees Report.
[b]"Effective taxable payroll" consists of total earnings subject to Social Security taxes, after adjustment to reflect the lower contribution rates on self-employment income, tips, and multiple-employer "excess wages." This adjustment is made to facilitate both the calculation of contributions (which is thereby the product of the tax rate and the payroll) and the comparison of expenditure percentages with tax rates.

Table 7.1

Projected Expenditures and Legislated Tax Income for Old-Age, Survivors, and Disability Insurance Program,[a] Expressed as a Percentage of Effective Taxable Payroll[b]

Calendar Year	OASDI Expenditures	OASDI Tax Income	Difference[c]
(1)	(2)	(3)	(4)
1979	10.31%	10.16%	−0.15%
1980	10.56	10.16	−0.40
1985	10.50	11.40	0.90
1990	10.70	12.40	1.70
1995	10.67	12.40	1.73
2000	10.65	12.40	1.75
2010	11.58	12.40	0.82
2020	14.29	12.40	−1.89
2030	16.44	12.40	−4.04
2040	16.29	12.40	−3.89
2050	16.15	12.40	−3.75
25-year averages:			
1979–2003	10.59	11.76	1.17
2004–2028	13.26	12.40	−0.86
2029–2053	16.30	12.40	−3.90
75-year average:	13.38	12.19	−1.20

[a]Projected under intermediate set of demographic and economic assumptions in 1979 Trustees Report. Figures for 1979 represent actual experience.
[b]"Effective taxable payroll" consists of total earnings subject to Social Security taxes, after adjustment to reflect the lower contribution rates on self-employment income, tips, and multiple-employer "excess wages." This adjustment is made to facilitate both the calculation of contributions (which is thereby the product of the tax rate and the payroll) and the comparison of expenditure percentages with tax rates.
[c]Negative figures represent deficits.

projected to exceed expenditures during the period from 1981 until the year 2015.[3] At this time the combined OASDI trust funds are projected to be equal to about three years' outgo. Thereafter outgo will exceed tax income, requiring that the interest earnings on the trust funds, and later the principal of the trust funds, be used to make benefit payments. By the year 2025, the trust funds are projected to fall to the level of one year's outgo, thus requiring an increase in taxes at that time in order to preserve the trust funds' ability to act as contingency reserves.

The actuarial balance of the OASDI program may be summarized during the next seventy-five years as follows: an actuarial surplus during the first twenty-five years of the seventy-five-year projection period, an approximately offsetting actuarial deficit during the second twenty-five-year period, and a substantial actuarial deficit during the latter third of the seventy-five-year period.

The average annual amount by which expenditures are projected to exceed tax income over the entire seventy-five-year projection period is 1.20 percent of taxable payroll. This actuarial deficit represents about 9 percent of average expenditures of 13.38 percent of taxable payroll.

Another way to express the actuarial deficit is as a single-sum amount—$800 billion as of January 1, 1979—determined by computing the excess of expenditures over tax income (sometimes positive and sometimes negative) in each of the next seventy-five years and discounting these amounts at interest[4] to the present time, and then reducing the sum of these amounts by the value of the trust fund at the present time.

If the actuarial deficit determined in 1979 is to be eliminated by the payment of additional taxes, it could be achieved, at least in theory, in one of two ways. A single-sum amount of $800 billion could be placed in the trust funds immediately, and the resulting trust funds together with interest thereon, supplemented by the currently scheduled Social Security taxes, would be sufficient to pay all benefits falling due in the next seventy-five years. At the end of that period, the trust funds would have returned to a relatively low level as at present.

As an alternative to this obviously impossible solution, additional taxes could be collected over the next seventy-five years. The average additional taxes would have to be equivalent to 1.20 percent of taxable payroll (approximately 10 percent of the average scheduled taxes of 12.19 percent). If it is desired that the trust fund be maintained at a relatively low level to serve as a contingency fund—as in recent years—the additional taxes would not be constant throughout the next seventy-five years but would be variable so as to approximately match emerging expenditures. In this event, average taxes (paid by the employee and employer combined) would be about 1 percent of taxable payroll less than already scheduled until the turn of the century, about 1 percent more than already scheduled during the first quarter of the next century, and about 4 percent more than already scheduled thereafter.

In summary, the actuarial deficit is simply the amount by which projected future expenditures for benefits and administration exceed the projected income and the value of the trust funds. The actuarial deficit can be stated in various ways, some of which make it appear more formidable than others. There should be no question, however, about the necessity of eliminating any significant actuarial deficit that may appear from time to time. Otherwise, scheduled benefits cannot be paid.

HI Deficit

In determining the actuarial balance of the Hospital Insurance program, projections have been made customarily during a twenty-five-year future period. There is no valid justification for limiting the projection period; it should be the same seventy-five-year period that is used in determining the actuarial balance of the OASDI program. Hospital Insurance is in effect a deferred retirement benefit commencing at age 65 (or after the receipt of twenty-four months of disability benefits). It is similar to an old-age retirement benefit except it is not paid in cash but in the form of partial provision of hospital services. The demographic changes in the population that will cause the OASDI program costs to increase rapidly after the turn of the century will also cause the HI program costs to increase rapidly.

Accordingly, the actuarial balance of the HI program is presented here for a seventy-five-year period. The figures for the first twenty-five years are based upon the 1979 Annual Report of the Board of Trustees,[5] and the figures for the ensuing fifty years are based upon information prepared by the Health Care Financing Administration actuaries but otherwise unpublished.

Chart 7.B shows graphically the projected expenditures and tax income under the HI program. Expenditures are based upon the "intermediate" assumptions employed by the trustees. Table 7.2 gives the corresponding numerical comparison of the expenditures and tax income, and the resulting differences, over various periods. For convenience of presentation both the chart and the table ignore the trust fund balances since they play a relatively small role in the financing of a current-cost system.

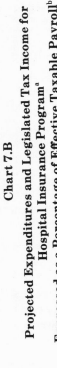

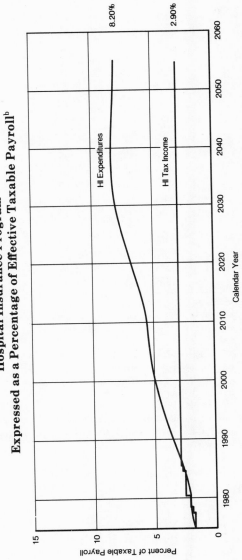

Chart 7.B

Projected Expenditures and Legislated Tax Income for Hospital Insurance Program[a] Expressed as a Percentage of Effective Taxable Payroll[b]

[a]Projected under intermediate set of demographic and economic assumptions in 1979 Trustees Report. After year 2000, unit-cost increases for medical care are assumed to increase at the same rate as average wages in covered employment. [b]"Effective taxable payroll" consists of total earnings subject to Social Security taxes, after adjustment to reflect the lower contribution rates on self-employment income, tips, and multiple-employer "excess wages." This adjustment is made to facilitate both the calculation of contributions (which is thereby the product of the tax rate and the payroll) and the comparison of expenditure percentages with tax rates. This effective taxable payroll is slightly different for OASDI and HI because of the tax treatment of self-employed persons; however, it does not materially affect the comparisons.

Table 7.2

Projected Expenditures and Legislated Tax Income for Hospital Insurance Program[a] Expressed as a Percentage of Effective Taxable Payroll[b]

Calendar Year	HI Expenditures	HI Tax Income	Difference[c]
(1)	(2)	(3)	(4)
1979	2.00%	2.10%	0.10%
1980	2.12	2.10	−0.02
1985	2.73	2.70	−0.03
1990	3.51	2.90	−0.61
1995	4.27	2.90	−1.37
2000	4.92	2.90	−2.02
2010	5.60	2.90	−2.70
2020	6.77	2.90	−3.87
2030	8.13	2.90	−5.23
2040	8.39	2.90	−5.49
2050	8.20	2.90	−5.30
25-year averages:			
1979–2003	3.64	2.78	−0.86
2004–2028	6.27	2.90	−3.37
2029–2053	8.28	2.90	−5.38
75-year average:	6.06	2.86	−3.20

[a]Projected under intermediate set of demographic and economic assumptions in 1979 Trustees Report. After year 2000, unit-cost increases for medical care are assumed to increase at the same rate as average wages in covered employment. Figures for 1979 represent actual experience.
[b]"Effective taxable payroll" consists of total earnings subject to Social Security taxes, after adjustment to reflect the lower contribution rates on self-employment income, tips, and multiple-employer "excess wages." This adjustment is made to facilitate both the calculation of contributions (which is thereby the product of the tax rate and the payroll) and the comparison of expenditure percentages with tax rates. This effective taxable payroll is slightly different for OASDI and HI because of the tax treatment of self-employed persons; however, it does not materially affect the comparisons.
[c]Negative figures represent deficits.

Tax income rises in steps in accordance with increases scheduled under the law. Expenditures rise throughout the period before leveling off after the children of the post-World War II baby boom have reached retirement age. An actuarial deficit first occurs in the mid-1980s when expenditures begin to exceed tax income. Thereafter, an actuarial deficit is projected to occur each year in the future.

The average annual amount by which expenditures are projected to exceed tax income over the entire seventy-five-year projection period is 3.20 percent of taxable payroll, or about 53 percent of average expenditures of 6.06 percent of taxable payroll. Expressed as a single-sum amount, this actuarial deficit is about $2,500 billion as of January 1, 1979.

Accordingly, if the HI actuarial deficit is to be eliminated by the payment of additional taxes it could be achieved by:

placing a single-sum amount of $2,500 billion in the trust fund; or

paying additional taxes that would average about 3.20 percent of taxable payroll over the next seventy-five years (an increase of approximately 112 percent of the average scheduled taxes of 2.86 percent).

Assuming the trust fund is to be maintained at a relatively low level to serve only as a contingency fund, the additional taxes would not be constant throughout the next seventy-five years but would be variable so as to approximately match emerging expenditures. In this event, average taxes (paid by the employee and employer combined) would be about 1 percent of taxable payroll more than already scheduled until the turn of the century, about 3.5 percent more than already scheduled during the first quarter of the next century, and about 5.5 percent more than already scheduled thereafter.

This is a formidable deficit no matter how it is presented: a lump sum of $2,500 billion, or increased taxes averaging more than 3 percent of taxable payroll. Furthermore, the HI actuarial deficit is three times the size of the OASDI actuarial deficit, yet it is not formally acknowledged by the Board of Trustees, the Congress, the Administration, or the Health Care Financing Administration which has administered the HI program since March 1977.

OASDI and HI Combined Deficit

The preceding discussions of actuarial deficits for OASDI and HI were based upon the intermediate set of demographic and economic assumptions used by the Social Security actuaries in making projections for the 1979 Trustees Reports. The actual situation could be better—or it could be worse. Chart 7.C depicts the projected expenditures for OASDI and HI combined under the optimistic and pessimistic assumptions as well as the intermediate assumptions used in the 1979 Trustees Reports. Tax income expressed as a percentage of taxable

Chart 7.C

Projected Expenditures for Old-Age, Survivors, Disability, and Hospital Insurance Programs Combined under Alternative Demographic and Economic Assumptions,[a] and Legislated Tax Income, Expressed as a Percentage of Effective Taxable Payroll[b]

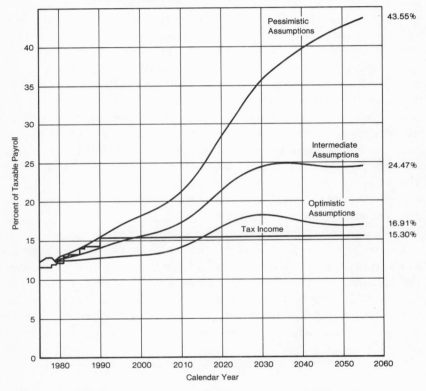

[a]See text and Appendix for discussion of alternative sets of assumptions.

[b]"Effective taxable payroll" consists of total earnings subject to Social Security taxes, after adjustment to reflect the lower contribution rates on self-employment income, tips, and multiple-employer "excess wages." This adjustment is made to facilitate both the calculation of contributions (which is thereby the product of the tax rate and the payroll) and the comparison of expenditure percentages with tax rates. This effective taxable payroll is slightly different for OASDI and HI because of the tax treatment of self-employed persons; however, it does not materially affect the comparisons.

payroll remains the same under all sets of assumptions. Table 7.3 gives the corresponding numerical comparison of the average expenditures and tax income, and the resulting deficits, over various periods for each of the three sets of assumptions.

Based upon the intermediate assumptions, the actuarial deficit for the OASDI and HI programs combined is 4.39 percent of taxable payroll on the average over the next seventy-five years (equivalent to $3,300 billion as of January 1, 1979). The optimistic assumptions produce an actuarial deficit of 0.38 percent of taxable payroll on the average over the next seventy-five years (equivalent to $300 billion as of January 1, 1979). The pessimistic assumptions produce an actuarial deficit of 12.00 percent of taxable payroll on the average over the next seventy-five years (equivalent to $6,800 billion as of January 1, 1979).

The taxes that are scheduled under present law (a tax rate for employees and employers combined that will increase by 25 percent from 12.26 percent in 1980 to 15.30 percent by 1990) will not be adequate to provide future benefits even under the optimistic assumptions. Under the pessimistic assumptions, scheduled future tax rates are woefully inadequate; that is, they are sufficient to provide only about half the benefits that will become payable during the coming seventy-five years.

At least one thing seems clear from examining these actuarial deficits. Only the foolhardy would continue to ignore the longer range financial problems projected for the Social Security program. It is not a question of whether future costs will be higher; it is a question of whether they will be so much higher as to be unaffordable. It is a question of whether we are making promises we will not be able to keep.

SMI Deficit

The question of the actuarial balance of the Supplementary Medical Insurance program is a difficult one because of the way in which the program is financed and the way in which future costs are presented (or not presented). Participants in SMI pay monthly premiums which account for about 30 percent of the current cost of the program. This percentage is expected to continue declining and to be about 10 percent by the year 2000. The amount of these premiums is determined for one year at a

Table 7.3

Projected Expenditures, Tax Income, and Deficits for Old-Age, Survivors, Disability, and Hospital Insurance Programs Combined, under Alternative Demographic and Economic Assumptions[a] Expressed as a Percentage of Effective Taxable Payroll[b]

Calendar Year	OASDHI Expenditures under . . .			Scheduled Tax Income	Tax Income Less Expenditures under . . . [c]		
	Optimistic Assumptions	Intermediate Assumptions	Pessimistic Assumptions		Optimistic Assumptions	Intermediate Assumptions	Pessimistic Assumptions
(1)	(2)	(3)	(4)	(5)	(6)	(7)	(8)
1979	12.31%	12.31%	12.31%	12.26%	−0.05%	−0.05%	−0.05%
1980	12.59	12.68	13.00	12.26	−0.33	−0.42	−0.74
1985	12.68	13.23	13.81	14.10	1.42	0.87	0.29
1990	13.11	14.21	15.38	15.30	2.19	1.09	−0.08
1995	13.34	14.94	16.89	15.30	1.96	0.36	−1.59
2000	13.41	15.57	18.42	15.30	1.89	−0.27	−3.12
2010	14.20	17.18	21.27	15.30	1.10	−1.88	−5.97
2020	16.91	21.06	28.16	15.30	−1.61	−5.76	−12.86
2030	18.50	24.57	35.66	15.30	−3.20	−9.27	−20.36
2040	17.34	24.68	39.66	15.30	−2.04	−9.38	−24.36
2050	16.78	24.35	42.52	15.30	−1.48	−9.05	−27.22
25-year averages:							
1979–2003	13.02	14.23	15.71	14.54	1.52	0.31	−1.17
2004–2028	15.84	19.53	25.73	15.30	−0.54	−4.23	−10.43
2029–2053	17.45	24.58	39.71	15.30	−2.15	−9.28	−24.41
75-year average:	15.43	19.44	27.05	15.05	−0.38	−4.39	−12.00

[a]See text and Appendix for discussion of alternative sets of assumptions. Figures for 1979 represent actual experience.

[b]"Effective taxable payroll" consists of total earnings subject to Social Security taxes, after adjustment to reflect the lower contribution rates on self-employment income, tips, and multiple-employer "excess wages." This adjustment is made to facilitate both the calculation of contributions (which is thereby the product of the tax rate and the payroll) and the comparison of expenditure percentages with tax rates. This effective taxable payroll is slightly different for OASDI and HI because of the tax treatment of self-employed persons; however, it does not materially affect the comparisons.

[c]Negative figures represent deficits.

time, approximately one year in advance. The balance of SMI costs is paid with general revenue.

Annual reports of the Board of Trustees on the financial condition of SMI include projections of income and expenditures for only three years. This limits any formal statement about the actuarial balance of the SMI program to a three-year period. SMI costs (relative to the payroll of active workers) may be expected to continue their rise until becoming nearly three times their current level early in the next century, yet no formal provision has been made to collect the taxes necessary to pay for these benefits. The theory seems to be "what we don't know won't hurt us."

Chart 7.D shows graphically the projected expenditures under the SMI program under the intermediate set of assumptions consistent with those used for the OASDI and HI programs. Also shown is the projected income from participants' premiums. Table 7.4 gives the corresponding numerical comparison of the expenditures and premium income, as well as the differences that must be drawn from general revenue during selected time periods. These amounts are expressed as a percentage of the payroll that is taxable for HI purposes even though the SMI program is not financed by payroll taxes. This is done to facilitate comparison with the other parts of the Social Security program. For convenience of presentation, both the chart and the table ignore the trust fund balances since they play a relatively small role in the financing of the SMI program.

The actuarial deficit could well be considered to be the amount by which projected future expenditures for benefits and administration exceed the projected income from premiums paid by the participants. Under this theory, future general revenue would not be taken into account since it has not been earmarked in any way to ensure its availability. Using such a definition, the actuarial deficit over the next seventy-five years would average approximately 1.78 percent of the payroll taxable for HI purposes. Expressed as a single-sum amount, this actuarial deficit is about $1,400 billion as of January 1, 1979. A range of possible future SMI costs is illustrated by Chart 7.E which shows projected expenditures under the three alternative sets of assumptions consistent with those used for

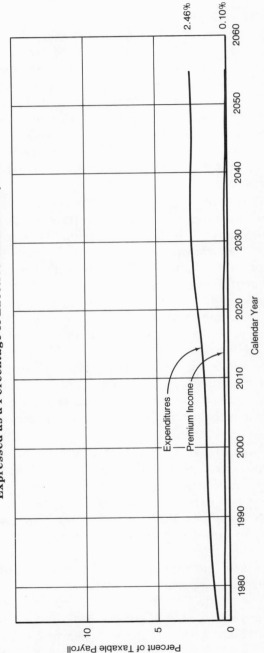

Chart 7.D

**Projected Expenditures and Premium Income
for Supplementary Medical Insurance Program
Expressed as a Percentage of Effective Taxable Payroll[a]**

[a] Although the SMI program is not financed by payroll taxes, its cost is shown for comparative purposes as a percentage of payroll that is taxable for HI purposes. Participation in SMI is optional and is financed by premiums paid by the enrollees, and by general revenue.

Table 7.4

Projected Expenditures, Premium Income, and General Revenue Requirements for Supplementary Medical Insurance Program[a] Expressed as a Percentage of Effective Taxable Payroll[b]

Calendar Year	SMI Expenditures	SMI Premium Income	Amount to Be Drawn from General Revenue
(1)	(2)	(3)	(4)
1979	0.88%	0.26%	0.62%
1980	0.95	0.26	0.69
1985	1.18	0.24	0.94
1990	1.39	0.21	1.18
1995	1.57	0.19	1.38
2000	1.60	0.16	1.44
2010	1.70	0.15	1.55
2020	2.11	0.14	1.97
2030	2.50	0.13	2.37
2040	2.48	0.12	2.36
2050	2.43	0.10	2.33
25-year averages:			
1979–2003	1.36	0.21	1.15
2004–2028	1.97	0.14	1.83
2029–2053	2.47	0.11	2.36
75-year average:	1.93	0.15	1.78

[a]Projected under intermediate set of demographic and economic assumptions in 1979 Trustees Report. Figures for 1979 represent actual experience.
[b]Although the SMI program is not financed by payroll taxes, its cost is shown for comparative purposes as a percentage of payroll that is taxable for HI purposes. Participation in SMI is optional and is financed by premiums paid by the enrollees, and by general revenue.

the OASDI and HI programs. There is no assurance, of course, that actual future costs will fall within this range.

The most important conclusions to be drawn from these statements about the actuarial deficit of the SMI program are that:

significantly larger costs can be expected for the future; and

these costs should be estimated, acknowledged, and some formal procedure adopted to assure their payment.

The present procedure of not formally acknowledging these future costs is unfair to present and future taxpayers and beneficiaries. It makes it too easy for us to make promises of future benefits that we may not be able and willing to finance.

Chart 7.E

Projected Expenditures for Supplementary Medical Insurance Program under Alternative Demograhpic and Economic Assumptions[a] Expressed as a Percentage of Effective Taxable Payroll[b]

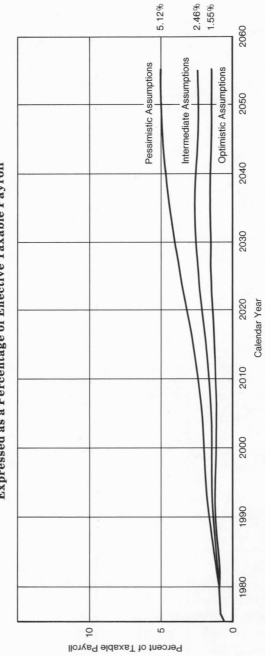

Pessimistic Assumptions — 5.12%

Intermediate Assumptions — 2.46%

Optimistic Assumptions — 1.55%

Calendar Year

Percent of Taxable Payroll

[a]See text and Appendix for discussion of alternative sets of assumptions.
[b]Although the SMI program is not financed by payroll taxes, its cost is shown for comparative purposes as a percentage of payroll that is taxable for HI purposes. Participation in SMI is optional and is financed by premiums paid by the enrollees, and by general revenue.

The Need to Eliminate Actuarial Deficits

Substantial actuarial deficits exist for all segments of the Social Security program. The OASDI deficit has been determined and acknowledged; but since it will not become significant until the children of the post-World War II baby boom begin to retire about twenty-five years from now, it has not yet been taken seriously. The HI deficit during the next twenty-five years has been determined but not very well acknowledged. The more significant HI deficit projected to occur early in the next century is not even computed and formally reported to Congress by the Board of Trustees. SMI deficits—or high future costs if you will—are not computed, they are not communicated to Congress, and they are not even worried about by anyone except a few knowledgeable and concerned individuals.

The total amount of these actuarial deficits for the Social Security progam (OASDI, HI, and SMI combined) is a staggering sum: $4,700 billion, or $4.7 trillion. These actuarial deficits must be eliminated. Indeed, they *will* be eliminated sooner or later. *It should be obvious that gaps between income and outgo (actuarial deficits) will be closed eventually by either raising taxes or lowering benefits.* It is simply a question of whether we plan in advance the best way to close these future gaps or wait until it is so late that we have no desirable options available to us.

The only prudent action is to eliminate the actuarial deficits now: to revise the benefits or the financing procedures, or both, so that anticipated future expenditures will equal anticipated future income on the basis of the best information available at this time. To do otherwise is to court disaster.

Accrued Liabilities

Once the actuarial deficits have been eliminated and Social Security is in actuarial balance—with anticipated future income equal to anticipated future expenditures—there is still the question of the "accrued liability." This is a completely separate issue from the "actuarial deficit." The existence and the amount of the accrued liability has no relationship whatsoever to the actuarial deficit, although these two terms are frequently confused.

The accrued liability can be defined as the present value of benefits that have been earned or accrued as of a given date but that will not actually be paid until a later date. This concept is discussed in the following sections for each major portion of the Social Security program.

OASDI Accrued Liability

At the beginning of 1979 there were 35 million persons receiving monthly Social Security benefits of about $105 billion per year under the OASDI program. All conditions had been met for these benefits to be payable in the future, thus the benefits may be considered to have been fully earned or accrued. The present value of these future benefits is estimated to be about $950 billion; that is, a fund of $950 billion invested at interest would be just enough to pay all the future benefits to these persons and the fund would be exhausted at the time the last benefit payment fell due. Accordingly, the accrued liability for benefits payable to these 35 million persons may be said to be $950 billion.

It is more difficult to define the accrued liability for the more than 100 million persons who have participated in the Social Security program at some time in the past and who are potential recipients of benefits at some time in the future. Because of their earlier participation, these persons may be considered to have earned or accrued a certain portion of the benefits that will be paid to them at some time in the future. It should be emphasized, however, that these benefits are not vested from a legal point of view because, in theory at least, the entire program could be terminated by Congress at any time. Section 1104 of the Social Security Act provides that "The right to alter, amend, or repeal any provision of this Act is hereby reserved to the Congress." As a practical matter, however, it is more reasonable to assume that Social Security will continue without abrupt change. A variety of methods can be used to calculate the amount of benefits and the value thereof that should be assigned to this earlier participation. According to a recent study made by the Office of the Actuary of the Social Security Administration,[6] it is reasonable to consider this accrued liability as of January 1, 1979 to be approximately $2,750 billion.

When that amount is added to the accrued liability of $950 billion for those persons already receiving benefits, the result is a total accrued liability of some $3,700 billion. Since the OASDI trust funds had assets of about $32 billion on January 1, 1979, the "unfunded accrued liability" could be considered to be about $3,668 billion, or $3.7 trillion. The unfunded accrued liability as of any given date may be viewed as the amount by which benefits, paid or promised with respect to earlier years of participation in the system, exceed the amount of taxes paid during those years by employees and their employers.

HI Accrued Liability

There has been little, if any, concern expressed about the accrued liability under the HI program. Yet, the HI program is similar to the OASDI program in most respects that are relevant to an accrued liability. Hospital Insurance is, in effect, a deferred benefit commencing at age 65 (or, if earlier, after the receipt of twenty-four months of disability benefits). The benefit is not paid in cash but rather in kind in the form of partial provision of hospital services. An individual may not be hospitalized and thus may not appear to receive tangible benefits; nevertheless, benefits are received just as surely as if cash benefits were paid to the individual in the amounts necessary to purchase the Hospital Insurance benefits. The program is financed by a portion of the Social Security taxes paid by active workers. To be eligible for HI benefits, a retired worker must be eligible for monthly old-age benefits, which in turn requires a certain minimum period of tax-paying participation in Social Security.

At the beginning of 1979, there were approximately 26.5 million persons eligible to receive partial reimbursement for hospital costs in the event of their illness. All conditions had been met for these benefits to be payable in the future, thus the benefits may be considered to have been fully earned or accrued without further payment of Social Security taxes by the individuals eligible for benefits. The present value of these future benefits is estimated to be about $400 billion; that is, a fund of $400 billion invested at interest would be just enough to pay all the future benefits to these persons and the fund would be exhausted at the time the last benefit payment fell due. Accordingly, the accrued liability for benefits payable to these 26.5 million persons may be said to be $400 billion.

Similarly, it is reasonable to assume that an accrued liability exists for the more than 100 million persons who have participated in the Social Security program at some time in the past and who are potential recipients of benefits at some time in the future. Because of their earlier participation, these persons may be considered to have earned or accrued a certain portion of the HI benefits that will be paid to them in the future, although these benefits are not vested from a legal point of view. No formal estimates have been made of this accrued liability by the actuaries of the Health Care Financing Administration; however, it is probably of the magnitude of $1,100 billion. When that amount is added to the accrued liability of $400 billion for those persons already eligible for HI benefits, the result is a total accrued liability of about $1,500 billion. Since the HI trust fund had assets of $11 billion as of January 1, 1979, this would still leave an "unfunded accrued liability" of $1,489 billion, or about $1.5 trillion. Just as with the OASDI program, the unfunded accrued liability as of any given date may be viewed as the amount by which benefits, paid or promised with respect to earlier years of participation in the system, exceed the amount of taxes paid during those years by employees and their employers.

SMI Accrued Liability

The accrued liability for the SMI program is somewhat more elusive and difficult to define because of two features that distinguish it from the OASDI and HI programs:

Participation is voluntary, although some 95 percent of those eligible are in fact participants.

Eligibility does not depend upon whether past Social Security taxes have been paid; rather, it depends upon whether "premiums" are paid after eligibility for benefits commences. Anyone eligible for the HI program is eligible for SMI, but anyone aged 65 and over with at least five years' residence in the United States is also eligible.

These differences are more of form than substance, however. Virtually everyone who becomes eligible will undoubtedly elect to participate in SMI, and participation will continue throughout his remaining lifetime. Furthermore, although eligibility does not depend upon the payment of Social Security taxes, the premiums required for eligibility are so insignificant it seems reasonable to assume that the right to receive SMI benefits after age 65 accrues ratably during a person's working lifetime prior to age 65.

At the beginning of 1979 there were approximately 26.3 million persons eligible to receive partial reimbursement for medical costs covered under the SMI program. All conditions had been met for these benefits to be payable in the future provided only that the participants continue to pay nominal premiums. For this group of participants, the premiums represent less than 20 percent of the total cost of future benefits; therefore, it is virtually certain that present participants will continue their eligibility by paying premiums.

The present value of the portion of these future benefits that will not be financed by the participants' premiums and thus will be paid from general revenue is estimated to be about $100 billion. This may be termed the accrued liability for these 26.3 million participants.

Similarly, it seems reasonable to assume that an accrued liability exists for the more than 100 million persons who are in the active work force paying taxes (personal income taxes, not payroll taxes) to support the SMI program and who will be eligible for SMI benefits when they reach age 65. Just as with the other parts of Social Security, from a strictly legal point of view there are no vested benefits or accrued liabilities because the entire program can be terminated at any time. It seems more reasonable, however, to assume that the SMI program will continue without abrupt change.

Although no formal estimates have been made of this accrued liability by the actuaries of the Health Care Financing Administration, it is probably of the magnitude of $300 billion. When that amount is added to the accrued liability of $100 billion for those persons already eligible for SMI benefits, the result is a total accrued liability of about $400 billion. Since the SMI trust fund had assets of $4 billion as of January 1, 1979, this would leave an unfunded accrued liability of $396 billion, or about $0.4 trillion. The unfunded accrued liability as of any given date may be viewed as the amount by which benefits, paid or promised with respect to earlier years of participation in the system, exceed the amount of premiums paid by participants and general taxes paid by all taxpayers (and allocated to the SMI program) during those years.

The Significance of the Accrued Liability

The total accrued liability as of January 1, 1979, under Social Security (OASDI, HI, and SMI combined) is some $5,600 billion, or about $6 trillion. The total assets of the Social Security trust funds are only $48 billion, thus the *unfunded* accrued liability is also approximately $6 trillion.

This unfunded accrued liability is based upon the intermediate set of demographic and economic assumptions used by the Social Security actuaries in making projections for the 1979 Trustees Reports. It would not be markedly different based upon the optimistic or pessimistic assumptions referred to previously. Compared with the actuarial deficit, there is relatively little variation in the unfunded accrued liability based upon the alternative assumptions. This is true, in part, because the unfunded accrued liability is related to a closed group of existing participants in Social Security and is thus independent of future birth rates.

As indicated in Chapter 6, if the Social Security program were a private system, it would be considered desirable to begin to collect more income than is necessary for current benefit payments and to accumulate a substantial fund in order to transform this *unfunded* accrued liability into a *funded* accrued liability. But, as also discussed in Chapter 6, it is not necessary to fund the Social Security accrued liability if it is assumed that Social Security will exist forever and that its promised benefits, together with other national commitments for the future, are consistent with the nation's ability to produce in the future. In other words, an unfunded accrued liability is not necessarily unacceptable for the Social Security program.

The existence of an unfunded accrued liability is significant, however, and should not be dismissed lightly—as some observers are wont to do. As already noted, an accrued liability represents the value of benefits that have been earned or accrued as of today but that will not be paid until a later date. A small part of the accrued liability is funded but most of it is unfunded. The unfunded accrued liability represents the value of benefits that have been promised as a result of service to date but that have not yet been paid for.

In other words, persons who have participated in Social Security the past forty years or so have received benefits (some of which will not be paid until later) of considerably greater value than the taxes they have paid. This excess value is equal to the unfunded accrued liability or approximately $6 trillion. Is it any wonder that we heard so few complaints about Social Security during its first forty years of existence? If taxpayers had paid the full cost of benefits accruing the past forty years, their taxes would have been about five times as much as were actually paid.

Some critics advocate terminating Social Security, part of their reasoning being that it will resolve its financial problems. If Social Security were terminated today *and* if we satisfied the promises made to date, we would have to pay benefits to millions of people currently receiving benefits or expecting to receive benefits in the future (only the benefits earned because of past service and excluding benefits that would have been earned in the future). This would require a lump sum amount today of $6 trillion (the unfunded accrued liability) or an equivalent amount spread over future years. The nation thus has a "hidden liability" of approximately $43,000 for every adult now between ages 20 and 65, or more than $24,000 for every living man, woman, and child regardless of age. This is seven times the estimated national debt of $800 billion as of January 1, 1979, the government's officially acknowledged liability.

The fact we must face is that we have made promises worth $6 trillion more than we have collected in taxes in the past. The choices are not many. We can make good on the promises by collecting higher future taxes than would have been required otherwise, or we can renounce some of the promises already made. Some would favor continuing to hide this unfunded accrued liability; but, whether hidden or explicitly acknowledged, it represents a significant lien on the nation's goods and services to be produced in the future.

Conclusion

We have seen that the existence of an unfunded accrued liability is not necessarily a sign of financial weakness in our Social Security system, provided we have arranged for future tax collections that are adequate to pay future benefits. In the final analysis, the future financial stability of Social Security depends upon the ability and willingness of the nation's workers and employers to continue to pay the taxes necessary to support the benefit payments.

The combined tax rate in 1980 was 12.26 percent of taxable payroll (6.13 percent from the worker and 6.13 percent from the employer). The combined tax rate is *scheduled* to rise to 15.30 percent by 1990, although the taxpayers have not yet demonstrated their willingness to pay these increased taxes.

The actuarial deficits under our present Social Security program imply *tax increases above and beyond those already scheduled.* To eliminate these substantial actuarial deficits, it seems likely that the combined tax rates under the OASDI and HI programs must rise to at least 24 percent within the next forty or fifty years: that is, double the present tax rates. Under more pessimistic assumptions, these tax rates must be triple the present rates. In addition, substantial but as yet unrecognized future taxes will be required to support the SMI program.

Painful as it may be to communicate this information to the taxpayer, it must be done. Since the financial stability of Social Security is based upon the taxpayer's *ability and willingness* to pay future taxes, we have a compelling obligation to keep the taxpayer informed about how high those taxes may be. If we are not willing to so advise the taxpayer, we have no right to use a current-cost financing method whose very foundation is the taxpayer's *ability and willingness* to make future tax payments.

Part Three
Commentary on
Selected Topics

Part Two contained basic descriptions of the Social Security program and the way it works. It gave the background information to permit a more informed discussion of Social Security—the way it is now and the way the reader may wish it to be in the future.

Part Three is designed to answer in a more direct way some of the questions that are frequently raised about Social Security. Also, it presents a commentary on aspects of Social Security that are ignored too frequently. In some cases the commentary will stand on its own; however, in others it will be more meaningful if Part Two has been read previously. To the extent the commentary on a topic is self-contained, it may duplicate other sections of the book.

8
Public Understanding of Social Security

The most important problem confronting Social Security in the immediate future is not the program's high cost, mismanagement, inappropriate benefits, unfair treatment of participants, or any of the other charges directed at it by critics. The major problem facing Social Security is the widespread lack of understanding of the program—its basic rationale, the type and level of benefits it provides, the method of financing, the significance of the high future cost, and the tenuous relationship between taxes paid and benefits received by an individual. The average individual does not know what Social Security is really all about. He does not know what to expect from Social Security. Should he expect it to meet all of his needs (and those of his dependents) in the event of old age, disability, death, or sickness? Or should he expect it to be merely a floor of protection in meeting these needs, a floor upon which he and his employer should build through supplemental private saving and insurance and some form of retirement program? Apart from his expectations, what type and level of benefits does Social Security actually provide in meeting these various needs? Most people don't know.

Social Security was enacted on August 14, 1935, some forty-five years ago. It is not a new program and no sudden and dramatic revisions have been made. The Social Security Administration has published millions of pamphlets explaining Social Security. The news media—radio, television, magazines, and newspapers—have issued billions of words and pictures on the subject. Hundreds of books have been written about every aspect of Social Security. So how did this public misunderstanding come about? It is probably a result of the following combination of factors.

First, in explaining Social Security over the years the government has employed certain rhetoric that has contributed to the confusion. The use of words and phrases like "insurance," "trust fund," "account," "contributions," and "earned right," while not necessarily wrong, has sometimes conveyed the wrong impression. Although the government may not have deliberately misled the public, it certainly has not been in the forefront of a movement to explain to the public the rationale of the Social Security program.

Moreover, during the first forty years of the program, the public did not devote very much effort to finding out what Social Security was all about. Taxes (euphemistically called "contributions") were fairly low; benefits to a retiring individual were high in relation to the taxes that had been paid; it almost seemed like something for nothing. That should have been reason enough to provoke a few more penetrating questions by the public than were actually asked. Over the past two or three years, however, this public apathy has evaporated just as rapidly as Social Security taxes have risen. An increasing number of people pay more in Social Security taxes than they do in federal income taxes. In 1980 an employee who earned $25,900 or more paid $1,587.67 in Social Security taxes. This was matched by his employer, resulting in total tax payments of $3,175.34. By the year 1990 this tax for a high wage earner will have increased to an estimated $4,039.20 for the employee and another $4,039.20 for the employer, or a total of $8,078.40. No longer will the public be indifferent to Social Security—the taxes paid and the benefits received.

Lastly, the media should assume some responsibility for the misunderstanding. It takes considerable time and effort to learn enough about Social Security to report on it in a meaningful way. Not enough people have been willing to invest that much time, and the result has been an undue amount of incomplete and confusing media coverage of the program.

If this general misunderstanding of Social Security continues, the inevitable result will be growing dissatisfaction and frustration among the taxpayers, and increasing reluctance to pay the taxes required to support the program. There is no excuse for permitting this lack of understanding to continue. Widespread understanding of the Social Security program may result in a certain amount of trauma and even disruption among the public, but even more disruption will result if the current misunderstanding is allowed to continue.

It is unlikely that rational changes can be made in the Social Security program as long as the present low level of understanding of the program exists. In the future, public understanding or misunderstanding will play a much more critical role in determining the shape of the program than it has in the past when the payroll tax was relatively low and when the taxpayer was in a less questioning frame of mind. If people understand Social Security, there is a much greater chance that the program will be modified to coincide with their desires and thus gain the public acceptance obviously necessary for a program that will pay benefits, and require tax collections, of almost three trillion dollars during the next ten years.

Accordingly, a careful analysis should be made of the Social Security program, as well as the various other governmental income maintenance programs, to determine exactly what policy is inherent in such programs. This rationale, once determined, should be explained clearly to the public. Everyone should understand the extent to which an individual is responsible for himself and his dependents in the event of his retirement, disability, death, or sickness and the extent to which the government (supported by the resources of the working segment of the population) is responsible.

In addition to the rationale, the cost of Social Security both now and in the future should be acknowledged and explained clearly to the public. No further attempts should be made to conceal the cost, to minimize the importance of the cost, or to apologize for the cost. Such efforts will not change the cost in any way.

After having been informed of the rationale, the cost, and other features of the Social Security program, the public will then be in a position to reaffirm the program or ask that it be revised. It seems likely that some change will be called for as the real cost and significance of Social Security become known. It is entirely possible that the public will reverse the trend in recent years of increasing governmental intervention in private affairs and decide that the "government should provide" only those benefits that can be provided in no other way, and that the individual should be responsible for himself and his dependents to the fullest extent possible.

9
The Need for a Periodic Benefit Statement

When you reach age 65 there is a good chance that you will be eligible for a monthly retirement benefit from one or more sources: Social Security, employer-sponsored retirement plan, personal insurance and annuity policies, and so on. If you become disabled prior to retirement, you may be eligible likewise for disability benefits from several sources. Moreover, if you die your spouse and children may be eligible for various "survivors benefits."

It is obviously important that you and your family know, at least approximately, the type and level of benefits that will be payable in these various events. Such knowledge will enable you to make private arrangements to fill any needs that may not be satisfied by Social Security and the various employee benefit programs in which you participate. Without full knowledge of the benefits that may be payable by programs outside your immediate control, it is almost certain that you will either overprovide or underprovide for your own future needs and those of your family.

It is difficult to obtain this information about your eligibility for future benefits. The prospects have brightened in recent years, however, and the future looks even better.

111

Private Pension Plan Benefits

Some employers have always done a good job informing employees about details of their employee benefit plans; others have not.

Congress passed the Employee Retirement Income Security Act (ERISA) in 1974 which required, among other things, that the administrator of a private pension plan make available to the employees copies of the plan and related documents as well as a summary of the essential features and provisions.

The Internal Revenue Code has long required that a qualified pension plan be reduced to writing and communicated by appropriate means to the plan participants and their beneficiaries. It was ERISA, however, that first required the plan administrator to furnish each participant and beneficiary a summary plan description written in a manner "calculated to be understood by the average plan participant or beneficiary." This is important since a plan document is usually complex and written in legal jargon.

The summary plan description must include the important plan provisions, a description of benefits, the circumstances that may result in disqualification or ineligibility, and the procedures to be followed in presenting claims for benefits under the plan. Upon the request of a plan participant or beneficiary, the plan administrator must provide, on the basis of the latest information available, the total benefits that have accrued in respect of the participant, as well as those that have vested, that is, become nonforfeitable. No more than one request per year may be made by a participant or beneficiary for this information. When an employee terminates from a plan with vested benefits, the employer is obligated to provide him without request a statement of the amount of his vested benefits.

This level of information disclosure is a vast improvement over practices that prevailed in the past. There is still much room for improvement, however, in providing information that is complete enough to be of value yet simple enough to be understood. Public employee retirement plans (covering employees of federal, state, county, and municipal governments) are not subject to these ERISA disclosure requirements;

hence, the amount of information disclosed varies considerably among public employee groups. Some public employees are well informed about their benefits; others are not.

Social Security Benefits

Social Security is another matter. Information is available (for those who seek it out) about the type and level of benefits that are payable in general. Very little information is available, however, about the benefits that may become payable to an individual in a particular situation. The average employee covered by Social Security does not know the amount of monthly benefits that would be payable to his spouse and children if he should die. Neither he nor his spouse realizes that some or all of these benefits may be lost if the surviving spouse works in paid employment after his death. Hardly any employee knows how much, if anything, would be payable in disability benefits if he should become unable to work any longer. This lack of information extends to almost every participant in Social Security and to every benefit provided.

In some instances, when employers provide estimates of private plan benefits that will be payable at retirement they also provide estimates of Social Security retirement benefits, particularly when there is an interrelationship between the benefits. Seldom, however, is detailed information provided about Social Security benefits that may be payable other than at retirement or, in some cases, disability.

Information Provided by the
Social Security Administration

Very little, if any, information is provided automatically to taxpayers about the specific benefits they may expect to receive from Social Security. It is possible for a taxpayer to go through life without receiving a single communication from the Social Security Administration (SSA) about his or her potential benefits.

This is not to say that the Social Security Administration tries to hide information about the program. Thousands of pamphlets are printed and distributed every year describing in general terms the benefits that are available. Radio, television, and newspapers often have public service announcements urging people to apply for benefits if they believe they are eligible. The Social Security Administration has hundreds of employees in offices throughout the country giving speeches to civic meetings and various groups of employees to explain Social Security. Nevertheless, this is a small effort compared to the large numbers of people who need more information: 35 million people currently receiving benefits and 115 million people (and their employers) paying taxes.

The Social Security Administration does make a concerted effort to see that benefits are paid to everyone who is eligible. District offices of Social Security throughout the country are responsible for developing and maintaining outreach activities with organizations and institutions having knowledge of potential claimants so they can be contacted by SSA representatives. In many cases a death claim is filed by a funeral home or other party that has paid the burial expenses. When such a claim is filed (the maximum death benefit is $255), SSA usually follows up to see if any survivors benefits are payable (sometimes worth hundreds of thousands of dollars). SSA representatives in many areas make routine visits to hospitals to determine whether anyone may be eligible for disability or other benefits.

The Medicare program poses a particular problem of making certain that everyone who is eligible for benefits actually receives them. Medicare becomes available at age 65 whether you are retired or still working. When you apply for retirement benefits, this is an automatic application for Medicare. If you do not retire by age 65, you must apply for Medicare separately. If someone is within three months of age 65 and has not applied for benefits, SSA has generally attempted to contact such person to advise of his eligibility for Medicare. SSA is handicapped in this area, however, since its records do not indicate current addresses (only the address at the time the Social Security number was issued). SSA used to obtain many of these addresses from the Internal Revenue Service files of individual income tax returns; however, recent privacy legislation prohibits sharing of personal information among the government agencies, and SSA no longer has access to current addresses of its taxpayers.

By one means or another most persons learn eventually of their eligibility and receive most of the benefits to which they are entitled. The most common loss is probably from filing a late application and losing benefits because of limits on making retroactive payments.

In contrast to the information it furnishes automatically, the Social Security Administration provides a much broader range of information to those who request it. Unfortunately, not enough people realize the burden is on them to ask for information and even fewer know how to articulate their requests.

Consider the following example of special information that can be obtained. You can file a form with SSA (Form OAR-7004, available at any Social Security office) and request "a statement of your Social Security earnings." You will then receive a statement showing the amount of earnings on which Social Security taxes have been paid in each of the past three years, as well as the total for your lifetime. It is important that you request this earnings statement and verify your records at least every three years so that any errors can be corrected. In general, an earnings record can be corrected at any time up to three years, three months, and fifteen days after the year in which earnings were received. SSA used to encourage people to check their earnings statements regularly but, for some reason, no longer does this.

There is not much use for the information in the earnings statement except to verify SSA's records of your earnings. It will not enable you to determine your current eligibility for benefits or to calculate the amount of such benefits. You can request additional information, however, when you file Form OAR-7004 by appropriately annotating the form. For example you could ask for:

The number of quarters of coverage on your record. This would help you determine whether you meet the requirements for various benefits.

An itemized record of your covered earnings by employer and calendar quarter beginning with your first quarter of employment and continuing to the present. This would help you compute the approximate amount of benefits to which you may become entitled (except

this is such a complicated calculation that it requires
an expert to do it).

An estimate of the amount of benefits you can expect to
receive at retirement. SSA frequently computes this
benefit estimate by assuming that you have no covered
earnings in the future—an assumption that tends to
underestimate your benefits. Furthermore, SSA pre-
fers to provide this information only for persons within
five years of retirement, that is, aged 57 or older.

Of course you can visit (or call or write) a local Social Security
office at any time and request any information you desire.
Chances are, if you have a reasonable request, it will be
satisfied. SSA offices are probably best equipped to help you at
the time you actually apply for benefits. It is in furnishing
information prior to eligibility for benefits that SSA is most
deficient.

The Need for More Information

The procedures currently followed by the Social Security
Administration fall short of satisfying the following reasonable
objectives:

A worker and family should know enough details about the
type and level of benefits to enable them personally to
provide such supplemental benefits as they believe
necessary in the event of retirement, disability, illness,
or death of the worker or the worker's spouse.

Workers and their employers should receive an accounting
that is compatible with the substantial amounts of
taxes they pay to support Social Security—total taxes
per person of as much as $3,175 in 1980 and $3,950 in
1981 (and an estimated $8,078 in 1990).

Some of the current public dissatisfaction with Social Security is because people do not fully realize the scope of benefits
payable. Better understanding would almost certainly result in
better acceptance of Social Security.

There are subtle yet important dangers of not providing
periodic benefit statements and not properly explaining Social
Security. One of these dangers is that a person may begin to
assume that "someone else" is making provision for his retire-

ment, disability, illness, or death. Then, when he actually needs the benefits he may find that "someone else" has not done the job to his satisfaction. The high taxes we are paying make it easy for us to build up unreasonably high expectations for benefits from Social Security. Such benefits are expensive, however, and the fact is that if Social Security met *all* of our economic security needs, substantially higher taxes would be required.

On the other hand, the opposite of unexpectedly small benefits may occur. "Someone else" may begin providing you with benefits that you do not particularly need or want and at a cost that you may not be willing to pay. As taxpayers, we need to assert more control over the size and shape of the Social Security program, and an important beginning step is to have a better understanding of the benefits being provided.

All of this points to a simple conclusion. The Social Security Administration and the Health Care Financing Administration should be providing all participants—taxpayers and benefit recipients alike—with comprehensive periodic benefit statements.

Each person who is receiving Social Security benefits should be given clear and simple information about:

> The amount of benefits and the conditions under which they will continue to be payable. Particular care should be taken in explaining how hospital and medical expenses will be shared by the beneficiary and the Medicare program.
>
> Events that will change those benefits (death of one of the beneficiaries, changes in the Consumer Price Index, remarriage, changes in average hospital and medical costs, earned income in excess of specified amounts, etc.). Increases in deductibles and coinsurance under Hospital Insurance, and increases in SMI premiums, should not come as a surprise. Reductions in monthly benefits because of earned income should not come as a surprise. In fact, nothing should come as a surprise to a beneficiary.
>
> The way in which such benefits are financed. If taxes (payroll or other) are increased to continue providing benefits, this should be noted. If benefits are increased

(or reduced), this should be explained and any associated increase (or decrease) in taxes should be noted. The status of the trust funds should be included in this financial report. Media headlines should not have to be relied upon for this information.

Each person who is paying Social Security taxes and who will not receive benefits until some future date should be given clear and simple information about:

The approximate amount of Social Security benefits that would be payable if the taxpayer should die or become disabled during the coming year, the conditions under which such benefits would continue to be paid, and the events that would change the benefits.

The approximate amount of Social Security benefits that would be payable when the taxpayer becomes eligible for retirement, the conditions under which the benefits would be paid, and the events that would change the benefits in any way.

The amount of Social Security payroll taxes paid by the individual taxpayer and the amount of earnings recorded for use in future benefit computations, for the most recent accounting period. This would permit ready verification by the taxpayer of information vital to the computation of future benefits.

The financial status of the various parts of the Social Security program. If Social Security payroll taxes were not adequate to pay benefits for the most recent accounting period and if general revenue were used, the amount should be noted. If the government borrowed money to pay current benefits, this should be noted and an explanation given of when and by whom the debt will be repaid. If tax increases (or decreases) or benefit increases (or decreases) are imminent, they should be reported and explained. The taxpayer deserves more than media headlines.

The preceding list of items for possible inclusion in a periodic benefit statement is not exhaustive. It is given to illustrate the kind of information that taxpayers and beneficiaries might find useful in evaluating Social Security and making personal plans for their future financial security.

Some may argue that providing this information is too costly—that it will require more government employees and thus will require higher taxes. This is true but is also largely irrelevant. Administrative expenses for Social Security currently amount to only about 2 percent of benefit payments. A relatively small increase in expenses in order to advise us about our benefits would not jeopardize the program; on the contrary, it would strengthen the program and make it more valuable to us.

Some may argue that Social Security is too large to permit the provision of individual benefit statements to 35 million beneficiaries and more than 100 million taxpayers—that the system would drown in its own paperwork. If this is true, and if Social Security has become so large and complex and difficult to administer that it cannot even provide taxpayers with details about what they are receiving for their tax dollars, then it should be transformed into a system that is manageable and understandable. There is a frightening possibility that this is, in fact, the situation and that in due time it will become evident to all concerned that Social Security has become so cumbersome that it cannot be administered—that an "administrative breakdown" is on the horizon.

These arguments notwithstanding, there is no excuse for the Social Security Administration not to provide periodic benefit statements that keep us informed about the benefits we can expect to receive in the future.

10
A Program of Future Promises— Fulfilled or Broken?

The actuary's job is to make forecasts about the future. Many other people do this in addition to the actuary: crystal ball gazers, seers, fortune tellers, economists, weathermen, and so on.

All of these people have one thing in common. When they forecast good news, their audience is grateful and happy. When they forecast bad news, their audience is unhappy and sometimes even belligerent. Moreover, people are so reluctant to believe bad news that they usually either refuse to listen or they label the forecaster as a panicmonger.

The actuary frequently has a thankless task. When he is making forecasts about possible future costs of pension benefits, his conclusion is almost always that future costs will be much higher than they are at present, that they will be much higher than most people expect, and that it may be difficult to pay for such pensions.

Why is it important to forecast the future costs of a program like Social Security? *Social Security is a program of future promises.*

Consider a retired man and his dependent wife who are both aged 65 and receiving a monthly Social Security check of $600.

Social Security promises to continue paying this monthly check as long as both the man and his wife are alive; the program also promises to pay $400 a month as long as the man lives after the death of his wife; or to pay $400 a month to the wife as long as she lives after the death of her husband.

But that is not all; Social Security promises to increase these monthly benefits so that they will keep up with the cost of living as measured by changes in the Consumer Price Index. If the cost of living increases 5 percent a year, in just fifteen years this $600 check will more than double to $1,247. If the cost of living increases 8 percent a year, this $600 check will more than triple to $1,903 within fifteen years.

This is a substantial promise which involves a lot of money (its "present value" is roughly $100,000) and a long period of years (benefits could still be payable thirty to forty years from now).

Let's take another example. Consider a male worker aged 20 who is just now entering the work force in employment covered by Social Security. The Social Security program makes the following promises:

If the worker dies at an early age, leaving behind a dependent wife and children, monthly benefits will be paid, not necessarily continuously, during the next fifty to seventy-five years.

If the worker becomes disabled at an early age, monthly benefits will be paid to the worker (and possibly to his wife and children) during the next fifty to seventy-five years.

If the worker lives to retirement at age 65 (forty-five years from now), monthly benefits will be paid to the worker for the remainder of his life (and possibly to his wife, if she survives him, for the remainder of her life), promises spanning the next seventy-five or more years.

In each of these cases, benefits will be related to the worker's average monthly earnings in the future, and benefits, once commenced, will be adjusted for changes in the cost of living.

Hundreds of other promises are made about benefits that will be paid during the next seventy-five to one hundred years. When we make these promises about the benefits Social Security will pay during the next seventy-five years or so, with respect to the millions of people now living and paying Social Security taxes, it is essential that we make every reasonable effort to determine whether we can make good on the promises. There are two basic approaches we can take.

The first one is what I call the "head-in-the-sand" approach. We can determine the type and level of benefits that we think people *need*. We can determine the costs of paying such benefits during the next *two or three years,* and if these costs don't seem too high, we can adopt the benefits and *let the future take care of itself.* Sad to say, many policymakers prefer this approach although they might not describe it in quite these terms.

The other approach is to make a reasonable effort to look ahead throughout the period over which the promises have been made and determine their likely future costs. It can then be decided whether or not we can afford the cost of such promises, not only for the next two or three years, but for the period of approximately seventy-five years during which we will have to make good on our promises.

This is the task of the actuary: to do the best job possible of forecasting future expenditures under the program over a long period of years to determine whether it seems reasonable to make such promises in view of the income that is similarly forecast over the same period. It cannot be concluded, of course, that today's projections of future Social Security expenditures will be highly accurate. The cost of the program will depend on a variety of changeable factors such as the rate of future economic growth and future fertility levels. Social Security actuaries realize this fact, however, and make projections on the basis of alternative sets of economic and demographic assumptions that span a range considered reasonable by most professional analysts.

Our knowledge of the future is limited, to be sure; but it is not as limited as many people assume. Consider the following:

Eighty-five percent of the people who are going to receive old-age retirement benefits at any time during the next seventy-five years are alive today.

These people will receive 96 percent of the total old-age retirement benefits that are paid during the next seventy-five years.

Of the total Social Security taxes that will be paid during the next fifty years, 81 percent will be paid by people who are now alive. For the first twenty-five years the figure is 99 percent.

Thus, while many of the projection factors are subject to substantial variation, the basic numbers of people who will be tomorrow's workers and beneficiaries can be determined today with reasonable certainty. The purpose of long-range projections is not to predict the future with certainty (no one, obviously, can do that) but rather to indicate how the Social Security program would operate in the future under a variety of economic and demographic conditions, any of which could reasonably be expected to occur. Such projections provide a valuable test of the reasonableness and long-range viability of the Social Security provisions that we enact today.

The extent to which we are interested in projections of future income and outgo of the Social Security program and the prospects for its continued financial health depends in part upon our own age. A person just now retiring at age 65 may be content to worry about Social Security's financial health for about the next twenty years or so. On the other hand, a person now aged 40 should be concerned about Social Security's financial health during the next fifty years at least. The Veteran's Administration is keenly aware of the long-range nature of pension promises. In mid-1979 the VA was still making monthly benefit payments to 103 widows and 142 needy children of Civil War veterans, both Union and Confederate.

The "head-in-the-sand" approach is taken by far too many people. I have watched in amazement as prominent politicians, policymakers, and labor leaders have taken this approach. It is understandable, perhaps even forgivable, for a layman to take this approach, particularly if he has never had the situation properly explained to him. It is completely irresponsible, however, for a politician or a labor leader or a policymaker to take such an approach, especially when he has been informed about the long-range consequences of promises inherent in a social insurance program. There is no excuse for persons in responsible positions not to familiarize themselves with the possible long-range consequences of their actions.

It is important to note that the Board of Trustees of the Social Security program has not been consistent in assessing our nation's ability to fulfill the promises we have made under the various parts of Social Security. Specifically, consider the following:

> *Old-Age, Survivors, and Disability Insurance Programs:* Projections are made for seventy-five years; however, there is steady pressure from the "head-in-the-sand" devotees to reduce this to as short a period as twenty-five years and thus to ignore the consequences of the inevitable transition from the present youthful population to a future older population.
>
> *Hospital Insurance Program:* Projections are made for only twenty-five years. Hospital Insurance benefits are paid principally for persons aged 65 and over; thus Hospital Insurance benefits may be viewed as a form of retirement benefit. Accordingly, it is just as important that seventy-five-year projections be made for these benefits as it is for the old-age benefits.
>
> *Supplementary Medical Insurance Program:* Projections are made for *only three years.* These benefits are paid for substantially the same persons who receive Hospital Insurance benefits and thus are just another form of retirement benefit; hence, it is as important that seventy-five-year projections be made for these benefits as it is for the cash old-age benefits and the Hospital Insurance benefits. Any report that the SMI program is in "sound financial health" is practically meaningless since projections are made for only three years.

It seems clear that we should do a better job of recognizing the cost implications of the longer term promises we have made under our Social Security program. As indicated in Chapter 4, the present Social Security program makes promises that we cannot keep unless tax rates are at least doubled within the working lifetime of today's young people. We must examine our Social Security program carefully in the light of its possible long-range costs and make whatever changes we believe are advisable.

The purpose of the long-range cost estimates made by an actuary is not to scare people or to cause unrest about the future viability of Social Security. The purpose is to provide the information necessary to ensure that we do not make promises we cannot keep. The purpose is to make certain that Social Security is a program of *fulfilled promises,* not a program of *broken promises.*

11
Do We Get
Our Money's Worth
from Social Security?

A question that is being asked more and more often is "Do we get our money's worth from Social Security?" This question can be answered from several different points of view and each produces a different answer.

Taxes, Benefits, and Administrative Expenses

First, consider the Social Security program from the viewpoint of the nation as a whole, taking into account only the dollars involved. The total income and outgo, including interest earnings and administrative expenses, of the trust funds since the program's inception are summarized in Table 11.1 for the three parts of Social Security that are supported primarily by payroll taxes. Table 11.1 shows that over the years about $1,000 billion has been collected in payroll taxes. Normally, as these taxes were collected, they were used almost immediately to pay benefits. This procedure is known as "current-cost" or "pay-as-you-go" financing and is one of the fundamental characteristics of our Social Security program, as discussed in Chapter 6. For a variety of reasons, the taxes collected plus other trust fund income are not exactly equal to benefits and administra-

127

Table 11.1

Summary of Cumulative Income and Outgo under the Old-Age, Survivors, Disability, and Hospital Insurance Programs, 1937–79
(Amounts in Billions)

	Old-Age and Survivors Insurance[a]	Disability Insurance[b]	Hospital Insurance[c]	Total
	(1)	(2)	(3)	(4)
Payroll Taxes	$796.0	$100.6	$127.7[d]	$1,024.3
Interest Earnings	32.4	4.7	5.5	42.6
General Revenue	6.1	0.9	8.4	15.4
Total Income	$834.5	$106.2	$141.6	$1,082.3
Benefit Payments	$796.8[e]	$ 97.0[f]	$125.2	$1,019.0
Administrative Expenses	13.0	3.6	3.2	19.8
Total Expenditures	$809.8	$100.6	$128.4	$1,038.8
Excess of Income Over Expenditures (Value of Trust Funds on 12-31-79)	$ 24.7	$ 5.6	$ 13.2	$ 43.5

[a]Taxes were first collected in 1937; monthly benefits were first paid in 1940.
[b]Taxes were first collected and benefits first paid in 1957.
[c]Taxes were first collected in January 1966; benefits were first paid in July 1966.
[d]Includes $1.3 billion in net transfers from the Railroad Retirement Fund and $0.06 billion in HI premiums paid by uninsured voluntary enrollees.
[e]Includes $14.6 billion in net transfers to the Railroad Retirement Fund and $0.07 billion in payments for vocational rehabilitation services.
[f]Includes $0.4 billion in net transfers to the Railroad Retirement Fund and $0.6 billion in payments for vocational rehabilitation services.

tive expenses paid in a given period. Any excess of income over expenditures is maintained in the appropriate trust fund for the payment of future benefits during periods when income is less than outgo. As indicated by Table 11.1, total income to the OASI, DI, and HI trust funds from 1937 through 1979 exceeded total expenditures by $43.5 billion—and this amount was present in the three funds at the beginning of 1980.

Trust fund assets are invested in U.S. Treasury securities, primarily special issues yielding interest at the same rate as the average of all outstanding long-term Treasury securities. During the twelve months ending June 30, 1979, the effective annual rate of interest earned by the combined assets of these three trust funds was approximately 7.5 percent. Total OASDHI interest earnings in 1937–1979 were $42.6 billion. The reason the interest earnings appear relatively small compared to the $1,000 billion in tax income is that the amount in the trust funds at any given time has been small relative to the total amount of benefit payments. The relatively low level of trust fund assets at any given time is consistent with the fund's purpose as a contingency reserve to cover any temporary short-falls that occur as a result of current-cost financing. Table 11.1 also indicates that administrative expenses have been low, amounting to only 2 percent of the benefit payments for all three trust funds combined.

Table 11.2 summarizes similar information on income and outgo for the Supplementary Medical Insurance trust fund. This program is not supported by payroll taxes, but rather by premiums paid by those electing to participate and by general revenue derived from all taxpayers (not just Social Security taxpayers).

Table 11.2

Summary of Cumulative Income and Outgo Under the Supplementary Medical Insurance Program, 1966–79 (Amounts in Billions)[a]

Premiums from Enrollees	$21.3
General Revenue	35.1
Interest Earnings	1.4
Total Income	$57.8
Benefit Payments	$48.3
Administrative Expenses	4.6[b]
Total Expenditures	$52.9
Excess of Income Over Expenditures (Value of SMI Trust Fund on 12-31-79)	$ 4.9

[a]Premiums were first collected in January 1966; benefits were first paid in July 1966.
[b]SMI administrative expenses are higher (relative to benefits) than under OASDI or HI due to the many benefit claims, often involving small amounts.

There is no mismanagement of the trust funds, there is no significant waste in administering the programs, and there is no significant misapplication of the funds. That is, benefits are generally determined correctly and are paid to those who are entitled to receive them according to Social Security law. Mistakes are made, of course, but most of the spectacular stories of fraud and abuse that have appeared in recent years are about Supplemental Security Income and Medicaid, welfare programs which are more difficult to administer than the Social Security benefits being discussed here. Accordingly, an examination of the past financial operation of the four major parts of the Social Security program could easily lead one to conclude that "Yes, we do get our money's worth from Social Security."

Individual Equity

A second viewpoint from which to consider whether we get our money's worth is the viewpoint of the individual. Chapter 3 explained the types of benefits that are payable under Social Security, and Chapter 5 explained how taxes are assessed in order to pay for those benefits. A careful reading of those sections will indicate that there is relatively little connection between what an individual pays in taxes and receives in benefits. The system was not designed to pay benefits to an individual that are equivalent to his tax payments. Accordingly, it is a futile exercise (perhaps even a waste of time) for individuals to attempt to determine whether they can expect to receive benefits from Social Security that are commensurate with their tax payments. The answer is "No." As illustrated below, many participants can expect to receive much more in benefits than can be provided by their taxes and many can expect to receive much less. This does not mean the system has failed because it is "unfair"; it means simply that the system was never designed on the principle of individual equity or "fairness" for each participant—even if many people thought it was.

Therefore, if one ignores the value to the nation as a whole of the existence of our Social Security program and is concerned only with the direct value a particular individual receives in terms of benefits or benefit protection, the answer to the question of whether we get our money's worth from Social Security is "No. Some get more and some get less."

Ample support for this conclusion is provided in a recent study by actuaries at the Social Security Administration. This study[1] considered the value of benefits payable under Social Security throughout the lifetime of more than 100 hypothetical workers. The study took into account only the principal benefits: those payable in the event of retirement, death, and disability, including benefits payable with respect to a spouse and children, as well as to the worker. "Secondary benefits" were not taken into account by this study; for example, benefits to dependent parents or divorced spouses. These secondary benefits, although valuable to those who receive them, are not a significant part of the overall cost of Social Security. Medicare benefits were excluded to simplify the calculations.

After the value of the benefits was computed, it was determined how much the worker and the employer would have to pay in taxes to finance such benefits. The cost was expressed as a level percentage of the worker's earnings that are subject to Social Security tax. Administrative expenses, which amount to less than 2 percent of benefit payments, were ignored.[2]

The results of this study are not surprising to anyone who understands how Social Security works; however, they will be astonishing to those who think "you get what you pay for" when you pay Social Security taxes. Table 11.3 briefly describes four hypothetical workers[3] and shows the tax rates that would be payable by each worker and his employer if total taxes were equivalent to the total benefits during the lifetime of the worker and his dependents. *The theoretical tax rate is as low as 2 percent of earnings for some workers and as high as 26 percent of earnings for others.* In each case the employee tax would have to be matched by an equal employer tax. By way of contrast, the actual tax rate for all employees is 5.35 percent for 1981 (with a matching employer tax rate) and is estimated to be about 8 percent by the end of the working lifetime of today's new entrant to the work force. Of course this tax rate excludes Medicare taxes since Medicare benefits were excluded from the benefit values used in preparing Table 11.3. While these examples may not be typical of persons covered by Social Security, they do show that it is only sheer coincidence when a worker receives benefits that are equivalent to the taxes that he or she pays. This statement is true whether we consider employee taxes only, employee and employer taxes combined, or taxes of the self-employed.

It should be noted that the calculations shown in Table 11.3 are strictly theoretical, and it cannot be assumed that an

Table 11.3

Theoretical Tax Rate Payable by Workers and Employers, Each, If Taxes Are to Be Equivalent to Benefits for Selected Workers Entering the Work Force[a] in 1978

Brief Description of Worker[b]	Tax Rate Payable by Worker (with Matching Rate Payable by Employer)
Unmarried male who enters work force at age 22, works in steady employment at the maximum taxable earnings under Social Security, remains single, retires at age 70	2%
Unmarried female who enters work force at age 25, works in steady employment at the average earnings level for all workers covered by Social Security, remains single, retires at age 65	6%
Married male with dependent wife and two children, who enters work force at age 22, works in steady employment at the federal minimum wage, retires at age 65	12%
Married male with dependent wife who enters work force at age 52, works in steady part-time employment at high salary (that produces same annual income as full-time employment at the federal minimum wage), retires at age 65	26%

[a]In employment covered by Social Security
[b]Retirement age shown in each example represents age at which worker is assumed to retire if he or she has not died or become disabled prior to that age.

individual or a group of individuals with the characteristics indicated in Table 11.3 can duplicate Social Security benefits by means of private savings and insurance for the costs that are shown. Many benefits provided under Social Security are virtually impossible to duplicate outside a system covering practically the entire working population and having the assured tax revenue inherent in such a system. Chapter 17 discusses this and related points in more detail.

Equity Among Generations

A third viewpoint from which to consider whether we get our money's worth is that of the various generations of persons covered by Social Security. Under the current-cost method of financing used for the Social Security program, the amount of taxes collected each year is intended to be approximately equal to the benefits and administrative expenses paid during the year plus a small additional amount to maintain the trust funds at an appropriate contingency reserve level. This means that the taxes paid by one generation of workers are used to provide the benefits to an earlier generation of workers. Therefore, the taxes paid by a particular generation of workers are not necessarily equivalent to the cost of the benefits that generation will eventually receive.

For example, if benefit levels are increased over time (in addition to adjustments made for inflation), then any particular generation may receive benefits of greater value than the taxes it paid to become eligible for such benefits. On the other hand, if benefits are decreased or "deliberalized" over time, any particular generation may receive benefits of lesser value than the taxes it paid to become eligible for such benefits.

Also, the size of the working population relative to the retired population, now and in the future, is an important determinant of whether a given generation will receive benefits equivalent to the taxes it pays. Even if benefits are not increased from their present levels in relation to preretirement earnings, current projections indicate that future generations of workers must pay considerably higher tax rates than today's workers (at least 50 percent higher) because in the future the ratio of beneficiaries to taxpayers will be higher.

From the viewpoint of one generation compared with another, past generations have done extremely well. The case of Miss Ida Fuller is one well-known and extreme illustration. The program's very first beneficiary, Miss Fuller paid only about $22 in Social Security taxes prior to her retirement but lived to collect more than $20,000 in retirement benefits. Most early participants, of course, did not receive "actuarial bargains" of this magnitude. Still, on average, they have done remarkably well. Specifically, during the first forty years of Social Security's existence, the total taxes paid by employees and employers combined have amounted to only one-fifth of the value of the benefits that have been paid or promised with respect to this period of participation. In other words, during the past forty years, if the Social Security tax rates had been five times what they were, they would have been adequate to pay for the benefits that were "earned" during that period. This concept is discussed in more detail in Chapter 7.

Present and future generations will not fare as well. Social Security actuaries have estimated that the generation of workers currently entering the work force will receive benefits that in total are roughly 15 percent greater than those that can be provided by their Social Security taxes and those of their employers (based upon taxes scheduled by present law and ignoring Medicare benefits and taxes). Future generations should probably expect to receive less in benefits than can be provided by the total of employee and employer Social Security taxes; however, this will depend to some extent upon the timing of future changes in the benefits and upon fluctuations in future birth rates.

This question of equity among various generations is not as simple as it seems and it should be considered from a broad point of view. In recent American history, for example, each generation has enjoyed a better standard of living than the prior generation. At least some of the credit for this steady improvement in the standard of living should be given to the work, savings, and sacrifice of prior generations. Thus, it could be considered that the receipt by today's beneficiaries of benefits of greater value than could have been provided by their past taxes is a partial repayment for the sacrifices they made which resulted in a higher standard of living for later generations of workers. The point in mentioning this question of intergenerational equity is not to resolve it but rather to note that any consideration of money's worth from Social Security should be viewed from a broad perspective, taking into account much more than Social Security taxes paid and benefits received by a particular individual or group of individuals.

Are Benefits Appropriate?

There is yet a fourth point of view from which to consider the question of money's worth: whether we are buying the proper benefits with our Social Security tax dollars. Just because there is no significant waste in administering the Social Security program, it does not follow automatically that we get our money's worth from our tax dollars. Similarly, just because we may not be discontent with questions of equity among generations or among individuals within each generation, it does not follow automatically that we get our money's worth.

Perhaps we are providing the wrong benefits to the wrong people. To the extent that this is true, it can be said we do not get our money's worth from Social Security. It is difficult, if not impossible, to find a simple answer to questions about whether we are collecting the right taxes from the right people and paying the right benefits to the right people. The answer depends upon one's philosophy of right and wrong and, for better or for worse, there is no agreement among all Americans as to exactly what this philosophy should be.

I would suggest that the answer to the question "Do we get our money's worth from Social Security?" depends upon the ultimate effect of Social Security on the American social and economic structure. Will the effect be favorable or unfavorable? Will the effect be what we intended or will there be unforeseen consequences? My opinion is that we will get our money's worth from Social Security if it is designed to be consistent with the following principles:

> An individual should have freedom of choice to the fullest extent possible consistent with the interest of the nation as a whole.
>
> An individual should be afforded maximum opportunity and incentive to develop and utilize his abilities throughout his lifetime.
>
> A government (federal, state, or local) should provide those benefits, and only those benefits, that an individual (acting alone or as part of a group of individuals utilizing some form of voluntary pooling or risk-sharing arrangement) cannot provide for himself. In meeting this responsibility, the government should become involved to the least extent possible consistent with the interest of the nation as a whole.

The development of a system like the Social Security program is a continuing and evolutionary process. A program that was appropriate for yesterday is not appropriate for today. A program that is appropriate for today will not be appropriate for tomorrow. The present Social Security program is a product of decisions made by past generations of policymakers who lived in a different social and economic environment and who were trying to resolve problems different from those that will exist in the future. When Social Security was enacted some forty-five years ago, the nation had been in a serious depression for almost six years. The social and economic conditions existing at that time included the following:

> More workers than jobs and a consequent high unemployment rate
>
> A small elderly population relative to the younger potential working population
>
> Relatively undeveloped reliable institutions through which an individual could invest and save for the future
>
> An almost completely undeveloped system of private pensions and other employee benefits provided by employers

When the bulk of today's population approaches retirement some thirty to fifty years in the future, social and economic conditions can be expected to be quite different from what they are now or were forty-five years in the past. Accordingly, the nation need not and should not be forever influenced by past decisions made to solve past problems. On the contrary, it is the responsibility of today's generation to begin now to make any changes that may be necessary so the Social Security program will be appropriate for the probable future social and economic environment. In designing a Social Security program for the future, full recognition should be given to the extent to which the design of the program itself will influence the future environment, to ensure that more problems will not be created than resolved. It must be borne in mind that a social insurance system, if not properly designed and communicated, can:

> effectively dictate the retirement age patterns followed by the nation and thereby encourage earlier retirement at a time when later retirement may be in the best interest of the nation;
>
> discourage individual initiative and private saving for retirement, yet fail to provide adequate retirement benefits; and

create unrealistic expectations for retirement which, when unfulfilled, will result in frustration and dissatisfaction.

In my opinion, our present Social Security program exhibits these unsatisfactory characteristics in varying degrees.

So, what is the answer? Do we get our money's worth from Social Security, from the viewpoint of whether the program is appropriate to society's needs? With regard to the past forty years: PERHAPS, but it does no good to worry about what is past. With regard to the next forty years: NO, not unless we change the program.

Even if the present Social Security program were appropriate for the conditions that existed in the past, it will not be appropriate for conditions that are likely to exist in the future when the young working population of today is ready to retire. Although the present Social Security program may have given us our money's worth in the past, it will not give us our money's worth in the future because, unless the program is changed, *we will be using our tax dollars to buy benefits that are inappropriate for the future.*

12
The Earnings Test

You work and pay taxes all your life and finally retire on Social Security and a company pension. Things are going all right until you encounter some unexpected medical expenses—and inflation. You locate a temporary job that will put your finances in order, but then learn that because of your new job you must forfeit some of your Social Security benefits and you will not be as much better off as you thought.

You are a widow with small children and are glad to be receiving Social Security benefits but would like to resume your career. This will give you extra money to send the children to college and will also make your future life happier. But then you find out that since you are so successful in your job, you will lose most of your Social Security benefits and you will not have as much extra money for the children's college as you had planned.

The culprit is the "earnings test," sometimes called the retirement test, an often misunderstood feature of Social Security designed to reduce or even eliminate benefits when a beneficiary has more than nominal earnings.

The earnings of a retired worker can reduce both his own benefit *and* the benefits of dependent beneficiaries, but the earnings of a dependent beneficiary or a survivor beneficiary can reduce only his own benefit and not the benefit of any other beneficiary. The earnings test does not apply to disabled beneficiaries; other standards are used to determine the continuance of disability. Also, eligibility for Medicare benefits is not affected by the earnings test.

The earnings test is complicated but its essential features can be summarized as follows:

The test applies only to beneficiaries under age 72 (age 70 beginning in 1982) whose benefits are not based on disability.

Certain types of income are not counted in applying the earnings test (investment earnings, rental income, pension benefits, etc.).

A beneficiary may have annual earnings up to a specified amount—the annual exempt amount—without having any benefits withheld:

For people aged 65 to 72 (70 starting in 1982), the annual exempt amount is:

$5,000 in 1980
$5,500 in 1981
$6,000 in 1982

automatically adjusted after 1982 to reflect increases in average wage levels.

For people under age 65, the annual exempt amount is $4,080 in 1981, automatically adjusted after 1981 to reflect increases in average wage levels.

If earnings of a beneficiary exceed the applicable annual exempt amount, $1 in benefits is withheld for each $2 of excess earnings. For example, a beneficiary over 65 who earned $6,000 in 1980 would have $500 withheld from his benefits because his earnings exceeded his annual exempt amount ($5,000) by $1,000.

Beneficiaries can have relatively high earnings and still get some benefits.

A beneficiary could earn an amount equal to the total of the applicable exempt amount and twice his annual benefit before all his benefits would be withheld.

A 65-year-old worker who elects to begin receiving benefits in 1980, having had average earnings during his career, could earn $16,724 in 1980 before all his benefits ($5,862) would be withheld.

If the above beneficiary has a spouse (also 65) receiving dependent's benefits, their combined benefits would be $8,793 and he could earn $22,586 before all their benefits would be withheld.

There is a provision that permits a person who retires to receive benefits in the remainder of the year regardless of his earnings before retirement. In the first year a beneficiary has a nonwork month, that is, a month in which he earns less than one-twelfth the annual exempt amount, and does not provide substantial services in self-employment, benefits are not withheld in any nonwork month even if annual earnings exceed the annual exempt amount. (Prior to 1978, the monthly measure applied in all years of benefit payment. It is currently applied in some years of benefit payment to certain types of beneficiaries such as children and young widows.)

Since the exempt amount of earnings is a flat amount for all beneficiaries, it favors the lower paid workers. For example, a worker who has always earned something less than the federal minimum wage is not affected by the earnings test and can continue working at the same earnings level after age 65 and receive full Social Security benefits. On the other hand, a worker who has always earned the maximum taxable amount under Social Security and who continues to work past age 65 at the same earnings level will receive no benefits at all while still working prior to age 72.

The reason for the earnings test lies in the traditional view of the purpose of the Social Security program; namely, to replace, in part, earnings that are lost when a worker becomes disabled, dies, or retires in old age. The earnings test is used as a measure of whether a loss of income has occurred. The test also applies to dependents and survivors who have earnings, although the rationale for this is not clear. It is sometimes stated that earnings of dependents and survivors offset partially the loss of a worker's income to the family. This reasoning is faulty, however, in the case of dependents and survivors who worked prior to becoming eligible for benefits. Perhaps the reasoning follows the general concept that Social Security benefits are based partly on "presumed social need." Thus dependents or survivors with significant earnings of their own are assumed not to need Social Security benefits as much as dependents or survivors without earnings.

The original earnings test in 1940 was simple but stringent: If monthly earnings in covered employment were $15 or more, the entire monthly benefit was forfeited. Over the years the retirement test has been liberalized continually as a result of public pressure for change.

There is no provision in the present Social Security law that is subject to such consistent public and Congressional criticism as the earnings test. In each session of Congress in recent years, well over 100 bills have been introduced to change the earnings test.

The reason for this public criticism and misunderstanding of the earnings test is not hard to find. For forty years the government has employed rhetoric to describe Social Security that has led people to believe that their "contributions" were placed in a "trust fund" under an "insurance program" to create an "earned right" to benefits payable upon old age, disability, death, or illness. Little emphasis was given to explaining that the "earned right" was to a benefit payable only if the beneficiary did not have substantial earnings. After awhile the public began to believe that they had in fact "bought and paid for" their benefits (as they believed them to be defined) and that it was inconsistent with forty years of rhetoric, if not downright unfair, to withhold benefits just because the beneficiary continued to work (particularly if the work was to supplement an inadequate benefit in a time of frustrating inflation).

The result of this misunderstanding of the nature of Social Security should not be surprising: pressure by the public to liberalize the earnings test, a yielding to this pressure by Congress, and a substantial change in the very nature of Social Security (to conform more with what the public thought Social Security was all along). This process will probably continue until the earnings test is eliminated altogether and the original design of this part of the Social Security program is transformed completely. There comes a time when misunderstanding is too deeply imbedded to be reversed.

In theory, at least, the original concept of the earnings test was a sound one. In effect, it provided for a flexible retirement age for each individual. Retirement benefits were not to be paid to everyone at an arbitrarily determined age; rather they were to be paid whenever a person was no longer both willing and able to work (but not earlier than age 65 originally, reduced later to age 62).

The purpose of the earnings test was to facilitate changes in the size of the work force as the nation's work opportunities vary. Such changes are necessary because of shifts in the relative size of the aged and young populations caused by fluctuations in the birth rate and because of changes in the nation's production needs. We shall see a striking need for higher effective retirement ages during the first half of the next century as today's youth reach their sixties and the size of the work force (as we now define it) declines relative to the total population.

It is tempting to suggest that the trend toward elimination of the earnings test be reversed and that the original concept of a strict earnings test be restored. This could be achieved simply by freezing the exempt amounts of earnings at present levels instead of raising them as average wages increase, and retaining age 72 as the maximum age for applying the earnings test instead of continually reducing it. In a relatively short time, inflation would effectively restore a strict earnings test to Social Security, which would then provide flexible retirement ages to accommodate the nation's changing needs. This would, of course, also reduce the high retirement costs after the turn of the century by reducing the ratio of beneficiaries to active taxpayers. It may be too late to restore a strict earnings test, however, since that would require the population to view Social Security in a considerably different way than they have become accustomed.

13
Sex and Social Security

What does sex have to do with Social Security? Plenty, according to those who complain that women are not being treated fairly by Social Security as a result of their sex. In reality, Social Security has discriminated in favor of women based upon their sex more often than it has discriminated against them. Paradoxically, however, Social Security satisfies income security needs less adequately for women than it does for men. To understand this situation requires some background explanation.

The overall social and economic environment in America makes it easier for independent men than for independent women to support themselves during their active healthy lifetimes, and it provides more support for independent men than for independent women in the event of their inability to work because of age or disability. This environment is a reflection of the different roles played by men and women in this country during the early twentieth century. A considerable amount of work and effort is required to sustain a family, and the roles traditionally played by married men and women in performing this work may be stated simply as follows:

The man works full time outside the home for cash wages which he uses to support himself and his family.

The woman works full time caring for the home and family and receives no cash wages.

145

This division of responsibilities, which used to be the norm, was a workable arrangement, particularly during a lasting marriage. Until recently, divorce was relatively infrequent.

When Social Security was designed and adopted in the 1930s it was intended to recognize and be compatible with this environment. By doing so it served to reinforce and perpetuate such an environment, even though it did not create the environment.

This environment has changed, however, and it will continue to change. Women are increasingly combining paid employment with family life. The percentage of married women in the labor force increased from 20 percent in 1947 to almost 50 percent in 1980. It has been estimated that by the end of the 1980s, two-thirds of all married women under age 55 will be working, including over half of all mothers with young children. Women in paid employment already outnumber women who work at home without pay—slightly more than half of the female population over age 15 is working for pay. As the frequency of divorce has increased, so has the number of women supporting themselves and their children.

Changes in the Social Security program have not kept pace with changes in the economic role of women and in the institution of marriage that have occurred since Social Security was enacted. This has led to charges that Social Security discriminates against women, or that it is unfair or inequitable in its treatment of women.

The women's issue is often misunderstood. There is no significant discrimination against women in the current Social Security program. Any discrimination, now as well as in the past, is more often against men than against women. The 1979 Advisory Council on Social Security, which devoted more time to women's benefits than any other issue, summarized their findings on discrimination as follows:[1]

> ... the social security law is largely sex-blind. With few exceptions (which the Administration and the council recommend be eliminated), benefits are not paid on the basis of sex, but rather on the basis of labor force attachment and family status. The council also notes that as a group, women get as good a return on

the social security taxes they pay as do men. Indeed, if separate systems were established for men and women, women workers would have to pay social security taxes that are about 9 percent higher than men would pay. Because the average wages of women are lower than men's, a greater portion of their wages is replaced by benefits because of the weighting in the formula for low-income workers. Also, because women tend to live longer, they collect more benefits than men. These two factors outweigh the fact that more dependents' benefits are paid on the basis of men's wage records than are paid on the basis of women's wage records.

It may be useful to list the circumstances in which men and women receive different treatment under the Social Security program. In some cases women are favored, while in others men are favored. This information was taken from the report of the 1979 Advisory Council on Social Security.[2]

Nine Remaining Gender-Based Distinctions

1. Divorced Men and Women. Although benefits are provided for aged divorced wives, aged divorced widows, and disabled divorced widows, the statute does not provide benefits for aged divorced husbands, aged divorced widowers, or disabled divorced widowers (*Social Security Act,* Sections 202(b)(1), (c)(1), (e)(1), and (f)(1)). (Although still in the statute, this provision is no longer implemented for aged divorced husbands because of a successful challenge in the courts, *Oliver v. Califano.*)

2. Young Fathers and Mothers. Benefits are payable to young wives, widowed mothers, and surviving divorced mothers who have children entitled to benefits in their care, but not to young husbands, widowed fathers, or surviving divorced fathers in similar circumstances (*Social Security Act,* Sections 202 (g)(1), (b)(1), and (c)(1)). (Although still in the statute, this provision is no longer implemented for widowers with an entitled child in their care because of a successful challenge in the courts, *Weinberger v. Wiesenfeld.*)

3. Remarriage of a Surviving Spouse Before Age 60. A widow who remarries before age 60 may receive benefits on a deceased husband's earnings if she is not married when she applies for benefits, while a widower who remarries before age 60 cannot get such benefits, even if the subsequent marriage has terminated (*Social Security Act*, Sections 202(e)(1) and (f)(1)).

4. Transitional Insured Status. When Congress enacted the transitional insured status provisions in 1965 to provide special payments for persons who had not been able to work in covered employment long enough to qualify for benefits, wife's and widow's benefits were included in the provisions, but husband's and widower's benefits were not *(Social Security Act,* Section 227).

5. Special Age-72 Benefits. When both members of a couple are receiving special age-72 payments, the wife's payment is equal to one-half of the husband's payment even though each member must qualify for the payment individually (*Social Security Act,* Section 228(b)).

6. Benefits for Spouses of Disabled Beneficiaries. If a disabled male beneficiary who is married to a dependent or a survivor beneficiary ceases to be disabled, the benefits of his spouse are terminated; however, if the disabled beneficiary is a female whose disability ends, the benefits to her spouse do not end (*Social Security Act,* Section 202(d)(5) et al.). For example, when two beneficiaries who have been disabled since childhood marry, their benefits continue; if the male recovers from his disability, both benefits are terminated, while benefits for the male continue if the female recovers. Similarly, when a disabled worker is married to an aged survivor and recovers from his or her disability, termination of the spouse's benefits depends on the sex of the worker.

7. Determination of Illegitimacy. In the few jurisdictions in which an illegitimate child does not have the right to inherit the intestate personal property of his mother, a woman's illegitimate child cannot qualify for Social Security benefits under the same conditions as a man's illegitimate child can (*Social Security Act,* Section 216(h)(3)).

8. Waiver of Civil Service Survivor's Annuity. A widow can waive payment of a federal benefit attributable to credit for military service performed before 1957 to be able to have the military service credited toward eligibility for, or the amount of, a social security benefit, but a widower cannot (*Social Security Act,* Section 217(f)).

9. Self-Employment in Community Property States. The income from a business operated by a husband and wife in a state which has a community property statute is deemed to belong to the husband unless the wife exercises substantially all of the management and control of the business (*Social Security Act,* Section 211(a)(5)(A)).

Although the number of gender-based distinctions in the present law is not large, it is obviously preferable that they be removed so as to eliminate any lingering confusion about discrimination in the Social Security program. In some cases it has not been feasible to correct, retroactively, past discrimination based upon sex. One example is the less liberal treatment of men than women born before 1913 in the computation of benefits and insured status (not mentioned in the previous listing of gender-based distinctions since it does not apply to those currently becoming eligible for benefits). No consideration is being given to correcting this discrimination because of the large short-term costs it would entail and because the courts have upheld the provision currently in the law.

If the Social Security program does not discriminate directly against women, why are there so many complaints about its unfairness? To some degree, the complaints are due to misunderstanding and lack of knowledge about program provisions. But valid reasons also exist for unhappiness concerning the design of Social Security in relation to the nature of women's careers. Women suffer certain disadvantages during their working life that result in lower benefits under Social Security. As a general rule, women earn less than men of comparable age, education, and prior experience. One reason for this is the historically weaker job commitment of women, e.g., working irregularly and changing jobs frequently. This was, of course, a natural consequence of fulfilling the role of motherhood and traditional family life. In addition, there has been an occupational segregation which effectively divides labor into that "typically" done by women (e.g., nurses, teachers, secretaries) and that done by men (e.g., doctors, professors, managers).

Much of the criticism of the way Social Security treats women is in reality a criticism of the way our social and economic environment treats women. Accordingly, it is inappropriate and probably even futile to attempt to use Social Security as a vehicle to achieve social, economic, and political parity of women and men. More appropriate tools for this purpose would appear to include the Equal Pay Act of 1963, Title VII of the Civil Rights Act of 1964, the Equal Employment Act of 1972, and various affirmative action programs.

This is not to say that the present Social Security program properly meets the needs of women and that no change is appropriate. It is to say, however, that much of the criticism regarding the benefits Social Security provides women is ill-founded. Rational changes can be made only in response to rational analysis and criticism.

One of the alleged inequities in the benefits provided by Social Security is not because of a conflict between men's and women's benefits. Rather, it is a conflict between benefits provided women who work in paid employment, and women who work at home and are married to a person covered by Social Security. The homemaker who pays no Social Security taxes may receive as much or more in Social Security benefits as the woman who works in paid employment and pays Social Security taxes. An alternative way to view this situation is that for many years women who were not in paid employment got something for nothing; that is, they received certain Social Security benefits without paying any taxes therefor. Now that they are in the paid work force, however, women are treated just like any other working person—except they receive the *larger* of benefits based upon their own work record and benefits based upon their being a dependent.

Since approximately half the married women are in paid employment and half are not, there are obvious difficulties in modifying Social Security to satisfy the desires and needs of all women simultaneously. Marriage as an institution is not dying, rather it is evolving. People still get married although perhaps at later ages. Most families still have children, even though a smaller number. The frequency of divorce has increased but most divorced people remarry. Accordingly, it would be ill-advised to revise Social Security dramatically so as to accommodate the needs of this relatively new female role, at the expense of the traditional female role. Any change in Social Security must make suitable provision for both extremes of the female role as well as the many variations in these roles that currently exist or that may develop in the future.

It is common to criticize Social Security on the grounds that benefits are disproportionate to taxes for certain taxpayer groups, e.g., women in two-wage earner families. As indicated in Chapter 11, Social Security was not intended to be a savings plan under which an individual receives benefits commensurate with his or her tax payments. Accordingly, it is not appropriate to use "individual equity" as a yardstick by which to measure Social Security's fairness to women or to any other group. Social Security will always fail this test, providing more than a fair return on taxes for some and less for others.

Women are coming to view their home and childcare activities as being as valuable as their husbands' work for cash earnings and to believe that disability and retirement benefits should be provided based on the value of such activities. The basic nature of Social Security—as presently constituted—is to provide benefits only when there has been a loss of cash earnings; hence, it will be a very difficult philosophical transition for Social Security to provide benefits based upon non-cash-earning activities, homecare or otherwise.

It is increasingly pointed out that Social Security gives insufficient protection for divorced women. Even though the law was recently changed to lower the number of years divorced wives must have been married to their former husbands (from twenty years to ten years) in order to receive benefits, the complaint still persists that ten years is too long a marriage prerequisite for receipt of benefits. A woman need be married to her husband for only one year (and sometimes less) in order to receive a wife's or survivor's benefit based on his record, yet a marriage that lasted nine years is of insufficient duration to allow for the payment of a similar benefit to a divorced wife. A complaint is sometimes made that the level of benefits for divorced women is inadequate since it is the same as the wife's benefit, which is intended as supplemental income for a second household member and not as sole support for a single household member.

In considering the appropriateness of these complaints, it should be noted that any deficiency in benefits is not the result of discrimination against women; on the contrary, in the areas just mentioned, any discrimination that exists is against men, not women, since divorced men generally receive less favorable treatment than divorced women. Furthermore, charges that benefits provided by Social Security are inadequate should be viewed in light of the premise that Social Security is intended to provide only a basic minimum benefit and is not intended to be sufficient by itself.

In summary, there is no overt discrimination against women in the Social Security program. On the other hand, Social Security is structured to reward work patterns that fit men better than women. Furthermore, Social Security is structured to reward life patterns (e.g., male breadwinner and female homemaker, and lifelong marriages) that are becoming much less representative of modern life. The net result is that Social Security is not meeting the income security needs of women in today's world as well as it did some forty years ago. The need for some kind of change is irrefutable.

14
Integration of Private Benefit Plans with Social Security

Social Security was *not* designed to meet all the financial needs that arise from a person's old age, disability, death, or illness. It is still necessary to supplement Social Security with personal savings and employee benefit plans. Supplemental employee benefit plans are sometimes designed without regard to the benefits provided under Social Security. It is preferable, however, to correlate any supplemental plans with Social Security so that the combined benefits from all sources will form a rational package. This process of correlation is usually called "integration."

In theory, integration is not very difficult. In practice, however, it is quite complicated, largely because of:

the design of the Social Security program itself; and

the requirements of the Internal Revenue Service that supplemental plan benefits be designed in certain ways in order to be a "qualified plan" and thus be accorded favorable tax treatment.

A discussion of the integration of supplemental retirement benefits and Social Security benefits upon retirement at age 65 will illustrate some of the problems.

153

Social Security retirement benefits are based largely upon the principle of "social adequacy" and thus provide benefits for persons with low average earnings that are higher, relative to preretirement earnings, than for persons with high average earnings. For example, consider four workers retiring in January 1980 at age 65 after a steady work history, each at a different level of earnings. A worker whose past earnings have always been at about the minimum wage level would receive benefits during the first year of retirement of approximately 71 percent of his or her average earnings in the three years prior to retirement. This percentage is frequently called a "replacement ratio" because it represents the proportion of average preretirement earnings that is replaced by the retirement benefit. This replacement ratio would be 55 percent for a worker whose past earnings have equaled the average earnings of all employees covered by Social Security, 39 percent for a worker whose past earnings have equaled the maximum taxable wage base in effect during prior years, and 20 percent for a worker whose earnings have been twice the maximum taxable wage base in effect during prior years. These replacement ratios represent the basic benefit payable to a worker alone. For a worker with an eligible spouse (also aged 65), the replacement ratios become 106 percent for the low wage earner, 83 percent for the average wage earner, 59 percent for the maximum wage earner, and 29 percent for the high wage earner (one earning twice the maximum taxable wage base). These replacement ratios for the various categories of workers retiring at age 65 in 1980[1] may be summarized as follows:

| | Annual Earnings in 1979 | Social Security Benefits as a Percentage of the Last Three Years' Average Earnings | |
		Worker Alone	Worker and Spouse
Minimum wage	$ 6,032	71%	106%
Average wage	11,479	55	83
Maximum taxable wage	22,900	39	59
High wage	45,800	20	29

An examination of these figures makes it obvious that income replacement needs at retirement are not met uniformly for all of the workers in the example and that for most workers some kind of supplemental plan is called for. This need for supplementation is not a deficiency of the Social Security program; it was always intended that Social Security provide a basic floor of protection upon which additional protection could be built. Furthermore, it has always been a characteristic of Social Security to provide more adequate benefits for workers earning lower than average wages than for workers earning higher than average wages.

It is not unusual to find a supplemental retirement plan that provides benefits that are a uniform percentage of average preretirement earnings and that are the same whether the worker does or does not have a spouse. Such a plan *supplements* Social Security, yet it is not *integrated* with Social Security. As an example, consider a supplemental plan that provides a career worker with retirement benefits of 60 percent of average earnings in the three years prior to retirement. The benefits under such a plan are summarized below for the same workers used as an example in the preceding table:

	Annual Earnings in 1979	*Supplemental Plan Benefits as a Percentage of the Last Three Years' Average Earnings*	
		Worker Alone	*Worker and Spouse*
Minimum wage	$ 6,032	60%	60%
Average wage	11,479	60	60
Maximum taxable wage	22,900	60	60
High wage	45,800	60	60

If this supplemental plan is superimposed on the Social Security program, the total benefits may be summarized as follows:

	Annual Earnings in 1979	*Total Benefits as a Percentage of the Last Three Years' Average Earnings*	
		Worker Alone	*Worker and Spouse*
Minimum wage	$ 6,032	131%	166%
Average wage	11,479	115	143
Maximum taxable wage	22,900	99	119
High wage	45,800	80	89

This table illustrates the wide discrepancy in benefits relative to preretirement earnings that can occur when a supplemental retirement plan is simply *added to* Social Security but not *integrated with* Social Security. Such a situation is not uncommon, particularly among supplemental plans covering public employee groups.

If a supplemental retirement plan is to be integrated with Social Security, the plan must comply with the Internal Revenue Code as well as with rules and regulations of the Internal Revenue Service if the plan and its participants are to be accorded favorable tax treatment. The Internal Revenue Service requirements for integration permit a supplemental plan to provide benefits, relative to preretirement earnings, that favor more highly paid workers in order to offset the effect of the Social Security program which favors lower paid workers.

Assume, for example, that the benefit level of 80 percent of the final three-year average earnings shown in the preceding table for a high wage worker with no spouse is considered to be the desired goal for all workers regardless of their earnings level. Assume further that the supplemental plan benefits are modified toward that goal within the limits of the integration rules of the Internal Revenue Service (using the "offset" method[2] of integration). The benefits under such a plan may be summarized as follows:

	Annual Earnings in 1979	Supplemental Plan Benefits as a Percentage of the Last Three Years' Average Earnings	
		Worker Alone	Worker and Spouse
Minimum wage	$ 6,032	18%	18%
Average wage	11,479	30	30
Maximum taxable wage	22,900	44	44
High wage	45,800	60	60

If these integrated supplemental plan benefits are added to Social Security benefits, the total benefits may be summarized as follows:

	Annual Earnings in 1979	Total Benefits as a Percentage of the Last Three Years' Average Earnings	
		Worker Alone	Worker and Spouse
Minimum wage	$ 6,032	89%	124%
Average wage	11,479	85	113
Maximum taxable wage	22,900	83	103
High wage	45,800	80	89

A review of this table indicates that it is not possible to achieve simultaneously for all employee categories the stated goal of replacing 80 percent of the final three-year average earnings. Even if a supplemental plan is integrated to the full extent permitted by Internal Revenue Service requirements for a tax-qualified plan, there is still a wide variation in benefits. Lower wage earners receive relatively larger benefits than high wage earners. Workers with spouses receive relatively larger benefits than single workers. If adequate benefits are provided the high-wage single workers, excessive benefits must be provided all other workers.

The problem is made even worse by a factor not yet mentioned in order to simplify the discussion. Death and disability benefits provided by Social Security favor the lower wage earner just as does the age-retirement benefit. Death and disability benefits provided under a supplemental retirement plan can be integrated with those provided under Social Security; however, if they are so integrated the permissible degree of integration of age-retirement benefits is lessened. This would further aggravate the imbalance in benefits illustrated in the preceding table.

Of course, not everyone would agree that the combined benefits from Social Security and a supplemental retirement plan should be a uniform percentage of gross preretirement earnings. Some would argue that it is "equitable" for such a percentage to decline as average earnings increase—to reflect, if for no other reason, the progressive nature of the federal income tax and the nontaxability of Social Security benefits. These features tend to make a declining replacement ratio for gross preretirement earnings equivalent to a level replacement ratio for net (after tax) preretirement earnings. In any event, it would seem that more uniformity of retirement benefits relative to preretirement earnings is desirable than is permitted by current integration requirements of the Internal Revenue Service.

This entire subject may seem complicated, and it is. Nevertheless, the following observations seem reasonable:

Social Security alone does not meet all the financial needs that arise from a person's old age, disability, death, or illness. It meets those needs more completely for lower wage earners than for higher wage earners and more completely for married workers than for single workers.

Supplemental plan benefits must be provided if income replacement needs are to be met adequately. Supplemental benefits should be *integrated with* and not just *added to* Social Security benefits. Otherwise, the unevenness with which financial needs are met will be continued but at a higher level.

Under present laws and regulations, it is not possible to integrate supplemental benefit plans with Social Security to the extent necessary to satisfy uniformly the financial needs of all workers at the various earnings levels. If appropriate benefits are provided for workers with average earnings, less than adequate benefits are provided for the more highly paid workers; if adequate benefits are provided for the more highly paid workers, excessive benefits will be provided for lower paid workers. This situation can be corrected only if the Internal Revenue Service integration rules are revised, or if the Social Security program is revised, or both.

Many employee groups that do not participate in Social Security (civilian employees of the federal government and a portion of the employees of state and local governments and nonprofit organizations) have established employee benefit plans that satisfy uniformly the financial needs of all participants regardless of their earnings level. If these employee groups elect to participate in Social Security or are required to do so, significant revisions will be necessary in their existing employee benefit plans if rational balance is to be maintained in the benefits provided employees at the various earnings levels. The extent to which these revisions can be implemented is seriously hampered by the Internal Revenue Service laws and regulations, assuming they are in fact applicable to public as well as private employee benefit plans.

Providing rationally correlated benefits under two systems, Social Security and supplemental employee benefit plans, is quite difficult in view of the nature of Social Security itself and the Internal Revenue Service rules for integration. Nevertheless, proper correlation of benefits is essential if income replacement needs are to be met at an affordable cost. To achieve this correlation within the framework of the present laws and regulations requires that:

tax-qualified supplemental employee benefit plans be integrated as completely with Social Security as is allowed by Internal Revenue Service rulings; and

death and disability benefits for all employees, and a portion of the retirement benefits for the more highly paid employees, be provided separately from tax-qualified retirement plans so as to minimize the limiting effect of integration rulings.

It is unfortunate that federal tax laws are not more consistent and are not more conducive to the formation of rationally conceived supplemental employee benefit plans. Many tax laws are designed to encourage the adoption of supplemental plans while others tend to discourage their adoption. The Internal Revenue Service integration rules in particular make it virtually impossible to design a supplemental retirement plan that fits together with Social Security to form a sensible combination of retirement benefits. On the other hand, many supplemental plans are not as completely integrated with Social Security as is permitted under existing tax laws, imperfect though such laws are.

15
Inflation and Automatic Benefit Increases

Social Security payments for 35 million beneficiaries were increased by 14.3 percent in June 1980. This benefit increase corresponded with the increase in the Consumer Price Index of 14.3 percent from the first quarter of 1979 to the first quarter of 1980 and was granted automatically in accordance with Social Security's automatic adjustment provisions. These provisions were enacted in 1972 and were scheduled to take effect in 1974, but it was 1975 before they were permitted to operate without modification. Increases in Social Security benefits in the course of payment for each year since 1974 are summarized in Table 15.1.

These benefit increases have provided valuable protection against inflation for Social Security beneficiaries. The cumulative increase in benefits during the seven-year period from 1973 to 1980 was 81 percent. At first glance, the automatic adjustment provisions may appear to have solved the problems of inflation. There are many factors to consider, however; and in attempting to alleviate the various problems caused by inflation, the government faces a dilemma because not all of these problems can be resolved simultaneously. In fact, resolving one problem often aggravates another—as indicated below.

Table 15.1

Automatic Increases in Social Security Benefits

Calendar Year of Benefit Increase	Percentage Benefit Increase
(1)	(2)
1974[a]	11.0%
1975	8.0
1976	6.4
1977	5.9
1978	6.5
1979	9.9
1980	14.3

[a]Automatic benefit increases were originally scheduled to become effective in 1974, with an indicated increase of 11 percent. The Congress overrode the automatic provisions and provided part of this increase earlier than scheduled and the balance at the regular time.

Responsibility and Opportunity

It can be argued that the government has a responsibility to maintain the purchasing power of any Social Security benefit it provides if the program is to carry out the purpose for which it was established. The individual pensioner did not cause the inflation which is robbing him of purchasing power. In most cases, at least some of the blame must be placed on governmental economic policies. To the extent that external forces or actions by the nation's active workers have caused inflation, it is true that the government may not have played a role—but then neither did the individual pensioner. Consequently, the government may still be considered responsible for finding a solution.

Moreover, the retired pensioner is out of the active work force and usually is powerless to protect himself against inflation. The government is the only logical protector of pensions provided by Social Security. The government enacted the Social Security law in the first place; it is the government that can and must amend the law as necessary to preserve the pensioner's standard of living. Finally, if the government does not protect pensioners against inflation, who will do so?

These are powerful arguments in favor of governmental action, and they do in fact usually lead to governmental intervention such as Social Security's 1972 automatic adjustment provisions. But what does governmental intervention entail? Can the government really solve the problems caused by inflation?

Who Bears the Burden of Inflation?

It is easy to make casual references to "governmental responsibility" or having the "government pay" for all or part of a social insurance program, without pausing to realize what this truly means. The government has no magic wand. If social insurance benefits are made inadequate by inflation and the government responds by increasing benefits, this simply means that the active workers and their employers must pay higher taxes to provide such benefits. Many analysts believe that higher payroll taxes result in more inflation and that increased benefits to pensioners will reinforce, if not aggravate, inflation. If this is true, the net result is still further increases in pensions and further increases in inflation, resulting in an ever-increasing upward spiral. This is particularly so if wages of active workers are adjusted for inflation. And if the government adjusts *pension benefits* for inflation, to be consistent it must endorse adjustment of *wages* for inflation.

The problem of maintaining the purchasing power of the active worker is a difficult one. It requires wage increases *in excess of the rate of inflation* to offset the progressive income taxes that must be paid on gross income. Social Security benefits are not taxable; therefore, if both wages and pensions are increased by the same percentage amount to compensate for inflation, the pensioners' standard of living will increase relative to the active workers' standard of living.

Table 15.2 compares the average increase in earnings of persons who pay Social Security taxes and the increase in the Consumer Price Index during recent years. Historically, average wages have increased faster than prices. This is a reflection of increased productivity of the nation's workers and thus an improved standard of living. For example, from 1952 through 1972, average wages increased faster than prices by an average annual amount of more than 2 percent. This was not true during the period 1973–1979 when, as indicated in Table 15.2, average earnings of Social Security taxpayers generally

Table 15.2

Comparison of Yearly Increase in Consumer Price Index and
Average Earnings of Social Security Taxpayers

Calendar Year	Percentage Increase in Consumer Price Index[a]	Percentage Increase in Average Earnings of Social Security Taxpayers[b]
(1)	(2)	(3)
1973	6.2%	6.9%
1974	11.0	7.5
1975	9.1	6.6
1976	5.8	8.4
1977	6.5	7.1
1978	7.6	8.1
1979	11.5	8.4[c]

[a]The figure for 1973 represents the relative increase in the average CPI for 1973 over the average CPI for 1972, and so on.
[b]The figure for 1973 represents the relative increase in the average earnings for 1973 over the average earnings for 1972, and so on.
[c]Preliminary estimate.

increased less than the Consumer Price Index (by an average annual rate of 0.6 percent). A comparison of the increase in net earnings after taxes (instead of gross earnings) with the Consumer Price Index would show a substantially larger gap, or loss of purchasing power among the active workers.

On the other hand, Social Security benefits have been adjusted fully to reflect increases in the Consumer Price Index—putting the Social Security recipient at an advantage over the active worker. If this phenomenon continues, the result will be an eventual conflict between the working and nonworking populations, since it will not be possible to protect the nonworking population against the ravages of inflation, except at the expense of the working population. Similarly, there can easily be a conflict among the various segments of the working population, since it is virtually impossible to distribute the burden of inflation "equitably." If inflation continues, these realities will be more widely recognized and strong efforts will be made to require all segments of the population to share more equally in bearing the cost of inflation. This could result in less than a full adjustment in Social Security benefits for inflation.

There are other problems in adjusting pensions and wages for changes in the cost of living. For example, some methods of compensating for inflation may, in fact, overcompensate and thus accelerate the very inflation for which adjustment is being made. In some cases this is because of faulty methods in designing the cost-of-living index; in other cases it may result from failing to apply different adjustments to the active and the retired populations, although there is little reliable information available on whether different adjustments should be applied. Accordingly, extreme care must be taken in constructing an index (or indices) to be used in adjusting pensions and wages.

The Real Solution

Although the problems posed by inflation are complex, it is clear they must be addressed in some way. It is becoming generally accepted that the purchasing power of social insurance pensions (and other benefits) should be restored if eroded by inflation. Increasing the benefits, however, should be viewed as a temporary stop-gap measure. A government cannot simply increase social insurance benefits and thereby presume to have resolved the widespread problems caused by inflation, or even to have alleviated them, except temporarily for a limited segment of the population.

In the final analysis, there is only one action a government can take that will be in the best interests of the most people and keep social and economic turmoil to a minimum. The government must identify the underlying *causes* of inflation, attack those causes, and keep inflation under control to the maximum possible extent. This is a large order, but to do otherwise will be to permit inflation to fester into such a complex problem that there will be no acceptable solutions.

16
Should Social Security Cover Everyone?

Approximately 75 percent of the nation's workers are in jobs automatically covered by Social Security and are therefore required to pay Social Security taxes. Of course this entitles them to receive Social Security benefits if they meet the eligibility requirements. Roughly 5 percent of the nation's workers are in jobs that are not covered by Social Security, hence they neither pay Social Security taxes nor receive its benefits. The remaining 20 percent of the working population have the option of paying or not paying Social Security taxes and thus receiving or not receiving its benefits. About three-fourths of the workers with this option have chosen to participate in Social Security. (Generally speaking, the option must be exercised by groups of employees and not by individuals.) The reasons for this varying treatment of different segments of the population are outlined in Chapter 2.

Is this situation of nonuniversal and partly optional coverage by Social Security a fair arrangement? Is it in the best interest of the nation?

The purpose of Social Security is to ensure that everyone with a significant work history is assured a basic standard of living in the event of retirement because of age or disability and that the dependents of every such worker are also assured a basic standard of living in the event of the worker's retirement,

167

disability, or premature death. In theory it may be acceptable to exclude a portion of the population from the protection offered by Social Security, provided there is reasonable assurance that this excluded segment will have alternative protection and thus not become a "charge on society." Most of the persons who do not participate in Social Security do in fact have a variety of employee benefit programs that provide much of the benefit protection offered by Social Security. Of course, no alternative system can be as financially stable as Social Security, publicity to the contrary notwithstanding. Furthermore, even though a person may be protected adequately under an alternative system, there is no assurance that such protection will continue as long as it is needed: either the system may change or employment may terminate. Accordingly, it should be anticipated that some of the persons who do not participate in Social Security and who rely upon other systems of benefit protection will die or become disabled or reach old age without receiving benefits equivalent to those that would have been afforded under Social Security. This will in turn create some situations in which society (more specifically, the taxpayers) will have to step in and provide financial support through one of the welfare programs—the very situations that Social Security was adopted to prevent.

Another point to consider is the fairness, actual as well as perceived, of a nonuniversal system. If Social Security were a system whereby an individual received benefits with a value approximately equal to his tax payments, then it might be considered fair, or "actuarially sound," to permit optional participation or to exclude certain groups from participation. As we saw in Chapter 11, however, this is not the case. Benefits are not equivalent to taxes. It is natural, therefore, for persons for whom participation is optional to select their options in such a way as to take maximum advantage of Social Security, leaving the bulk of the taxpayers—who have no choice in the matter—to make up any extra cost this may entail. This is in fact what is happening. When a group of municipal employees opt out of Social Security, they take with them the right to receive future benefits of considerably greater value than the taxes paid to the date of withdrawal. When a career federal civil servant takes a part-time job in employment covered by Social

Security, he receives benefits of considerably greater value than his tax payments. When a policeman or fireman retires at age 50 and then works in a job covered by Social Security, upon his "second" retirement he receives benefits of much greater value than his tax payments. This is not the fault of the municipal employee or the career federal civil servant or the policeman or fireman; it is the fault of the Social Security system which was designed to cover all of the nation's workers but which, because of a series of "loopholes," leaves out a significant portion of the population.

If groups of employees in different parts of the nation were given the option of continuing to support the national defense effort by electing either to continue paying the necessary taxes or to discontinue paying such taxes, it would be reasonable to expect that certain groups would "opt out" of paying the taxes used to support the defense effort. Similarly, if persons were given the opportunity to "opt out" of providing any support for the nation's educational system, it would be reasonable to expect that some persons would elect to discontinue paying taxes that are used to educate our youth. In both of these cases, persons who elected to discontinue tax payments would nonetheless receive benefits, admittedly indirect and difficult to perceive, from the national defense effort and the national educational effort, since both of these efforts would be continued by other taxpayers—perhaps at a slightly reduced level because of slightly reduced tax receipts. The difference between these examples and the option for certain groups of persons to withdraw from Social Security is not very great. Although a person who opts out of Social Security and discontinues paying Social Security taxes may suffer a reduction in benefits, it is not a complete cessation even though the payment of taxes ceases completely. First, the withdrawing employee will in most cases receive at least some Social Security benefits in the future as a result of the payment of Social Security taxes in the past. Second, there is an indirect, although substantial, benefit by virtue of the Social Security system's continuing to pay benefits to some 35 million persons—retired and disabled persons and their dependents, as well as widows and orphans. Were it not for the Social Security program, the burden of supporting a large proportion of these beneficiaries would fall directly upon all taxpayers regardless of whether they paid taxes to the Social Security program.

Social Security was not designed to be a neatly defined package of benefits that a particular group of persons could elect to buy or not buy in exchange for the payment of Social Security taxes. It was designed to provide a wide range of benefits to the bulk of the nation's workers and their dependents based upon their presumed need. The benefits are based upon prior earnings levels, the worker's type and number of dependents, the ability of the beneficiary to work, and so on. Benefits are not related, except incidentally, to the taxes paid by the participant. Since the program is operated on a pay-as-you-go basis, the taxes paid by one generation of workers are used to provide benefits for an earlier generation of workers. Therefore, the taxes paid by a particular generation of workers are not equivalent to the cost of the benefits that will be provided eventually to that generation of workers.

These characteristics of Social Security result in a significant redistribution of income: intragenerational transfers as individuals within each generation receive benefits with a different value than the taxes paid by such individual, and intergenerational transfers as benefits received by one generation taken as a whole are more or less than the value of the taxes paid by such generation.

The provisions regarding optional participation for certain groups of workers were designed as if the employee group concerned would pay taxes equivalent to the benefits it receives. This is obviously not the case under our present Social Security program; hence such provisions are poorly conceived and inappropriate. Apparently when the provisions were designed it was presumed that most persons for whom participation is optional would elect to participate and that they would not decide to withdraw at a later date.

One of the reasons frequently given for requiring everyone to participate in Social Security is that it will solve Social Security's financial problems. This is not an appropriate reason. For one thing, if more people are added to Social Security, they will not only pay more taxes but will also receive more benefits. The net effect of bringing everyone into Social Security would be to decrease the required tax rate paid by employees and employers by less than ½ percent each on the average over the next seventy-five years. This is not very much compared with the present tax rate of 6.65 percent and the much higher tax rates of 8 to 12 percent that will be required during the early part of the next century if no changes are made in the program. But this phenomenon of reduced payroll tax rates deserves closer study. Even though universal coverage may result in slightly lower payroll tax rates, and thus may appear to alleviate Social Security's financial problems, *it would not reduce the total tax burden—direct and indirect—imposed on present participants to support Social Security.* On the contrary, it would most likely *increase* the tax burden.

This paradox may be explained as follows by considering the effect of bringing federal employees into Social Security. Federal employees would pay the same Social Security tax rate as all other participants; however, because of the characteristics of federal employees, their Social Security taxes relative to their benefits would be higher than the average for all other participants, yielding a "gain" to Social Security. This gain would result in lower average benefit costs relative to taxable payroll and lower average tax rates for all participants. It should be obvious, however, that the cost of benefits for present participants would not be lowered by adding federal employees; it is simply that "excess" Social Security taxes paid by federal employees would permit slightly reduced taxes by present participants. But who pays the Social Security taxes for federal employees, including any "excess" taxes? It is the taxpayers of the nation. Accordingly, any reduction in Social Security payroll taxes made possible by including federal employees would be offset by an exactly corresponding increase in general revenue paid by all taxpayers.

One might argue that the federal employee—not the general taxpayer—would pay half the Social Security tax, hence there would be a saving to the general taxpayer. Any such tax saving would be unlikely for the following reasons. Federal employees already contribute 7 percent of their salary to their own retirement system. Inclusion of federal employees in Social Security would almost certainly be made on the basis of no increase in employee cost; hence existing employee contributions to the civil service retirement plan would be reduced by the amount of

any Social Security taxes imposed on federal employees. Therefore, federal employees would not pay any more under Social
Security and the civil service retirement plan combined than
they now pay under the civil service retirement plan alone. (A
minor exception, perhaps, is with respect to short-term
employees, since Social Security taxes are not refundable as are
contributions to the civil service retirement plan; therefore,
some short-term employees would in effect pay higher contributions if participating in Social Security.) Any diversion of
present employee contributions from the federal civil service
retirement plan to Social Security would have to be restored by
added general revenue paid by the nation's taxpayers.

One might argue that civil service retirement plan benefits
could be reduced by the amount of any Social Security benefits
newly provided, resulting in a saving to the general taxpayer. It
is true that the substitution of pay-as-you-go financed Social
Security benefits for advance-funded civil service retirement
plan benefits may give an apparent reduction in costs in the
short run, but it cannot reduce costs in the long run; it can only
shift part of the costs to later generations. Providing identical
benefits through different vehicles cannot change the cost,
taking into account the time-value of money.

Finally, universal coverage would actually increase the total
tax burden because civil service retirement plan benefits can be
reduced by some but not all the benefits provided by Social
Security. This is because Social Security provides some benefits
that are not provided by the civil service retirement system.
Therefore, if federal employees are included in Social Security
on the basis of not receiving lower total benefits than the
present benefits provided under the civil service retirement
system, it follows that there would be an increase in total
benefits (to the extent Social Security provides benefits not
provided by the civil service retirement system). This increase
in benefits for federal employees would result in increased costs
for the general taxpayer.

The same general reasoning concerning the financial implications of requiring federal employees to participate in Social
Security also applies to the inclusion of employees of state and
local governments, although the particular taxpayers affected
may be different. For example, lowered Social Security taxes

may be offset by increased state and local income taxes or increased real estate or other taxes. Inclusion of employees of nonprofit organizations in Social Security could result in lower Social Security costs for existing participants if the characteristics of such employees result in a "gain" to Social Security. This would be true because employer-paid and employee-paid Social Security taxes of nonprofit organizations would not be provided from general revenue. The financial impact of including all nonprofit organization employees is minor, however, compared with the financial impact of including all federal, state, and local government employees.

In summary, with regard to the financial aspect of universal coverage, although there are certain financial inequities in nonuniversal coverage, which should probably be corrected, universal coverage cannot possibly reduce the total tax burden—direct and indirect—of supporting Social Security (unless, in the process, someone suffers a benefit reduction). Universal coverage can result only in the shifting of Social Security costs among taxpayers brought about, generally speaking, by substituting general revenue for part of the payroll tax. In addition, universal coverage could result in a shift among generations of some of the costs of the affected public employee retirement systems. This would result from substituting part of the Social Security benefits for part of the public employee retirement system benefits, which could in turn cause a change in the financing patterns since Social Security is financed on a pay-as-you-go basis (for all its participants) and a given public employee retirement system may be financed on a pay-as-you-go basis (for its particular participants) or some form of advance-funded basis. Universal coverage could also result in higher long-range total costs of benefits for public employees since they would, in some cases, receive a broader array of benefits by participating in Social Security.

Universal coverage would, of course, pose many problems. Most employee groups not now covered by Social Security have their own employee benefit programs. These programs would need to be revised in the event of universal coverage so that the employees affected would receive neither smaller nor appreciably larger benefits after inclusion in Social Security than before inclusion. There would also be certain technical as well as legal problems in revising existing employee benefit plans. All of these problems can be resolved, however, should coverage under Social Security become universal.

Based upon the present design of Social Security, there should be no optional participation: everyone should participate in both the payment of its taxes and the receipt of its benefits, direct and indirect. If it is desired that participation be optional, one of the following types of change should be made:

> The Social Security program should be redesigned so that the benefits paid to each group of workers are approximately equivalent to the taxes paid by such group.

> The provisions regarding optional participation should be revised so that a group of workers electing first to participate and then to opt out would receive benefits more closely related to the taxes paid during its period of participation in Social Security.

Unless one of these basic changes is made, there can be no satisfactory basis for optional participation. On the other hand, compulsory participation of all federal, state, and local government employees and employees of nonprofit organizations does not appear likely in the near future because of the strong opposition to mandatory participation by government employees not now participating, as well as legal questions regarding the constitutionality of mandatory participation of state and local government employees. Accordingly, the debate over this issue can be expected to become more and more heated and confused and acrimonious. This issue cannot be resolved to the mutual satisfaction of everyone involved based on the present design of Social Security.

17
Should You Opt Out of Social Security If You Can?

As indicated in Chapter 2, there are about 10 million employees of state and local governments and 4 million employees of nonprofit organizations who participate in Social Security on a voluntary basis. These employees can elect to withdraw from, or "opt out" of, Social Security. The decision to opt out cannot be made on an individual basis but must be made for groups of employees.

An increasing number of these voluntary participants have considered opting out of Social Security as taxes have continued to rise, as misunderstanding of Social Security has increased, and as more people have become disenchanted with the federal government and its huge programs that, to some people, are unnecessarily paternalistic.

This chapter presents some of the many considerations to be taken into account by employee groups that are considering opting out of Social Security. In order for the chapter to stand on its own as much as possible, there is some duplication of material contained in other parts of the book.

General Background Information

The Social Security Act originally excluded from Social Security coverage all employment for state and local governments because of the question of whether the federal government could legally tax such employers. Also excluded was work for most nonprofit organizations, which were traditionally exempt from taxes.

Legislation enacted in 1950 (and later) provided that employees of such organizations could be covered by Social Security on a voluntary basis under certain conditions. For example, Social Security coverage is available to employees of state and local government systems on a group voluntary basis through agreements between the Secretary of Health and Human Services (formerly Health, Education, and Welfare) and the individual states. After coverage of the employees of a state or of a political subdivision of the state has been in effect for at least five years, the state may give notice of its intention to terminate the coverage of such employees. The termination of coverage becomes effective on December 31 of the second full calendar year after such notice is given, unless the state withdraws the notice of termination within such period. However, once the termination becomes effective, it is irrevocable and the same group cannot be covered under Social Security again. Nonprofit organizations may terminate coverage similarly except that the notice of intention to terminate cannot be given until coverage has been in effect for at least eight years and termination of coverage becomes effective at the end of the calendar year quarter occurring two years after the notice is given.

Approximately 75 percent of the 13 million state and local employees and 90 percent of the 4 million employees of nonprofit organizations are covered by Social Security under these voluntary participation arrangements.

In the past few years there has been an increase in the number of terminations of coverage among state and local government employees. Table 17.1 compares the number of newly covered employees with the number of terminations during each of the past seven years. The number of employees who terminated during the seven-year period 1973–1979 was 113,423, compared with total terminations of about 130,000 employees during the program's entire history through June 1980. Coverage groups in Alaska, California, Louisiana, and Texas account for 86 percent of the terminations.

Table 17.1

**State and Local Government Groups and Employees—
Comparison of Number Newly Covered and Terminated during
the Period 1973–1979**

Year	Newly Covered		Terminated	
	Number of Groups	Number of Employees	Number of Groups	Number of Employees
(1)	(2)	(3)	(4)	(5)
1973	709	20,231	32	4,287
1974	821	21,281	68	8,680
1975	1,057	17,010	46	13,014
1976	762	20,000	54	7,940
1977*	675	17,000	137	25,242
1978*	722	17,050	112	20,515
1979*	601	13,293	79	33,745
Total	5,347	125,865	528	113,423

*Estimates prepared by the Social Security Administration.

As of early 1980 there were 255 coverage groups representing 77,289 employees who had given their two-year notice of intention to terminate but had not yet terminated. The filing of such a notice by a state does not necessarily mean that coverage will be terminated, however, since the state may withdraw the notice at any time before the termination becomes effective. Coverage groups in four states account for most of these potential employee withdrawals: California (16,301), Georgia (14,436), Louisiana (9,109), and Texas (25,147).

The State of Alaska is the first and only state to withdraw all of its employees from Social Security. The termination of the coverage agreement for Alaska state employees became effective December 31, 1979 and ended participation for about 14,500 employees.

The increasing attention given in recent years to the question of Social Security coverage, how widespread it is and how widespread it "should be," was reflected in the Social Security Amendments of 1977. In these amendments Congress directed the Secretary of Health, Education, and Welfare to undertake a study of the feasibility and desirability of covering federal employees, state and local government employees, and employees of nonprofit organizations under the Old-Age and Survivors Insurance, Disability Insurance, and Hospital Insurance programs on a mandatory basis. The final report on this study was issued on March 25, 1980. Although the report did not make a definite recommendation, it concluded that universal coverage was feasible and at least implied that it was desirable. The chairman of the study group, in his letter of transmission to the Secretary of HEW, clearly supported universal coverage as both feasible and desirable. Furthermore, universal coverage was considered by the 1979 Advisory Council on Social Security, which issued its final report on December 7, 1979. The Advisory Council found that "our nation's income security goals can be achieved fully and equitably only if all employment is covered by social security." Universal coverage will probably be considered by other recently appointed income maintenance study groups, and it appears likely that they, too, will support universal coverage or, at least, not be opposed to it.

Financial Importance to Social Security of Participation by Groups Not Now Covered or for Whom Participation Is Optional

In fiscal year 1979, Social Security taxes received by the Old-Age and Survivors Insurance, Disability Insurance, and Hospital Insurance trust funds representing amounts paid with respect to coverage of state and local government employees amounted to $12.1 billion, about 10 percent of the total taxes received. If a large proportion of such employees should withdraw from the system, tax income would be reduced substantially and immediately. There would be little immediate reduction in benefit payments to such employees; however, over a period of time (twenty-five years or so) the reduction in liability would be more substantial.

Because outgo now exceeds income under the Social Security program and the trust fund balances are relatively small, the withdrawal of a large number of state and local employees would have a significantly adverse effect on the system, especially in the short term, thus requiring relatively large immediate tax increases in one form or another.

Over the long term, however, the average cost of the Social Security program would be affected relatively less than in the short term by changes in participation among persons not now covered or for whom participation is optional. It is estimated that the average seventy-five-year cost of the cash benefits part of the Social Security program (OASDI) will be about 13.4 percent of taxable payroll under present law (assuming that all presently participating groups continue to participate). If all state and local groups that now participate should withdraw from the program, the average seventy-five-year cost would increase to about 14.3 percent of taxable payroll (a relative increase of 7 percent). On the other hand, if all state and local groups, as well as federal employees, not now participating should become participants in the program, the average seventy-five-year cost would decrease to about 12.8 percent of taxable payroll (a relative decrease of 4 percent).

The Hospital Insurance portion of Social Security would also be affected financially by increased or reduced participation by groups for whom participation is optional. It has been estimated by the Health Care Financing Administration actuaries that if all state and local government and nonprofit organization employees who now participate should withdraw from coverage, the average twenty-five-year cost of the Hospital Insurance program would increase by about 0.4 percent of taxable payroll (a relative increase of 10 percent). Alternatively, if all employees not currently covered should become participants in Social Security, the average twenty-five-year cost of the Hospital Insurance program would decrease by about ¼ percent of taxable payroll (a relative decrease of approximately 6 percent). The longer range effect has not been calculated, but it would probably be less significant.

Changes in the level of participation in Social Security by groups for whom participation is optional would have a financial impact on the entire economy, not just on Social Security costs, as indicated in Chapter 16. It is not possible to describe the exact financial impact on every aspect of the economy. It is possible, however, to conclude—as explained in detail in Chapter 16—that the inclusion in Social Security of all federal, state, and local government employees would not decrease the total tax burden of supporting Social Security. Generally speaking, it would only substitute general revenue for part of the payroll tax.

The financial impact on the Social Security program of participation or nonparticipation by groups for whom participation is optional is probably less important than the effect on the employees themselves of gaining or losing the diverse benefit protection offered by the program.

Difficulties in Making Cost Comparisons of the Social Security Program with Alternative Private Systems

Social Security provides many benefits and has many characteristics that are difficult, if not impossible, to duplicate for subgroups of the population. It is only through a mandatory program with practically universal coverage that it is feasible to provide many of the benefits that are available under Social Security. Therefore, it is almost impossible to make a valid comparison of the cost of Social Security benefits as provided under:

the Social Security program financed through its payroll taxes; and

a private program providing the "same benefits" but financed in a different way.

Some of the characteristics of the Social Security program that make it virtually impossible to duplicate are listed below.

Benefits increase automatically as increases occur in the Consumer Price Index, in the average wages of the nation's employees, and in the average covered wages of a particular employee.

Benefits in course of payment increase with the CPI.

Survivorship benefits, as well as benefits that may become payable upon future age-retirement or disability-retirement, increase automatically:

Benefit formula is revised as changes occur in the average wages of the nation's employees.

Average earnings of a particular employee for purposes of computing benefits ("indexed earnings") change as his own earnings change and as average wages of the nation's employees change, usually resulting in eligibility for increased benefits.

Type and level of benefits change automatically as an employee's family status changes (without any change in the Social Security taxes payable). For example:

Single male marries.

Family has children.

Couple divorces after ten years of marriage (former wife continues to be eligible for certain benefits).

All of these changes—and others—result in automatic extensions in benefit protection. Certain other changes in family status result in contractions in benefit protection.

When an employee changes employers, he takes his "accrued benefits" with him regardless of his length of service. If he has satisfied part but not all of the participation requirements for a particular benefit (say the disability benefit) and his new employment is covered by Social Security, his previous participation will be added to his new participation in determining eligibility for future benefits. Changes back and forth between employed and self-employed status have no effect on benefits (but do affect Social Security taxes paid).

Survivorship protection and disability protection are provided without regard to an individual's health, occupational and avocational hazards, or other factors affecting his "insurability status." The same amount of Social Security tax is paid by an individual regardless of any of these factors.

Medicare benefits are payable to persons aged 65 and over who are entitled to monthly cash benefits under Social Security and to disabled persons under age 65 after they receive disability benefits for twenty-four months. Special medical expense benefits are payable to an insured person or to his dependents in the event of kidney disease.

Social Security benefits are not subject to federal income tax and are usually not subject to state and local income tax. The value of this tax-free feature to the individual depends upon the type and amount of his other income.

Social Security benefits for retired and disabled persons, their dependents, and their survivors are, in general, either reduced or not paid when the beneficiary is engaged in substantial employment or self-employment. Whether benefits are eliminated completely or simply reduced depends upon the individual's level of earnings. Different earnings levels apply for persons under age 65 than apply for persons between ages 65 and 72. This "earnings test" is no longer applied after an individual reaches age 72. (After 1981 references to age 72 will become age 70.) There are special rules, which include medical considerations, for disabled beneficiaries who work.

The Social Security program has experienced dramatic changes over the years with the addition of survivors benefits, disability benefits, Medicare, automatic adjustment provisions, and so on. Although future changes are certain to occur, they cannot be predicted with certainty.

Nature of Social Insurance: Social Adequacy

Because of the characteristics of Social Security listed above, it is probably possible to find a group of employees who could rightfully maintain that they receive less in benefits relative to their Social Security taxes than some other group of employees. For example, compare the following two hypothetical Groups A and B. (This example is for illustrative purposes only; it is not suggested that groups having precisely these characteristics exist.)

Group A

Women employees married to men who are in employment covered by Social Security.

Relatively high salaries for the husbands and low salaries for the wives.

Relatively small number of children.
Short working career for the wife.

Group B

Male employees.
Hazardous working conditions.
Nonworking wives with a relatively large number of children.
Relatively low wages.

Obviously more will be paid in benefits with respect to Group B relative to their Social Security taxes than will be paid with respect to Group A. Is this fair? It depends upon your standard, the yardstick by which you measure.

According to social insurance standards, it is fair and just that Group B receives relatively more from the program than does Group A. Social Security is a program of social insurance. It emphasizes social adequacy. It pays benefits according to presumed need: A married male who dies leaving behind a wife and three young children is presumed to have a need for survivorship benefits; a single person who dies—male or female—is presumed not to have a need for survivorship benefits (unless there are dependent parents). Yet, the Social Security tax rates paid by single and married persons are the same. That is social insurance.

It costs more to provide survivorship protection and disability protection for persons in Group B than it does for persons in Group A, yet the Social Security tax rates are the same for Group A and Group B. That is social insurance.

In a social insurance program that emphasizes the principles of social adequacy, no attempt is made to relate the benefits that a particular group of persons receives to the taxes paid by that group of persons to become eligible for such benefits.

There is, of course, a relationship between the taxes an individual pays and the benefits he receives since benefits are related to the earnings on which taxes are paid—among numerous other factors. But this relationship is more tenuous than most people have realized and this misunderstanding contributes materially to the public's current dissatisfaction with the Social Security program.

Can a Particular Group of Persons Duplicate Their Social Security Benefits at a Lower Cost than Their Social Security Taxes?

It follows from the preceding comments that some groups of employees could argue that they could obtain the same benefits that are provided by the Social Security program but at a lower cost than their Social Security taxes. While this seems reasonable, and while it may be true in theory (because of the way in which a social insurance program works), as a practical matter it is not true because it is not possible for a small group of employees to obtain many of the benefits that are available under the Social Security program.

If a group of employees drops out of the Social Security program, at least some of the employees will lose some benefits because some Social Security benefits are irreplaceable. The value of the benefits that are lost may well be offset by the reduced cost for the group as a whole; however, with respect to the individuals who are affected by the lost benefits, the reduced cost may not offset the value of the lost benefits.

Furthermore, just because the Group A employees may receive less in benefits than the Group B employees, it does not necessarily follow that Group A can duplicate its benefits at a lower cost than the Social Security taxes that it currently pays or will pay in the future (including the taxes paid on behalf of the employees by the employer).

Under the current-cost method of financing used for the Social Security program, the amount of taxes collected each year is intended to be approximately equal to the benefits and administrative expenses paid during the year plus a small additional amount to maintain the trust funds at an appropriate contingency level. This means that the taxes paid by one generation of workers are used to provide the benefits to an earlier generation of workers. Therefore, the taxes paid by a particular generation of workers are not necessarily equivalent to the cost of the benefits that will eventually be paid to it.

For example, if benefits are liberalized over time (in addition to adjustments made for inflation), then any particular generation may receive benefits of greater value than the taxes it paid to become eligible for such benefits. On the other hand, if benefits are deliberalized over time, any particular generation may receive benefits of lesser value than the taxes it paid to become eligible for such benefits.

Also, the size of the working population relative to the retired population, now and in the future, is an important determinant of whether a given generation receives benefits equivalent to the taxes it pays. Even if benefits are not increased from their present levels in relation to preretirement earnings, current projections indicate that future generations of workers must pay considerably higher tax rates than today's workers (at least 50 percent higher) because in the future the ratio of beneficiaries to taxpayers will be higher.

Relative Financial Stability of Social Security Program and Private and Public Systems

Despite the financial problems—specifically the need for additional income—the Social Security program will face during the coming years, there is little reason to expect that private and public employee benefit systems will not also face difficult financial problems, particularly if they attempt to provide benefits roughly comparable to those provided under the Social Security program. The financial problems of many of these private and public systems have become evident recently as a result of the maturing of some of the systems and as a result of the preparation of appropriate actuarial studies for others.

It stands to reason that a national social insurance program supported by the taxes of and operated for the benefit of 90 percent of the working population has greater financial stability and has a greater chance of meeting any financial challenge it may face than any smaller system covering only a few hundred or a few thousand employees in a limited geographical area or in a single industry.

Dilemma of Irrevocability of Election to Discontinue Participation

If a group of employees opts out of the Social Security program, the decision is irrevocable and future employees of this group will never again be eligible for coverage under present law.

It may be advantageous to the present employees of a particular group to opt out if they have sufficient quarters of coverage to be permanently and fully insured. The reduction in benefits may be more than offset by the exemption from future taxes (because of the weighted benefit formula, the minimum benefit, and the eligibility for Medicare benefits). For new employees of the group who have *no* Social Security coverage, however, the benefits that are relinquished may be equal to or greater than the taxes not required to be paid.

In other words, while it may be advantageous to present employees in a particular group to opt out of the Social Security program, it may *not* be advantageous to future employees to relinquish participation in the Social Security program. It is natural for present employees—or their representatives—to make decisions on opting out based on their own self-interest. But what about future employees whose self-interest is to participate in the Social Security program? Are they to be banned from participation in a program that provides benefits they need (and will probably desire) just because of action taken by their predecessor-employees? The government would undoubtedly come under pressure to permit any disadvantaged group of future employees to participate in the Social Security program, present law notwithstanding.

Another possibility to keep in mind is that a portion of the cost of the Social Security program may be financed by general revenue at some future time. If so, the general revenue paid by all segments of the population will be used to provide benefits to a limited segment of the population (participants in the Social Security program). In this event, also, the government would come under pressure to permit groups that had opted out to participate again in the Social Security program.

For these and related reasons, it seems unlikely that a group that opts out and is thereby irrevocably ineligible for future participation will in fact be forever excluded from the Social Security program. This means that a group that opts out now in accordance with present law will have been given advantages not afforded similar groups at other points in time—and thus could be considered to have received unfair advantage.

Better from Whose Point of View?

Consideration of whether a particular group of employees should opt out of Social Security should take into account the viewpoints of a number of interested parties, some of whose preferences can be expected to be conflicting:

Employer

Present employees with past Social Security coverage and their families

Future employees with no Social Security coverage and their families

Taxpayers and financial supporters of nonprofit organizations

Nation as a whole

Miscellaneous Considerations

The provision that enables a group of employees to "opt in" for a few years and then "opt out" creates a one-time opportunity for such a group to take advantage of the program—and of the participants for whom participation is compulsory. This is because of the "inequity" of the present law which pays to short-term participants benefits that are disproportionate to their period of participation, when compared with benefits earned and taxes paid by persons who participate in the program throughout their entire working career. This feature of the law also makes it possible for persons whose primary employment is not covered by Social Security—and who thus participate for a relatively short period—to receive benefits that are relatively large compared with their tax payments. To the extent that flaws in the design of the program create opportunities for the Social Security program to be taken advantage of, it is likely that the program will be redesigned. The Social Security Amendments of 1977 took limited steps in this direction by modifying the minimum benefit as well as certain dependent's benefits.

At the time a group of employees elects to participate in Social Security the individual employees usually have a voice in the decision; however, a subsequent decision to "opt out" of Social Security can be made unilaterally by the employer, at least in theory, without obtaining consent of the employees (present and future) who are affected. It would seem imprudent for an employer to make a unilateral decision to "opt out" of Social Security without consulting the employees who would be affected. On the other hand, even if all employees should favor "opting out," it may well be imprudent for the employer to honor the employees' wishes because of gaps that may then occur in employee benefit protection—as a result of the adverse impact on future employees who would be deprived of Social Security benefits as well as the possible long-range adverse, but unforeseeable, effect on present employees.

By one means or another it appears likely that virtually all persons will be covered by the Social Security program within ten to fifteen years and possibly sooner. If this is true, then a group that opts out of Social Security now and makes the necessary changes in its employee benefit program (not only the retirement plan but also the various death and disability benefit plans) will be faced with still further turmoil when it reenters the Social Security program and must again redesign its employee benefit program. Employee benefit programs that provide age-retirement, disability, and survivor benefits are long-range programs that need not and should not be revised frequently and substantively.

Conclusion

Groups of persons for whom participation in the Social Security program is optional face a predicament: whether to discontinue participation, if they are currently covered by Social Security, or to initiate participation, if they are not currently covered by Social Security. The problem is complex and its resolution depends upon diverse factors and future events, many of which cannot be predicted with certainty. Furthermore, because of the different interests of the various parties involved, a decision that appears to be advantageous for one party may not be advantageous for another party. Accordingly, there can be no assurance that a particular decision will turn out to be "correct" in the long run for the majority of persons much less for each person affected.

With respect to the original question posed in this chapter, "Should you opt out of Social Security if you can?": If a one-word reply is required I would answer "No." If a two-word reply is required I would answer "Probably not." If a one-sentence reply is desired, I would answer "No, but in the case of some employee groups, it may be preferable to opt out, taking into account the average of all points of view; however, if a group opts out, some individuals and their families will lose some benefits and thus be worse off."

It is vexatious to ponder a question with no clearly preferable answer. As indicated in Chapter 16, this dilemma arises because Social Security was designed to be compatible only with universal, mandatory participation. The imposition of optional participation on such a system cannot have been expected to work for very long—and it did not.

18
Should You Opt
Into Social Security
If You Can?

There are almost four million workers whose present jobs are not covered by Social Security—jobs that could be covered if the workers and their employers so desired. For the most part these are employees of state and local governments and non-profit organizations. They include all state employees in Colorado, Louisiana, Maine, Massachusetts, Nevada, and Ohio, and all state teachers in Alaska, California, Colorado, Connecticut, Illinois, Kentucky, Louisiana, Maine, Massachusetts, Missouri, Nevada, Ohio, and Puerto Rico. State employees of Alaska are not covered by Social Security, but they are not eligible to elect coverage because they were once covered and elected to withdraw.

On the other hand, there are approximately ten million state and local government employees, including state teachers, and almost four million employees of nonprofit organizations who *are* covered by Social Security.

Which group made the correct decision—the fourteen million workers who decided to participate in Social Security or the four million workers who decided not to participate? The total benefit protection—in the event of retirement, disability, or death—enjoyed by each of these two groups is different since, as was indicated in Chapter 17, it is virtually impossible to duplicate the benefits provided under Social Security.

Should these decisions, many of which were made some thirty years ago, be reevaluated? Just as a significant portion of the fourteen million workers are considering whether to opt out of Social Security, perhaps many of the four million workers should be considering whether to join Social Security.

Chapter 17 outlines the many factors to be considered in deciding whether to opt out of or continue to participate in Social Security. These same factors should be studied by groups that wish to consider joining Social Security. In addition, it is possible to make "quantitative studies" that will compare the benefits and costs of various alternative benefit programs for a particular group of employees considering joining (or opting out of) Social Security. Although these studies will give important guidance for making such decisions, they will not eliminate the role of judgment—as well as a certain amount of luck—in predicting the future course of Social Security and the actions and needs of the particular employees affected. The following miscellaneous comments may give added perspective to the question of whether to elect participation in Social Security.

Social Security has changed considerably in the thirty years since optional participation first became possible. These changes may make participation more desirable than it was when the last serious consideration was given by a particular group to joining Social Security. Disability and Medicare benefits have been added. A new method of determining benefits (based on indexed earnings) has been adopted and benefits in general have been increased. Automatic cost-of-living benefit adjustments have been in effect since 1974—a significant change in this era of inflation. Some of Social Security's benefits may be more important now than they were in the past; for example, benefits for divorced wives and tax-exempt benefits in a time of high taxation. All things considered, Social Security offers a very different package of benefits now than it did several years ago.

For some groups of employees it may be desirable to replace an existing system of employee benefits—partially, if not completely—with the Social Security program. Characteristics of the employee group may have changed since the decision not to participate was made. The financial situation of the employer may have changed. And, as already noted, Social Security has changed.

Despite the adverse publicity in recent years, Social Security is a good buy for many groups. For some employees, it may provide almost all the employee benefits that are needed. Also, there are some employee groups that still have no pension plan and would be well-advised to consider Social Security along with the other systems available. A small group of employees, most of whom have average earnings or less, should look seriously at the option of joining Social Security. If the group has a limited number of employees with higher earnings and special needs, supplemental benefits outside of Social Security can be arranged easily.

Groups with a relatively large number of employees nearing retirement age would probably find Social Security a particularly good buy. Some groups may find it advantageous to join Social Security for a few years and then opt out after a majority of employees have acquired certain minimum benefit rights. Some risk would be involved in such a course since Congress may change the law permitting withdrawal, particularly if the trend toward opting out accelerates.

Not participating in Social Security is sometimes a handicap in hiring the more experienced and mature employees who are employee-benefit-plan conscious and whose former jobs were covered by Social Security.

Most employees of employers whose jobs are not covered by Social Security have had some covered employment in the past and are thus entitled to some Social Security benefits. An employer that wants to integrate its supplemental plan benefits with these Social Security benefits may have difficulty in justifying such procedure if not participating in Social Security and may thus have to provide larger benefits than otherwise necessary.

Every year Congress considers financing some part of Social Security with general revenue. If and when this happens, and it almost certainly will, more of the cost of Social Security will be borne by the general body of taxpayers and less of the cost will be borne directly by the participants themselves. In such an event, Social Security will become a much better buy for the participants (considering only the direct payroll taxes). In fact, if a large enough portion of Social Security is financed by general revenue, the only sensible course of action for an employee group—from an economic viewpoint—would be to participate in Social Security.

In view of the above commentary, it would seem desirable for each employee group to reevaluate its position regarding participation in Social Security—the four million nonparticipants as well as the fourteen million participants. It would be unfortunate if sheer inertia prevented a group of employees from modifying past decisions—made under past conditions to solve past problems—and thus prevented the group from more appropriately satisfying the employee benefit needs of tomorrow.

A final word to prevent any misunderstanding: The reader can conclude fairly that I would recommend participation in Social Security for many employee groups not now covered. Later in the book I recommend significant change in Social Security so it will better serve our future needs. There is no conflict in these recommendations. Social Security should be changed; but until it is, we should take maximum advantage of the present system.

19
The Fortunate Eight Percent

This chapter is for a limited audience: the approximately 10 million men and women who will pay the maximum taxes and receive the maximum benefits under Social Security. All the comments and examples in this chapter apply to persons who have always had earnings equaling or exceeding the maximum earnings base used in computing benefits and taxes under Social Security and who will continue to do so in the future. By thus limiting the applicability of the chapter, we can reduce the number of examples and figures that you, the fortunate eight percent of Social Security participants, must examine in order to know how you personally—not someone else—will be affected by Social Security. Of course there will be some duplication of other sections of the book.

Your Taxes

Table 19.1 shows for an individual the maximum amount of earnings that have been subjected to tax for selected years since tax collections began on January 1, 1937. This is also the maximum amount of earnings used in determining benefits; hence the maximum is referred to as the "contribution and benefit base." Table 19.1 also shows the tax rates and the maximum taxes during these selected years. Figures are shown

Table 19.1

Contribution and Benefit Base, Tax Rate, and Maximum Tax for Selected Years

| Calendar Year | Contribution and Benefit Base | Employees[a] | | Self-Employed[b] | |
		Tax Rate	Maximum Tax	Tax Rate	Maximum Tax
(1)	(2)	(3)	(4)	(5)	(6)
1937	$ 3,000	1.0%	$ 30.00	—	—
1950	3,000	1.5	45.00	—	—
1960	4,800	3.0	144.00	4.5%	$ 216.00
1970	7,800	4.8	374.40	6.9	538.20
1980	25,900	6.13	1,587.67	8.1	2,097.90
1981	29,700	6.65	1,975.05	9.3	2,762.10
1990	52,800[c]	7.65	4,039.20[c]	10.75	5,676.00[c]

[a]A matching amount of taxes is paid by the worker's employer.
[b]Self-employed persons were not covered by Social Security prior to 1951. In 1951 the tax rate was 2.25%, and the maximum tax was $81.00.
[c]Amounts for 1990 are estimates prepared by the Social Security Administration.

separately for employed persons and for self-employed persons. In the case of employed persons, a matching employer tax is also payable. Figures for 1990 are on an estimated basis (the tax rate is specified in law but the contribution and benefit base will depend upon future changes in average wages). The Social Security taxes shown in Table 19.1 represent combined OASDI and HI taxes.

Table 19.1 indicates that the annual taxes for an employee have grown from $30.00 in 1937 to $1,587.67 in 1980 and that they will increase to an estimated $4,039.20 by the year 1990. For a self-employed person taxes have risen from $81.00 in 1951 (the first year the self-employed were covered) to $2,097.90 in 1980, and they will grow to an estimated $5,676.00 by the year 1990. These figures demonstrate, if nothing else, why the fortunate eight percent of Social Security taxpayers are paying more attention than ever before to Social Security.

This dramatic increase in taxes during the next ten years will be caused by two factors. First, the tax rate itself is scheduled to increase from 6.13 percent in 1980 to 7.65 percent in 1990 for employees as well as for their employers (a relative increase of 25 percent). For self-employed persons the tax rate is scheduled to increase from 8.10 percent in 1980 to 10.75 percent in 1990 (a relative increase of 33 percent). Second, the maximum taxable wage base is scheduled to increase from $25,900 in 1980 to $29,700 in 1981, and it is scheduled to increase thereafter at the same rate that average wages increase for the nation's workers.

For the next ten years or so following 1990, it is unlikely there will be significant increases in the amount of taxes relative to earnings. The maximum taxable wage base during this period is scheduled to rise in direct proportion to the rise in average earnings; hence, this will not result in any "real" increase in taxes. The tax rate for employees (and employers) will probably have to be increased from the scheduled rate of 7.65 percent in 1990 to about 8.0 percent by the year 2000, a relative increase of only 5 percent. Thus, the bulk of the tax increases for the remainder of this century will probably take place within the next ten years—that is, by 1990. The next round of substantial tax increases will not be required until some twenty-five years hence, around the year 2006, when the post-World War II baby boom begins to reach age 60. During the twenty-year period from 2006 to 2025, as this generation reaches retirement age, the tax rate for employees will have to increase from about 8 percent to about 12 percent. The tax rate for self-employed persons must increase from 10.75 percent in 1990 to about 11 percent in the year 2000 and to about 16 percent in the year 2025.

Please remember that these taxes for the future are estimates based upon the intermediate assumptions mentioned in Chapter 4. Actual future tax rates could be lower or higher than these estimates, depending upon actual experience. It seems more likely, however, that they will be higher than lower.

There has been increasing resistance among taxpayers to these higher payroll tax rates. This has resulted in proposals that payroll tax rates be held down and that more general revenue be used to finance Social Security. This procedure would not reduce the total taxes collected for Social Security purposes; it would simply redistribute the tax burden. Lower *payroll tax rates* would result in higher *total taxes* for persons with above-average earnings. The reasoning for this statement is as follows. General revenue consists primarily of personal and corporate income taxes. Personal income tax rates increase as income increases, while Social Security payroll tax rates are constant and are not even applied to an individual's income in excess of the contribution and benefit base. Accordingly, the use of general revenue to raise a given amount of taxes would result in higher taxes for high wage earners than would the use of payroll taxes.

The effect on employer costs of substituting general revenue for payroll tax is more complex. Employers with above-average profits could expect to pay higher total taxes; employers with above-average labor costs could expect to pay lower total taxes; nonprofit organizations and state and local governments participating in Social Security would pay none of the added general revenue, yet would benefit from the reduced payroll tax. Using general revenue would result in a further redistribution of the tax burden since it would impose taxes for Social Security purposes on individuals not covered by Social Security and thus not benefiting directly from Social Security. These and other effects of introducing general revenue and thus redistributing the tax burden are seldom mentioned when the panacea of general revenue is proposed.

Questions are frequently asked about the total Social Security taxes that have been paid in the past. An employee who paid the maximum tax from Social Security's inception on January 1, 1937 through December 31, 1979 would have paid a total of $11,203. This same amount would have been paid by the employer. A self-employed person would have paid total taxes of $14,987 during this period. In considering the value of Social Security taxes paid in the past, it is more appropriate to assume that they were invested and earned interest. In making calculations that involve interest, Social Security actuaries usually assume that funds can be invested to yield 2½ percent more than the rate of inflation each year (although this is relatively more difficult to achieve in years of high inflation). Based upon this assumption, the cumulative employee taxes of $11,203 augmented by interest become $27,760 (not including employer taxes which would have accumulated an equal amount). The cumulative self-employed taxes of $14,987 augmented by interest become $32,820.

Table 19.2 summarizes these figures as well as similar figures for more recent periods. Because of the relatively higher taxes

Table 19.2

**Maximum Cumulative Taxes Paid during Selected Periods by
Employees and Self-Employed Persons**

Period	Total Taxes		Taxes Accumulated With Interest[b]	
	Employees[a]	Self-Employed	Employees[a]	Self-Employed
(1)	(2)	(3)	(4)	(5)
1937–1979	$11,202.97	$14,987.10	$27,760	$32,820
1960–1979	10,056.97	13,920.60	19,550	27,530
1970–1979	7,811.77	10,619.70	12,150	16,620

[a]An equal amount of employer taxes was paid during this period.
[b]An interest rate of 2½ percent more than the Consumer Price Index increase during each year was assumed for this purpose.

in recent years, the bulk of the tax has been paid during the past ten years. As will be indicated later, extreme care must be taken in interpreting these accumulated taxes lest erroneous conclusions be drawn.

Your Benefits

Contrary to popular belief, your benefits are not based primarily upon the Social Security taxes you have paid. Taxpayers have been led to believe that there is a strong connection between their tax payments and their benefits because of forty years of propaganda about "contributions" paid to a "trust fund" under an "insurance program" thus creating an "earned right" to benefits payable upon old age, disability, death, or illness. The fact is that benefits are based upon many factors, principally the following:

The average earnings upon which you have paid Social Security taxes, excluding earnings for certain years and adjusted for changes over the years in national average earnings. (But benefits are not uniformly proportional to earnings. Benefits relative to earnings are higher for low wage earners than for high wage earners.)

Your need as measured by your earning power after becoming eligible for benefits.

The number and kind of your family members, including their need as measured by their earning power after becoming eligible for benefits.

The following sections give examples of benefits payable under various circumstances. Not every benefit is mentioned, just the principal benefits most often payable. Keep in mind that Social Security benefits are not subject to federal, state, and local income taxes. On the other hand, Social Security taxes paid by individuals are not tax deductible; that is, they are paid from earnings on which normal federal and state income taxes have been paid.

Retirement Benefits

Social Security retirement benefits can begin as early as age 62 or as late as age 70 (age 72 until 1982), depending upon the circumstances. Examples are given first for retirement at age 65; then earlier and later retirements are discussed.

To be eligible to receive retirement benefits, you must be "fully insured." You obtain "insured" status by earning "quarters of coverage." In 1981, one quarter of coverage is obtained for each unit of $310 that you earn in covered employment and pay Social Security taxes on during the year. (No more than four quarters of coverage can be earned in any given year.) In future years this amount will increase automatically in step with increases in average wages. Prior to 1978 a quarter of coverage was obtained for each quarter in which you had wages of at least $50. If you were self-employed prior to 1978, you earned one quarter of coverage for each unit of $100 of self-employment income (maximum of four per year). To be "fully insured," you must have as many quarters of coverage as there are years in the period beginning with 1951 (or the year you became age 22, if later) and ending with the year before the year in which you become age 62. This period is inclusive: for example, a worker reaching age 62 in January 1980 would need 29 quarters of coverage to be fully insured for retirement benefits (one quarter for each of the years 1951 through 1979).

If you quit working at the end of 1979 and attained age 65 in January 1980, you were eligible for a retirement benefit of $572.00 payable each month from January 1980 until your death (no benefit is payable for the month in which death occurs). This monthly benefit will be increased automatically to take into account increases in the Consumer Price Index. Generally speaking, benefit increases are made in June each year if an increase of at least 3 percent is indicated. This automatic adjustment feature has considerable value. With inflation of 5 percent per year, the $572.00 monthly benefit would become $730.30 after five years and $932.30 after ten years. With inflation of 10 percent per year, the $572.00 monthly benefit would become $921.50 after five years and $1,484.40 after ten years—and $2,390.90 after fifteen years.

These full benefits may not be paid, however, if you continue to work after age 65 and receive earned income (as distinguished from investment income, rental income, and the like). In 1980 you can receive earned income of $5,000 without affecting your retirement benefits; however, benefits will be reduced by $1 for every $2 you earn over $5,000. Therefore, if your earned income is $19,873 or more in 1980 you would not receive any Social Security retirement benefit for 1980. (This computation is based on total benefits in 1980 of $7,436.60 reflecting the June 1980 cost-of-living benefit increase.) Earned income of more than $5,000 and less than $19,873 would result in the loss of some but not all Social Security retirement benefits. The "earnings limitation" increases from $5,000 in 1980 to $5,500 in 1981 and $6,000 in 1982. Thereafter the earnings limitation is increased to keep up with increases in average wages of all the nation's employees. After you reach age 70 there is no earnings limitation, and you will receive your total Social Security retirement benefit no matter how much you earn. During the calendar year in which you reach age 70, your earnings during the month of your 70th birthday and thereafter are excluded in determining your benefits for the year. (Until 1982 the earnings limitation applies until age 72.)

This example makes it clear that Social Security does not make an unconditional promise to pay benefits beginning at age 65. If you continue working at full salary, benefits will not commence until age 70 (age 72 until 1982). A substantial reduction in salary may entitle you to receive partial Social Security benefits; however, full benefits are payable prior to age 70 (age 72 until 1982) only if your paid employment virtually ceases.

Just as Social Security does not unconditionally provide benefits at age 65, it does not specify the age at which you must retire to receive Social Security retirement benefits. Benefits may commence as early as age 62 or as late as age 70 (72 until 1982). However, age 65 is the "normal retirement age." If benefits commence prior to age 65, they are reduced; and if benefits commence after age 65, they are increased.

Benefits commencing earlier than age 65 may be smaller for several reasons. First, you may have smaller average earnings as a result of not working until age 65. Second, a reduction factor will be applied to the benefits otherwise payable because you will receive more monthly benefit checks since they will begin sooner. This reduction factor is $5/9$ of 1 percent for each month that you receive your benefits before age 65. If benefits begin at age 62, for example, they will be reduced by 20 percent. Furthermore, the annual amount of earned income you can have between ages 62 and 65 without giving up Social Security benefits is only $3,720 (in 1980), in contrast to the $5,000 earnings limit after age 65. This may result in a further effective reduction in benefits commencing earlier than age 65.

Benefits commencing later than age 65 may be larger for two reasons. First, you may have larger average earnings as a result of working beyond age 65. Second, an increase factor will be applied to the benefits otherwise payable to reflect your expectation to receive fewer monthly benefit checks since they will begin later. If you reach age 65 before 1982, the increase factor is 1 percent of your benefit for each year after age 65 that you postpone receipt of your benefit ($1/12$ of 1 percent for each month). If you reach age 65 in 1982 or later, the increase factor is 3 percent of your benefit for each year ($1/4$ of 1 percent for each month). The increase factor, be it 1 percent or 3 percent, is much less than it would be if full adjustment were made to compensate for the later commencement of benefit payments.[1]

Money-Saving Hints

If you reach age 65 in January 1980 and plan to work until March 1, 1980, you should still apply for Social Security retirement benefits as of January 1, 1980. If your earned income for January and February combined is less than $5,000, you can still receive Social Security benefits for January and February ($1,144 of tax-free income you might otherwise overlook). Even if you retire later than March 1, 1980, and your earned income exceeds $5,000, it may still work to your advantage to apply for benefits as of January 1. You may want to take into account the offsetting effect of the increase for delayed commencement of benefits which you will forego; however, in most cases it is to your advantage to start your benefits as soon after age 65 as possible.

Even if you do not start your retirement benefits at age 65, you should apply for Medicare benefits at age 65. Medicare is available at age 65 even if you continue working after age 65, *but only if you apply for the benefits.*

Benefits for Family Members When You Retire

When you retire and begin receiving benefits, other members of your family may also be entitled to benefits based upon your participation in Social Security, even though they may not have paid Social Security taxes. As in the above example, it is assumed that you quit working at the end of 1979, and attained age 65 and began receiving a monthly retirement benefit in January 1980 of $572.00.

If your spouse were aged 65 or older in January 1980, he or she is eligible for a benefit of $286.00 payable each month that both of you are alive. This benefit, too, will increase automatically as the cost-of-living increases. After your death, your spouse's benefit will increase to your basic benefit of $572.00 per month (plus any cost-of-living benefit increases that have been granted) and will be payable for his or her remaining lifetime.

If your spouse is between age 62 and 65, there is a choice to make:

Defer commencement of benefits until age 65, in which event the full $286.00 will be payable (adjusted for cost-of-living increases that have occurred in the interim).

Start receiving benefits immediately on a permanently reduced basis. (For example, if benefits commence at age 62 they would be reduced by 25 percent and would be $214.50.)

If your spouse is not yet age 62, you can arrange for benefits to commence at any time between ages 62 and 65. The exact amount will depend upon the age at which benefits commence and the cost-of-living increases that have occurred in the interim.

If your spouse has had government employment in a position not covered by Social Security, his or her spouse's benefit from Social Security will generally be offset by the amount of any pension benefit derived from such employment. An exception is made that permits the payment of spouse's benefits without the offset if the spouse were eligible for the noncovered-employment pension prior to 1983 and would have been eligible for the spouse's benefit under the law in effect in January 1977. (This is a situation where precise details should be furnished the local Social Security office for a determination of the exact benefits payable.)

Your spouse will be eligible to receive benefits *prior to age 62* if he or she is caring for an "eligible child" under age 18 (or any age if disabled before age 22). The benefit would depend on how many children were also receiving benefits. If there is one such child, the spouse's benefit would be $214.30 per month payable until the child reaches age 18. Your spouse's benefits would then stop, and start again any time your spouse elects between ages 62 and 65.

Each eligible child will also receive benefits until reaching age 18, or age 22 if a full-time student, or until death if disabled before age 22. An eligible child must be one of your natural children (legitimate or illegitimate), adopted children, dependent stepchildren or dependent grandchildren (if their parents are deceased or disabled), and must be unmarried. The amount of the benefits payable to your children depends on how many of your family members are eligible to receive benefits. For example, if only one child is eligible for benefits as your dependent, and no one else, his or her benefit would be $286.00 per month. If there are additional beneficiaries, the amount per beneficiary would be lower because of the limit on the total amount of benefits payable in any month to members of one family. For a worker retiring in January 1980 at age 65, this maximum family benefit was $1,000.60. Benefits for family members other than the primary beneficiary are reduced proportionately to the extent necessary to stay within the family maximum.

The examples of monthly retirement benefits given above are summarized in Table 19.3 along with the "replacement ratio" corresponding to each of the illustrative monthly dollar benefits. The replacement ratio is defined here as the ratio of the total benefits payable for 1980 (including the benefit increase for June and later) to the average annual maximum taxable earnings (gross earnings before taxes) during the three-year period 1977–1979. This is an arbitrary definition; average preretirement earnings could have been net of taxes, or they could have been averaged over a longer or shorter period than three years.

A projection of future replacement ratios gives an indication of the extent to which Social Security will replace preretirement income, and thus the extent to which Social Security must be

Table 19.3

**Estimated Social Security Retirement Benefits for
Workers Retiring at Age 65 in January 1980,
Having Had Maximum Career Earnings**

Beneficiary[a]	Monthly Benefit Amount	Replacement Ratio[b]
(1)	(2)	(3)
Worker only	$ 572.00	39%
Worker and spouse aged 65	858.00	59
Worker and one child	858.00	59
Worker and two children	1,000.60	68
Worker, spouse, and one or more children	1,000.60	68

[a]Benefits shown in family examples assume that each family member is dependent on the retired worker for support. See text for discussion of benefit eligibility requirements for family members.

[b]This figure is the ratio of the total benefits for 1980 to the average annual maximum taxable earnings during the three-year period 1977–1979; thus, it is the percentage of the final three-year average earnings that is replaced by Social Security benefits during 1980.

supplemented (by private savings and employer-provided pensions) to sustain any given standard of living. If the Social Security law is not revised, the replacement ratios shown in Table 19.3 will decline somewhat for persons retiring in the near future but will then rise and eventually stabilize at about 85 percent of the amounts shown in Column (3). This information is quite valuable in making advance provision for retirement. It should be kept in mind that the replacement ratios in Table 19.3 relate to the maximum taxable earnings covered by Social Security and not to actual average earnings, which may be larger.

The payment of benefits shown in Table 19.3 is subject to the earnings test mentioned earlier. Earnings of the worker may reduce benefits of both the worker and family members. Earnings of individual family members may reduce only their individual benefits.

The benefits payable to family members will be increased to reflect changes in the Consumer Price Index in the same way that benefits payable to the retired worker are increased.

Your divorced spouse (or spouses) may be entitled to benefits as early as age 62 if married to you for at least ten years. Benefits will not be payable unless you are also receiving benefits. In some cases remarriage of your spouse will disqualify him or her from benefits.

The benefit examples outlined above for family members by no means cover all the possible cases. A spouse may have earned benefits based on his or her own work record. If so, this benefit or the benefit payable as a family member, whichever is larger, will be payable. To be eligible for a wife's benefit, a woman must have been married to a retired or disabled worker for at least one year, but there are exceptions. There are countless fine points to consider in determining benefits. While this section provides information on the general level and nature of Social Security retirement benefits, your local Social Security office should be consulted once you near retirement age for a complete analysis of the various benefits payable and the particular rules involved.

Disability Benefits

To be eligible for Social Security disability benefits, you must be unable to engage in any substantial gainful activity because of some medically determinable physical or mental impairment that can be expected to result in death or has lasted, or can be expected to last, for a continuous period of at least twelve months; or, after age 55, if blindness prohibits you from engaging in substantial gainful activity requiring skills or abilities comparable to those of any gainful activity in which you previously engaged with some regularity over a substantial period of time.

In addition, you must have acquired quarters of coverage—that is, paid Social Security taxes—for a specified period of time which varies with your age. To be eligible for benefits in 1980: if you were born after 1956, you must have acquired at least six quarters of coverage in the last three years; at the other extreme, if you were born before 1930, you must have twenty-nine quarters of coverage, twenty of which were acquired in the last ten years; and if you were born between 1930 and 1956, inclusive, the required number of quarters of coverage falls within these extremes. For blind persons the requirements are somewhat less stringent.

There is a waiting period of five full consecutive calendar months before disability benefits begin. For example, if you became disabled in July 1979, benefits would first be payable for January 1980. (The benefit check would actually be received approximately February 3.)

Just as for retirement benefits, your basic disability benefit depends upon the average earnings upon which you have paid Social Security taxes—with certain adjustments. Your average earnings for this purpose vary with your attained age; therefore, benefits vary somewhat depending upon your age at disability. Accordingly, disability benefits for a person first eligible to receive them in January 1980 could be as low as $498.00 or as high as $552.40 depending upon the age at disability—the higher the age, the lower the benefits. If you became eligible for disability benefits payable beginning in January 1980, and you were then aged 35, your monthly disability benefit would be $528.90.

Monthly disability benefits are increased automatically to take into account increases in the Consumer Price Index, just as the age-retirement benefit is increased, and the benefits are also tax free. The payment of benefits ends with the earliest of:

the month in which you die;

the third month following the month in which disability ceases; and

the month in which you attain age 65.

At age 65, normal old-age retirement benefits become payable in an amount that is usually equal to the disability benefit.

The earnings limitation that applies to age-retirement benefits does not apply to the payment of disability benefits; however, other restrictions apply. A disabled person may be offered rehabilitation services by a state vocational rehabilitation agency. If so, benefits may be denied for any month in which such rehabilitation services are refused. There is a certain amount of judgment involved in determining when disability ceases. To encourage rehabilitation, earnings of up to $300 per month (as of 1980) are generally allowed without affecting the payment of disability benefits. Furthermore, a disability beneficiary is allowed nine months of trial work without affecting the right to benefits.

After you have received disability benefits for twenty-four months you will be eligible for Medicare benefits. Hospital Insurance benefits (Part A of Medicare) are provided free of charge. Supplementary Medical Insurance benefits (Part B of Medicare) are optional and require a monthly premium of $9.60 after July 1, 1980 (subject to annual increases as average medical expenses increase). If you or your dependent has chronic kidney disease requiring dialysis or kidney transplant, Medicare is available without the twenty-four-month waiting period.

Money-Saving Hints

Benefits are not paid automatically, they must be duly applied for. If you make late application for benefits, they can be paid retroactively but only for twelve months, beginning with the months after the five-month waiting period. In some cases where a disabled worker dies without having filed for disability, benefits may be claimed retroactively.

As early as possible you should establish the fact that disability has begun in order to minimize any dispute about when the disability has lasted five full months.

Disability benefits may begin with the first full month of disability if it arises within five years after an earlier qualifying disability has ended.

Benefits for Family Members If You Become Disabled

If you become disabled and begin receiving benefits, other members of your family may also be entitled to benefits based upon your participation in Social Security, even though they may not have paid Social Security taxes. In general, the rules for payment are the same as if you receive age-retirement benefits. As in the above example, assume that you became eligible for disability benefits payable beginning in January 1980, that you were then aged 35, and that your monthly disability benefit is $528.90.

If you are married but have no eligible children (defined later), no spouse's benefit will be paid until he or she reaches age 65. At age 65, your spouse's benefit would be $264.50 adjusted for cost-of-living increases granted between January 1980 and the spouse's attainment of age 65. Stated another way, your spouse's benefit at age 65 will be 50 percent of your benefit at that time. Your spouse may elect to receive benefits as early as age 62, in which event the benefits would be actuarially reduced to take into account the longer period over which they would be payable.

If your spouse has had government employment in a position not covered by Social Security, his or her spouse's benefit from Social Security will generally be offset by the amount of any pension benefit derived from such employment. An exception is made that would permit the payment of spouse's benefits without the offset if the spouse were eligible for the noncov-ered-employment pension prior to 1983 and would have been eligible for the spouse's benefit under the law in effect in January 1977.

If you should die—again, with no eligible children—a monthly benefit would be payable to your spouse when he or she reaches age 65. The benefit would be $528.90 adjusted for cost-of-living increases granted between January 1980 and the spouse's attainment of age 65. In other words, your surviving spouse's benefit at age 65 would be the same as would have been payable to you had you survived. Your surviving spouse may elect to receive benefits as early as age 60, in which event the benefits would be actuarially reduced to take into account the longer period over which they would be payable.

If you have eligible children, additional benefits may be payable not only to the children but also to your spouse regardless of age. An eligible child must be one of your natural children (legitimate or illegitimate), adopted children, dependent stepchildren or dependent grandchildren (if their parents are deceased or disabled), and must be unmarried. The amount of the benefits payable to your children and your spouse depends on how many of your family members are eligible to receive benefits since there are limits to benefits payable to a single family.

The following examples assume, as before, that you became eligible for disability benefits payable beginning in January 1980, that you were then aged 35, and that your monthly disability benefit is $528.90.

If you have a spouse who is caring for an eligible child under age 18 (or any age if disabled before age 22), each of them will be eligible for monthly benefits of $198.40, or a total of $396.80. This amount, together with your monthly benefit of $528.90, totals $925.70, which is the maximum family benefit in January 1980. If there is more than one child, the $396.80 payable to your family members would not be increased; rather, each family member would receive a smaller portion of the total. The spouse's benefit will cease when the child reaches age 18. The child's benefit will cease at age 18 except that if the child is a full-time student, benefits will continue through the semester or quarter the child reaches age 22 provided he has not yet received an undergraduate degree. If the child is a full-time student, the child's benefit would increase to $264.50 at age 18 (when the spouse's benefit ceases) because the family maximum would no longer be limiting.

If you should die while these benefit payments are being made to your spouse and child, the benefits would continue just as if you were still alive and disabled, except they would be larger: $396.70 for your spouse and $396.70 for your child, or a total of $793.40 per month. Benefits to your spouse would cease when the child reaches age 18 and would resume when the spouse reaches age 65 (or age 60 if reduced benefits are selected). The spouse's benefit at age 65 would be $528.90 adjusted for cost-of-living increases granted since January 1980. Benefits to your child would cease at age 18 (22 if a full-time student).

Table 19.4 gives examples of monthly disability benefits payable in several situations along with the replacement ratio corresponding to each of the illustrative monthly dollar benefits. For workers only, these replacement ratios will not change significantly unless the law is amended; hence, they can serve as a guide to how much Social Security benefits must be supple-

Table 19.4

Estimated Social Security Disability Benefits for Workers Becoming Eligible for Disability Benefits in January 1980 at Various Ages, Having Had Maximum Career Earnings[a]

Beneficiary[b]	Monthly Benefit Amount	Replacement Ratio[c]
(1)	(2)	(3)
Worker becoming disabled at age 25:		
Worker only	$552.40	44%
Worker, spouse, and one or more children	966.80	76
Worker becoming disabled at age 35:		
Worker only	528.90	42
Worker, spouse, and one or more children	925.70	73
Worker becoming disabled at age 55:		
Worker only	498.00	39
Worker, spouse, and one or more children	871.60	69

[a]Public Law 96-265 (enacted June 9, 1980) made a number of changes in the way benefits are calculated for disabled workers and their families. The disabled workers in this example would not be affected; however, benefits would be reduced somewhat for persons becoming eligible for family disability benefits in the future.

[b]Benefits shown in family examples assume that each family member is dependent on retired worker for support. See text for discussion of benefit eligibility requirements for family members.

[c]This figure is the ratio of total benefits for 1980 to the average annual maximum taxable earnings during the three-year period 1976–1978, the last three full years of earnings prior to disablement. In each example the worker is assumed to become disabled in July 1979 and to begin receiving benefits in January 1980.

mented to sustain any given standard of living. For workers becoming disabled after June 1980 and becoming eligible for *family benefits*, however, replacement ratios would be somewhat smaller than indicated here. Please note that the replacement ratios relate to the maximum taxable earnings covered by Social Security and not to your actual average earnings, which may be larger.

The payment of the benefits shown in Table 19.4 is subject to the continued disability of the worker as well as to the continued eligibility of the spouse and children. The earnings test, which applies to retired workers, does not apply to a disabled worker. The earnings test does apply, however, to family members, whose benefits are thus subject to reduction if their earnings exceed certain specified amounts.

Your divorced spouse (or spouses) may be entitled to benefits as early as age 62 if married to you for at least ten years. Benefits will not be payable unless you are also receiving benefits. In some cases remarriage of your spouse will disqualify him or her from benefits.

The benefit examples outlined above for family members by no means cover all the possible cases. A spouse may have earned benefits based on his or her own work record. If so, this benefit or the benefit payable by virtue of being a family member, whichever is larger, will be payable. To be eligible for a wife's benefit, a woman must have been married to a retired or disabled worker for at least one year, but there are exceptions. There are numerous details to consider in determining benefits payable in a particular situation. A thorough consultation with your local Social Security office is highly recommended.

Survivors Benefits

A variety of benefits may be payable under Social Security in the event of your death. To be eligible for some benefits you must be "currently insured"; for others you must be "fully insured."

You are currently insured if you have acquired at least six quarters of coverage—that is, paid Social Security taxes—in the thirteen-calendar-quarter period ending with the calendar quarter of death.

You are fully insured if you have as many quarters of coverage as there are years in the period beginning with 1951 (or the year you become age 22, if later) and ending with the year before your year of death.

You are eligible for a lump sum death benefit of $255 if you are *either* currently insured or fully insured. The benefit will be paid to your surviving spouse if living in the same household at your death; otherwise it will be paid to the funeral home director or such other person who paid the funeral expenses.

Upon your death one or more of the following types of monthly survivors benefits may become payable:

Mother's or father's benefit. A monthly benefit payable to a widow or widower, regardless of age, who is caring for at least one of your children under age 18 or disabled before age 22. A divorced wife can qualify for this benefit if the child in her care is her natural or legally adopted child. You must have been either currently insured or fully insured.

Child's benefit. A monthly benefit payable to a child who is under age 18, or over age 18 but disabled before age 22, or between ages 18 and 22 and a full-time student. The child must have been considered your dependent and must be unmarried. You must have been either currently insured or fully insured.

Widow's or widower's benefit. A monthly benefit payable to a widow or widower aged 60 or older who is not entitled to an old-age or disability benefit that is larger than the widow's or widower's benefit. A divorced wife can qualify for this benefit if married at least ten years before the divorce. In some cases a widow or widower who is disabled can start receiving survivors benefits at any time after reaching age 50. You must have been fully insured.

Parent's benefit. A monthly benefit payable to a parent aged 62 or older who was dependent upon you for support and who is not entitled to an old-age or disability benefit that is larger than the parent's benefit. You must have been fully insured.

The monthly survivors benefits outlined above have many

other conditions governing their initial and continued payment. The amount of the benefits depends upon a variety of factors, including the average earnings on which you have paid Social Security taxes (which is related, in part, to your age at death), the maximum benefits payable to a family, and the earnings of the beneficiaries once they are eligible for benefits. There are so many possible combinations of benefits that it is not feasible to cover all of them here.

Table 19.5 gives numerical examples of benefits payable in selected cases. The initial monthly benefit amount is stated in dollars. The total benefits payable for 1980 are stated as replacement ratios: that is, the benefit in relation to the average annual maximum taxable earnings during the three years preceding death. Also shown is the actuarial present value of these survivors benefits (explained later in this chapter in more detail). Consider the middle example in Table 19.5 of a worker who died in January 1980 at age 35, having had maximum career earnings and leaving as survivors a spouse aged 35 and two children aged 5 and 10. Assume that you, the worker, were a male and the spouse a female. (The actuarial present values are different for male and female spouses; for the other figures in the table, the sex of the spouse is irrelevant.) Based on all these assumptions, your wife and children would receive a monthly benefit of $928.80, or 63 percent of your average gross earnings during the three years prior to your death. Ignoring cost-of-living adjustments for the moment, this amount would continue for twelve years; that is, until your older child reaches age 22 (assuming the child was a full-time student). It would then reduce to $796.20 and continue for another year until your younger child reaches age 18. Monthly benefits for your wife would stop at this time (your wife would then be aged 48). Your younger child, if a student, would receive $398.10 for another four years, until age 22. When your wife reaches age 65, monthly benefits of $530.70 would be payable to her for the remainder of her life. Alternatively she could elect to receive reduced monthly benefits beginning anytime between age 60 and 65. If benefits commence at age 60, they would be $379.50 per month. All of these benefits would be increased to reflect changes in the Consumer Price Index, a very important feature.

Table 19.5

Estimated Amount and Value of Social Security Survivors Benefits for Survivors of Workers Dying in January 1980 at Various Ages, Having Had Maximum Career Earnings

Beneficiary[a]	Monthly Benefit Amount	Replacement Ratio[b]	Actuarial Present Value of Future Benefits[c]
(1)	(2)	(3)	(4)
Worker dying at age 25:			
Spouse aged 25 with one child	$849.00	58%	$189,800[d]
Spouse aged 25 with two or more children	990.60	68	221,300[d]
Worker dying at age 35:			
Spouse aged 35 with one child	796.20	54	155,100[e]
Spouse aged 35 with two or more children	928.80	63	172,000[e]
Worker dying at age 55:			
Spouse aged 55 with one child	739.20	50	100,100[f]
Spouse aged 55 with two or more children	862.50	59	103,000[f]

[a]Benefits shown in family examples assume that each family member is dependent on retired worker for support. See text for discussion of benefit eligibility requirements for family members.

[b]This figure is the ratio of the total benefits for 1980 to the average annual maximum taxable earnings during the three-year period 1977–1979; thus, it is the percentage of the final three-year average earnings that is replaced by Social Security benefits during 1980.

[c]This figure represents the amount that, if placed in an interest-bearing account on January 1, 1980, would be just sufficient to pay all monthly benefits as they fell due. It assumes that the family members have average life expectancies and that interest will be earned at a rate equal to the cost-of-living increases each year plus 2½ percent.

[d]Estimate assumes children are ages 1 month and 2 years as of January 1, 1980, and will remain in school until age 22. Single-child estimate assumes child is at lower age. Estimate includes present value of future widow's benefits to spouse, beginning at age 60, of $30,000.

[e]Estimate assumes children are ages 5 and 10 years as of January 1, 1980, and will remain in school until age 22. Single-child estimate assumes child is at lower age. Estimate includes present value of future widow's benefits to spouse, beginning at age 60, of $36,300.

[f]Estimate assumes children are ages 15 and 20 years as of January 1, 1980, and will remain in school until age 22. Single-child estimate assumes child is at lower age. Estimate includes present value of future widow's benefits to spouse, beginning at age 60, of $58,900.

The value of all these future benefits payable to your widow and children is approximately $172,000 as of January 1980 when they commence. In other words, a lump sum amount of $172,000 invested to earn interest (at 2½ percent more than the increase in the Consumer Price Index) would be sufficient, on the average, to provide the future monthly income outlined above. These survivor benefits, therefore, may be viewed as a death benefit of $172,000. As indicated in Table 19.5 for other examples, the effective death benefit ranges from some $100,000 to $221,000. Of course, a worker with no survivors would have no death benefit (except for the $255 lump sum benefit).

There are several factors that could affect the payment of these future benefits and thus decrease (in some instances, increase) their value. If the children do not continue as full-time students, their benefits will stop at age 18. If one of the children marries, the child's benefit will stop. If one of the children becomes disabled before age 22, the child's benefit and the mother's benefit will continue indefinitely (so long as your wife is caring for the disabled child). If your wife becomes disabled, she may qualify for benefits as early as age 50 (otherwise, between ages 48 and 60 she would not be receiving benefits). If your wife remarries after age 60, it has no effect on her benefits; but, if she remarries before age 60, in most cases she would forego all future benefits (but the children's benefits would not be affected). If your wife or either of your children should work, their earnings could result in a reduction of their Social Security benefits—because of the earnings limitation discussed previously. It is important to note, however, that the earnings of a particular survivor affect only his or her benefit and not the benefits of any other survivor. If your wife has government employment in a position not covered by Social Security, her survivors benefit will generally be offset by the amount of any pension benefit derived from such employment. An exception is made that permits payment of benefits without the offset to widows (and widowers) *if* they were eligible for their noncovered-employment pension prior to 1983 and meet all the requirements for entitlement to survivors benefits that existed and were applied in January 1977.

Money-Saving Hint

When a retired worker and spouse apply for benefits, the spouse will automatically be paid the higher of the benefits he or she would receive as either a spouse or as a retired worker. The spouse cannot apply only for spouse's benefits or only for retired worker benefits—the application for either is treated as an application for any and all benefits payable. In the case of a widow or widower, however, the applicant can choose to apply for either survivors benefits *or* retirement benefits. If the widow(er) is retiring before age 65 and is in good health, it could be greatly to her or his advantage to apply for reduced widow(er)'s benefits only, and then at age 65 apply for *unreduced* retirement benefits. In some cases the reverse procedure may yield greater value; that is, an application for reduced retirement benefits followed by an application at age 65 for unreduced widow(er)'s benefits.

An example will illustrate the potential windfall from restricting one's application. Suppose a male worker died in January 1980 at age 62, leaving a widow the same age. Assume that both the husband and wife had maximum career earnings in Social Security covered employment. The widow could begin to receive a monthly survivors benefit of $408.60 based on her husband's work record. She would also be eligible for a *reduced* retirement benefit of $402.80 based on her own work record—*but she doesn't have to apply for it at this time.* Instead she can collect the reduced widow's benefit of $408.60, plus cost-of-living adjustments, for three years and then apply for her *unreduced* retired worker's benefit of $503.40 per month, plus any intervening cost-of-living benefit increases. The actuarial present value of her net gain (or loss, if she simply continues to receive reduced widow's benefits) is approximately $15,000.

In other examples where there is a difference between the husband's and wife's earnings, it could still be to the surviving spouse's advantage to file for reduced benefits of one type and then convert to unreduced benefits of the other type at age 65. Of course, this assumes that the surviving spouse intends to retire prior to age 65 anyway—it would not necessarily be an advantage to stop working before age 65 just to receive three years of extra benefits. Careful examination of the facts is necessary in many of these cases to determine the best procedure since it is not always obvious.

There are many types of survivors benefits payable, and the preceding paragraphs merely summarize the more common ones together with the basic rules governing their payment. Social Security is obviously a very complicated program. If you are in doubt about your family's eligibility for Social Security benefits in the event of your death, you should consult with a local Social Security office—and do some studying on your own.

Medicare Benefits

You become eligible for Medicare benefits once you reach age 65 and fill out the appropriate applications. You are also eligible for Medicare benefits—even if you are under age 65—if you have been receiving Social Security benefits as a disabled beneficiary for at least twenty-four months, or if you or a dependent has chronic renal disease requiring dialysis or kidney transplant.

The Medicare program consists of Hospital Insurance (HI) and Supplementary Medical Insurance (SMI), frequently referred to as Part A and Part B, respectively. Hospital Insurance provides partial reimbursement for the cost of inpatient hospital services as well as a number of other services such as those provided by a skilled nursing facility or a home health agency. Supplementary Medical Insurance helps pay for the cost of physician services plus certain other expenses such as outpatient hospital care and home health agency visits. Not all medical services are covered by Medicare; the principal exclusions are routine care, outpatient drugs, eyeglasses, and dental care.

HI benefits are provided automatically once you reach age 65 as long as you are entitled to a Social Security benefit as a retired worker, spouse, widow(er), or other beneficiary. HI benefits are available even if your monthly cash benefit is completely withheld because of "excess earnings" under the retirement test. The SMI program is optional and requires premium payments of $9.60 per month after July 1, 1980. These premiums are subject to increase each July 1 in the future as the cost of medical care increases. If you are receiving a Social Security monthly benefit, the SMI premium will be deducted automatically from your benefit unless you specifically elect not to participate in SMI.

Under the HI program, the cost of a hospital stay is reimbursed once certain deductible and coinsurance requirements are met. Hospital services for up to 90 days in a "spell of illness" are covered; in addition you have a "lifetime reserve" of another 60 days that can be drawn on if you stay in a hospital for more than 90 days during one spell of illness. A "spell of illness" ends once you have remained out of the hospital or skilled nursing facility for 60 days. The hospital is usually reimbursed directly for any costs in excess of the amount you are required to pay. You must pay the first $180 of expenses (the "deductible") plus "coinsurance" of $45 per day if your hospital stay lasts longer than 60 days and $90 per day for any "lifetime reserve" days that you use. These deductible and coinsurance amounts apply to 1980 and will increase in future years as average hospital costs increase. In addition you must pay for certain costs not covered by the Hospital Insurance program: for example, the extra cost of a private room as distinguished from a semiprivate room.

If you have been hospitalized for at least three days and then enter a skilled nursing facility for follow-up care within two weeks after leaving the hospital, the services provided by the facility will be covered in part by the HI program for up to 100 days in a spell of illness. Days 21 through 100 will require that you pay a daily coinsurance amount of $22.50 (subject to future increase). After discharge from a three-day stay in a hospital or from a skilled nursing facility, up to 100 home health agency visits are provided under HI.[2]

The SMI program pays the "reasonable charges" for physician services, outpatient services by hospitals and clinics, and home health visits, after you have paid the first $60 of such services (this $60 deductible amount is *not* subject to automatic increase). You must also pay 20 percent of expenses in excess of the deductible as well as all expenses not considered "reasonable charges."

This is not a complete description of the benefits provided by the Medicare program. Chapter 3 contains somewhat more detail. You should consult with your local Social Security office (or your hospital and physicians) if you have particular questions.

All participants in the Medicare program are eligible for the same benefits regardless of the level of earnings on which they have paid Social Security taxes or the length of time such taxes have been paid. Approximately 70 percent of the cost of the SMI portion of Medicare is financed by general revenue which is paid by all taxpayers, including those not participating in Social Security. Accordingly, there is virtually no "individual equity," or relation between taxes paid and benefits received, under the Medicare program.

Money-Saving Hints

You should contact your local Social Security Administration office a few months before you reach age 65 and apply for benefits even if you have no intention of retiring at 65 and will not be able to receive cash benefits for some time. The application will ensure that you are eligible for Medicare benefits immediately at age 65. If your spouse is older than you and not eligible for retirement benefits based on his or her own earnings record, you should apply for cash benefits when he or she is about to reach age 65 (provided you are at least age 62). This action would establish your spouse's entitlement to Medicare benefits even if you yourself are not yet eligible. Medicare protection for your spouse could be valuable should hospital insurance coverage provided by your employer terminate or reduce upon a spouse's attainment of age 65.

Medicare does not pay for hospital and medical care outside the United States (except in Canada for U.S. residents living nearby and in a few other limited cases). Accordingly, if you depend normally upon Medicare and you plan to travel abroad, you should make alternative arrangements for temporary health insurance.

You should definitely enroll in the optional SMI program unless you have similar coverage provided without charge. As a taxpayer, you are already paying for most of the cost of SMI, whether or not you elect to receive its benefits. Currently only about 30 percent of the program's total costs are met from enrollees' premiums—the balance is paid from general revenue, the bulk of which comes from personal and corporate income taxes. In the future, premiums will represent an even smaller portion of total costs, probably no more than 10 percent by the year 2000.

You have a lifetime reserve of 60 hospital inpatient reserve days. Reserve days can be used one time only and are not renewable for a second benefit period as are the first 90 days of benefits. If you have other hospital insurance, you may want to save your reserve days for a later time when such other insurance may not be available. If you do not want to use your reserve days, you must notify the hospital before the end of your first 90 days of hospitalization.

Many private insurance companies have policies designed to complement Medicare by covering the cost of Medicare deductibles and coinsurance. Unless you are in poor health, it probably would be to your advantage to self-insure for these relatively small amounts rather than buy the complementary insurance policies. You should, however, consider such an auxiliary private policy if it includes reimbursement for costs in excess of "reasonable charges" and if it includes "catastrophic coverage" for hospital stays lasting longer than 150 days (or 90 days if you have used your lifetime reserve days under HI). Extended, high-cost illnesses are rare, but they can be financial catastrophes when they do occur.

Do You Get Your Money's Worth?

This is an easy question to ask but a difficult one to answer. Chapter 11 discusses this subject and concludes that the answer may be yes or no depending upon the viewpoint from which the question is being asked. The present chapter considers the question only from the viewpoint of the benefits received compared with the taxes paid for a given individual—a narrow yet quite legitimate viewpoint.

It is always tempting to compare the retirement benefits one may expect to receive with the taxes that have been paid. This is an interesting exercise, but much more complex and sophisticated studies are required to answer the money's worth question. Just to satisfy our curiosity, however, here are a few incomplete comparisons of the type sometimes made.

As shown in Table 19.3, a person retiring at age 65 in January 1980, having had maximum career earnings, would receive a monthly benefit of $572 payable for life. The value of these future benefits depends upon whether the retired person is male or female, the health status, and so on. For an average male, the present value of this benefit when it commences at age 65 is $77,800. In other words, this amount, if placed in an interest-bearing account on January 1, 1980 to yield the Consumer Price Index increase each year plus 2½ percent, would be just sufficient on the average to pay lifetime monthly benefits of $572, increased as the Consumer Price Index increases.

If this same illustrative male worker had a wife aged 65, the monthly benefit would be $858 during their joint lifetime and $572 during the remaining lifetime of the survivor. The present value of these benefits when they commence at age 65 is $143,100. If this couple also had two children, aged 16 and 18, who continued as full-time students until age 22, the monthly benefits would be even higher. The present value of such benefits would be $158,800.

The big question then is how do these present values ranging from $77,800 to $158,800 compare with the taxes that have been paid. Reference to Table 19.2 will provide the answers. An employee would have paid total taxes of $11,202.97, at the most, from 1937 through 1979. Invested to yield the Consumer Price Index plus 2½ percent, these taxes would have amounted to $27,760.00. Total taxes paid by employee and employer combined would have been at most $22,405.94, or $55,520.00 accumulated at interest. For a self-employed person, total taxes accumulated at interest would have been $32,820.

Accordingly, no matter what tax payments are considered they are substantially less than the value of the retirement benefits for persons and their families who live to age 65. But that is not the entire story. If you continue working full time after age 65, no retirement benefits will be paid until age 72 (or when you stop working, if sooner); this would cause a substantial reduction in the large present values of retirement benefits just illustrated. If you die just before reaching age 65 and have no dependents, only $255 would be payable. On the other hand, if you die at a young age and leave several survivors, total benefits worth more than $200,000 could be payable. The value of disability benefits and Medicare benefits must be considered—and a host of possible benefits to dependent parents, a divorced spouse, disabled children, and so on.

So, it is interesting to make these simple comparisons of retirement benefits and taxes, but they should not be mistaken for more thorough actuarial studies comparing all potential benefits with all potential taxes.

A recent study[3] on this subject by the actuaries at the Social Security Administration considered the value of the principal benefits payable under Social Security throughout the lifetime of several hypothetical workers. These values were then compared with the value of payroll taxes scheduled in present law. Standard actuarial procedures were employed, taking into account interest earnings, probabilities of death and disability, and so forth. To simplify the calculations, Medicare benefits and taxes were excluded from the comparison (although this is a significant benefit which should also be studied). Here is a summary of the results for several hypothetical employees entering the work force in 1978 at age 22. In each example, the person's status—married or single—is assumed to remain unchanged (except if affected by death). As in the rest of this chapter, the examples are for persons who receive maximum taxable Social Security earnings throughout their career.

An unmarried male employee could expect, on average, to receive benefits equivalent to 92 percent of his taxes (but only 46 percent of the combined taxes paid by his employer and himself). Unmarried self-employed males could expect, on average, to receive benefits equivalent to 61 percent of their taxes.

An unmarried female employee could expect, on average, to receive benefits equivalent to 125 percent of her taxes (63 percent of the combined taxes paid by her employer and herself). For an unmarried self-employed female, the expected value of benefits is equivalent to 83 percent of her taxes.

A married male employee (with a wife the same age and not in paid employment, and two children, 25 and 27 years younger) could expect to receive benefits equivalent to 210 percent of his taxes (105 percent of the combined taxes paid by his employer and himself). Such a married self-employed male could expect to receive benefits equivalent to 140 percent of his taxes.

A married couple, both of whom work and are the same age, with two children of ages 25 and 27 years younger, could expect to receive benefits equivalent to 125 percent of their own taxes (and 63 percent of the combined taxes paid by their employers and themselves).[4]

Whether persons currently entering the work force get their money's worth depends on which of the above categories they fit into, and whether they consider just their own taxes or those of their employer as well. Furthermore, it is difficult to be sure that a person now in one of these categories will remain permanently in that category; hence, a final answer to the money's worth question can be given only in retrospect after all the facts are in. Among the simplifying assumptions used in the above examples is that retirement occurs at age 65. If retirement should occur later than age 65 (a more likely assumption for persons entering the work force today) the ratio of benefits to taxes would be much lower than stated above.

Generally speaking, highly paid employees entering the work force today—and their employers—cannot expect to receive their money's worth from Social Security; that is, the value of their benefits will probably be less than the value of the taxes they and their employers will pay. On the other hand, persons retiring throughout the past forty years of operation of Social Security generally received much more than their money's worth. For the generations between these two extremes, the answer to the money's worth question is also in between. As discussed in earlier chapters, Social Security significantly redistributes income, not only within each generation but also from one generation to another. Accordingly, the younger members of the fortunate eight percent of Social Security participants to whom this chapter is addressed must look elsewhere for satisfaction than to an equitable return of benefits for their Social Security tax dollar. Chapter 11 mentions some of the broader issues to consider when asking the money's worth question.

20
Is Social Security Enough?

Social Security is a complex program providing a vast array of benefits which very few people comprehend. It is costly and will become even more costly. Accordingly, much of the public has come to believe that the government (through Social Security) is providing, or should provide, for most of our needs in the event of retirement, disability, sickness, or death.

Despite its complexity and cost, however, Social Security does not meet all of these needs uniformly for all sectors of the population. Some needs are met more adequately than others; for example, retirement needs are better satisfied for low income workers than for high income workers. Some needs are not met at all; for example, income maintenance during short-term illness and long-term partial disability. Some needs that appear to be satisfied may not be met in reality; for example, survivors benefits which are forfeited if the survivor has earnings in excess of the "earnings limitations."

It should be noted again, of course, that there are some eight million employees who are not covered by Social Security except through occasional employment (mainly, employees of federal government, state and local governments, and non-profit organizations; low-income, self-employed persons; and farm and domestic workers with irregular employment). This discussion of whether Social Security by itself provides adequate benefits obviously does not apply to these eight million employees.

For an individual to determine the status of his protection, a careful analysis of benefits from all sources—not just Social Security—is necessary. This is a difficult task, however. The Social Security Administration can provide valuable information on Social Security benefits, but it is not prepared to do so routinely for all participants. The personnel department of your employer can usually give information about employer-provided benefits (group life insurance, disability and sickness benefits, retirement benefits, etc.) but may or may not be equipped to provide detailed information about Social Security benefits. Your employer may also be able to give you information about benefits under programs it does not directly administer such as workers' compensation and state cash sickness plans. Your life insurance agent can provide information about any individual life insurance, disability insurance, health insurance, or retirement policies you may have. Putting all this information together is not an easy matter, but it is something you must do if you are to meet your various needs and those of your family on the most economical basis possible.

Where do you start? If your income is high, you may want to hire a financial advisor—a new breed of consultant specializing in analysis of your total financial picture. Some life insurance agents are qualified to help you organize your financial affairs. You stand a better chance with an experienced, well-trained agent—perhaps one who has completed the study program offered by the American Society of Chartered Life Underwriters and has thus received the C.L.U. designation. It is reasonable to expect your employer—probably through the personnel department—to provide some help in comparing your financial needs with coverage offered under employer-provided plans. In the final analysis, however, you will have to get heavily involved in comparing what you have with what you need, and thus be able to fill any voids that may exist. The following sections of this chapter are intended to help you identify these voids in income security for you and your family. Although the emphasis is on gaps in protection, in some cases there may be duplications that can be eliminated. The threats to income security are presented under four general headings: sickness, disability, death, and retirement.

Sickness

It is possible, of course, for you and members of your family to become ill or suffer an accidental injury at any time throughout life. This can result in loss of income because of inability to work, as well as hospital and medical expenses. This section deals only with the expenses of illness or injury; loss of income is covered in the following section on disability.

It should not be surprising that Social Security provides less protection against expenses of illness or injury than it provides against loss of income upon retirement, disability, or death. Social Security, as originally designed, was intended to replace a portion of lost income upon retirement and not to provide any reimbursement for expenses of illness. It was only when Medicare was added in 1965 that Social Security began to pay any of the costs of illness. Medicare benefits are provided only in the following relatively limited circumstances:

For a person after he or she reaches age 65 if entitled to cash payments under the Social Security (or Railroad Retirement) program.

For the spouse (aged 65 or older) of a person entitled to such cash payments, or the widow or widower of someone who had been entitled to such payments.

For a disabled person less than age 65 after having been entitled to Social Security benefits for twenty-four months. (This could be a disabled worker, a disabled widow or widower, or a person receiving childhood disability benefits. A person who has received a disability annuity under the Railroad Retirement Act for twenty-nine months is also eligible.)

For a person of any age with chronic kidney disease who is fully or currently insured under Social Security (including the afflicted spouse or dependent child of a person so insured).

Generally speaking, therefore, you and your spouse will be eligible for Medicare benefits after each of you reaches age 65 but not before. Your healthy children will never be eligible for Medicare benefits. This leaves many circumstances in which hospital and medical expenses are not covered by Social Security and in which supplementary health care arrangements may be advisable for you or your family members. Here are a few examples:

> If either you or your spouse is less than age 65 and you do not have adequate employer-provided health insurance (covering family members as well as yourself).
>
> If you are older than age 65, but your spouse is less than age 65 or you have dependent children.
>
> If you are younger than age 62, but your spouse is aged 65 or older and is excluded from employer-provided health insurance yet ineligible for Medicare.
>
> If you are older than age 65 and you live outside the United States or travel abroad.
>
> If you are older than age 65 and are an alien with less than five years' permanent residence in the United States (and thus are ineligible for Part B of Medicare).
>
> If you retire earlier than age 65 and your employer-provided health insurance terminates.
>
> If you become disabled earlier than age 65 and your employer-provided health insurance terminates.
>
> If you are a federal employee covered by a government-provided health insurance plan (under the Federal Employees Health Benefits Act of 1959).

In most of these situations you would be well-advised to make arrangements for supplementary health care coverage. This could be in the form of individual or group health insurance, Blue Cross-Blue Shield coverage, or group prepaid health care such as is offered by a health maintenance organization. If you are a regular full-time employee of an established company, you probably have such health insurance as one of your fringe benefits. Supplemental coverage is sometimes advisable even if health care benefits are provided by your employer, particularly to protect you in the event of a catastrophic or extended and high-cost illness.

After you reach age 65 and are covered by Medicare (Supplementary Medical Insurance as well as Hospital Insurance) you will probably still need to make special provision for the expense of illness. This is because Medicare does not pay the total health care expenses of those who participate. By way of example, here are just a few of the expenses *not* paid by

Medicare (the dollar amounts apply in 1980 and are subject to increase as average costs increase):

The first $180 of hospital expenses.

$45 per day for hospital charges for the 61st day through the 90th day and $90 per day for the 91st through the 150th day, and all costs thereafter plus all hospital room charges that exceed the cost of a semiprivate accommodation. (If you have previously exhausted your lifetime reserve of 60 days, you must pay all hospital costs after the 90th day.)

$22.50 per day for skilled nursing facilities charges for the 21st day through the 100th day, and all costs thereafter.

The first $60 of covered medical expenses plus 20 percent of subsequent covered medical expenses and all costs in excess of "reasonable charges" as determined by the Health Care Financing Administration.

The cost in excess of $250 per year of outpatient treatment for a mental illness.

These hospital and medical expenses that are not covered by Medicare can easily amount to thousands of dollars, particularly in an extended illness. Accordingly, even if you are covered by Medicare it is advisable to obtain supplemental protection against catastrophic illnesses.

Furthermore, you will still need a cash reserve to pay for part of the expenses of illness, even if you are covered by Medicare and even if you have appropriate supplemental health insurance coverage. Most insurance programs have features of "noncovered services," "deductibles," and "coinsurance" which require that you pay at least a portion of the costs.

Social Security is not intended to provide for all hospital and medical expenses in your old age. Furthermore, it provides for virtually none of those expenses for you and your family during your working years. In order to protect yourself and your family against the high costs of illness, as well as to ensure that proper medical care is available, it is essential that you make appropriate arrangements for supplemental health care insurance of one kind or another and that you accumulate a suitable cash reserve.

Disability

The financial problems caused by disability, particularly long-term permanent disability, are sometimes more severe than those accompanying death, or even old age. Yet, acquiring protection against disability usually receives the lowest priority. In this section, disability means the inability to perform part or all of one's normal work as a result of sickness or injury; hence, disability may be partial or total. Also, it may be temporary, lasting only a few days or weeks, or it may be permanent, lasting a lifetime.

Social Security began providing disability benefits in 1957. Since then eligibility for benefits has changed from time to time. Currently, the provisions may be summarized as follows (stated in a negative way to highlight the conditions under which benefits will *not* be available):

Disability benefits will not be paid unless you are so severely disabled that you cannot perform any substantial gainful work, and the disability is expected to last at least twelve months or result in death.

Disability benefits will not be paid until you have been disabled for five full consecutive months. Since the benefit for a particular month is not paid until the end of that month, the first benefit payment will not be made until sometime between six and seven months after the disability begins.

Disability benefits will not be paid unless you have paid Social Security taxes for a specified number of quarters, the number varying based upon your date of birth and disability. This is usually referred to as acquiring "quarters of coverage." For example, if you become disabled in 1980 the approximate requirements are:

Age at Disability	Quarters of Coverage Required
50	29 with 20 earned in last 10 years
40	20 earned in last 10 years
30	19 earned after age 21
20	6 earned in last 3 years

Therefore, you will not be eligible for disability benefits until you have paid Social Security taxes for at least one and one-half years and, possibly, as long as seven and one-fourth years. For disabilities occurring after 1980, even more quarters of coverage may be required.

You can see that there are many circumstances in which you could become disabled without being eligible for Social Security benefits. These voids in disability income protection may or may not be filled by other disability benefit programs in which you participate.

Many employers have formal or informal sick-pay plans which continue part or all of one's pay in the event of short-term sickness or disability. Some employers have sick-pay plans that provide benefits for six months, after which Social Security is presumed to be effective—at least for severe and probably long-lasting disabilities. Still other employers have comprehensive arrangements that meet a large proportion of the financial needs of a disabled person throughout his lifetime. The period of time during which employer-provided disability benefits are payable usually increases as the employee's service with the employer increases.

Five states (California, Hawaii, New Jersey, New York, and Rhode Island) and Puerto Rico require that employers participate in mandatory state-operated cash sickness benefit programs or establish comparable programs on a private basis. Employees are usually required to pay a large part of the cost of such plans. These programs provide cash payments for short-term periods (up to twenty-six weeks) in the event of sickness or injury that is not work connected. All fifty states require that employers participate in state-operated workers' compensation programs, or otherwise provide comparable benefits to compensate employees for job-related injuries, sickness, or death.

Few plans that provide disability benefits take into account the number and type of dependents of a worker. Social Security is a notable exception. Furthermore, hardly any program except Social Security provides disability benefits for members of a worker's family who become disabled.

Even after you meet all the eligibility requirements for Social Security disability benefits, you may still need to make special provision for supplemental disability benefits. This is because Social Security benefits are sometimes adequate but sometimes not. It depends upon your earnings level, family responsibilities, and—to a certain extent—your age at disability.

Table 20.1 illustrates the wide range of benefits payable under various circumstances. In each case it is assumed the worker becomes disabled in July 1979 and begins receiving benefits for January 1980. Benefits are not shown in dollar amounts, but rather as a percentage of average earnings during the three full years of work prior to commencement of benefits (1976–1978). This percentage is referred to as the replacement ratio. Since Social Security disability benefits are not taxable

Table 20.1

Ratio of Initial Social Security Disability Benefits to Average Earnings Prior to Disability for Illustrative Workers[a]

Earnings Level of Worker[c]	Replacement Ratio[b] When Disability Began at. . .	
	Age 25	Age 50
(1)	(2)	(3)
	Single Worker	
Minimum	70%	70%
Average	54	53
Maximum	44	39
Twice Maximum	22	20
	Married Worker with Eligible Family[d]	
Minimum	110%	110%
Average	99	97
Maximum	76	69
Twice Maximum	38	34

[a]Public Law 96-265 (enacted June 9, 1980) made a number of changes in the way benefits are calculated for disabled workers and their families. The disabled workers in this example would not be affected; however, benefits would be reduced somewhat for persons becoming eligible for family disability benefits in the future.

[b]Replacement ratio equals the disability benefits payable in the first year divided by the average of the last three full years of earnings prior to disablement. In each example the worker is assumed to become disabled in July 1979 and to begin receiving benefits in January 1980.

[c]"Minimum" denotes earnings equal to the minimum wage in each year. "Average" means earnings in each year equal to the average wages of all covered employees. "Maximum" and "Twice Maximum" refer to the level of the maximum contribution and benefit base under Social Security.

[d]Family is assumed to consist of worker, spouse, and one or more children.

and since many work-related expenses are eliminated, a replacement ratio of less than 100 percent will usually maintain the pre-disability standard of living (depending, of course, upon the level of medical care required).

Assume, for example, that you are a single worker who becomes eligible to receive disability benefits in January 1980 at age 50. Assume further that you have participated in Social Security throughout your adult lifetime and have always had maximum earnings covered by Social Security. Your monthly disability benefit during the first year would average $539.60, or about 39 percent of your average earnings during the three full years prior to disability. This benefit, taken by itself, is probably *not* adequate to support you and it will certainly not preserve your pre-disability standard of living; therefore, supplemental disability benefits should be provided through a pension plan, group or individual disability insurance plan, accumulation of personal savings, or by some other means. If your average earnings during the three-year period prior to disability had been $33,000 (twice the average maximum amount taxable for Social Security earnings), your disability benefit would be the same dollar amount but would be only 20 percent of your pre-disability average earnings. In this example, supplemental disability benefits are essential unless a substantial decrease is made in the standard of living.

In other situations, the Social Security disability benefit— once it commences—may be adequate, or even more than adequate, to continue the pre-disability standard of living. Consider a worker who earned the minimum wage and who becomes disabled at age 25 with a spouse and one or more small children. Social Security disability benefits during the first year would average $460.20 per month, or about 110 percent of average earnings during the three years prior to disability, assuming the spouse and children did not have earnings at a high enough level to forfeit any of their benefits because of the "earnings limitation."

For a person who begins to receive Social Security disability benefits in January 1980, the monthly benefit could be anywhere between $122.00 and $966.70, depending upon the circumstances.

An examination of the figures in Table 20.1 indicates a need to revise the Social Security benefit structure to eliminate inconsistencies and provide more equitable treatment of various categories of workers. There is no good reason an older worker should receive lower benefits than a younger worker if both of them have had the same level of pre-disability earnings. And the differentiation between benefits paid a single worker and a married worker with dependents appears to be greater than is reasonable. Recent amendments made a number of changes in the way benefits are calculated for disabled workers and their families (Public Law 96-265, enacted June 9, 1980). These amendments have no significant effect on the benefits shown in Table 20.1 for a single worker becoming disabled in the future. For married workers with families, however, benefits for future disabilities will be reduced about 15 percent, relatively speaking, from those shown in Table 20.1 (except for minimum wage earners, for whom the reduction is only 5 percent).

It is a rare case when an employee is adequately protected, from the first day of employment, against the various kinds of disability he may suffer. It is even more rare for family members to be protected against the possibility of their becoming disabled. The risk of loss of income because of disability may well be the most neglected area of personal financial planning. It is time-consuming and difficult, but not impossible, to summarize the benefits provided from all sources in the event of disability: Social Security, employer plans, workers' compensation, personal insurance, etc. Such a survey must be made, however, to identify gaps in coverage and enable you to obtain the supplemental disability insurance and plan the personal savings program necessary to protect you and your family from the catastrophe of disability.

Death

When someone who has been contributing to the support of a family dies, a variety of expenses may have to be met: burial costs, liquidation of personal debt (including home mortgage repayment), estate taxes, transitional costs while the surviving family adjusts to a different standard of living, and so on. If the decedent provided the principal support to a family, it may be necessary to replace part or all of the lost income for an extended period.

Social Security, as originally enacted in 1935, provided no death benefit except a guaranteed return of employee-paid Social Security taxes. In 1939, this type of death benefit was eliminated; instead, a lump-sum benefit and monthly benefits to survivors were adopted. Subsequent legislation broadened and extended these benefits so that, today, Social Security provides much more in death benefits than is commonly realized. In fact, the value of the death benefit ranges from $255 to $200,000 or more, depending upon the circumstances.

The lump-sum death benefit paid by Social Security is $255. This was the maximum benefit payable in 1954 and was intended to cover only the expenses of a modest funeral; however, the benefit has not been increased since then.

Survivors benefits, on the other hand, are relatively substantial and can be paid to:

a spouse caring for an eligible child;

a divorced spouse caring for an eligible child;

an eligible child;

a spouse aged 60 or older (50 or older, if completely disabled);

a divorced wife aged 60 or older (50 or older, if completely disabled), if the marriage lasted at least ten years; or

dependent parents aged 62 or older.

The amount of the benefits and the conditions for payment are based upon a seemingly endless set of conditions. These conditions are discussed briefly here and in more detail in Chapter 3. Eligibility for some death benefits requires that you be "currently insured," while eligibility for others requires that you be "fully insured."

To be currently insured, you need six quarters of coverage during the last thirteen quarters ending with the quarter in which you die. This would qualify your survivors for the lump-sum death benefit and monthly benefits for an eligible child and a spouse (or divorced spouse) caring for an eligible child.

To be fully insured, you must have between six and forty quarters of coverage depending upon when you were born and when you die. This requirement is not difficult to meet if you have been working in fairly steady employment. Fully insured status would qualify your survivors for monthly benefits for a spouse or a divorced wife and dependent parents, as well as the benefits mentioned above for currently insured participants.

Table 20.2 presents examples of benefits for several illustrative workers and their families. Benefits are expressed as replacement ratios; that is, the ratio of the first year's benefits to the average earnings in the three years prior to death. Consider, for example, a 25-year-old worker who has always had

Table 20.2

Ratio of Initial Social Security Survivors Benefits to Deceased Worker's Average Earnings Prior to Death for Illustrative Surviving Families

Earnings Level of Worker[b]	Replacement Ratio[a] Where Worker's Death Was at...	
	Age 25	Age 50
(1)	(2)	(3)
	Surviving Spouse and Two or More Children	
Minimum	101%	100%
Average	90	88
Maximum	68	59
Twice Maximum	34	29
	Surviving Spouse and One Child (or Two Surviving Children)	
Minimum	95%	95%
Average	75	73
Maximum	58	50
Twice Maximum	29	25
	One Surviving Child	
Minimum	48%	48%
Average	37	36
Maximum	29	25
Twice Maximum	14	13

[a]Replacement ratio equals the survivors benefits payable in the first year divided by the deceased worker's average earnings in the last three years prior to death. In each example the worker is assumed to die in January 1980.

[b]"Minimum" denotes earnings equal to the minimum wage in each year. "Average" means earnings in each year equal to the average wages of all covered employees. "Maximum" and "Twice Maximum" refer to the level of the maximum contribution and benefit base under Social Security.

earnings equal to the average amount earned by those covered under Social Security and whose family consists of a spouse (who is not currently working in paid employment) and two children. Such a worker who has at least six quarters of coverage would be both currently insured and fully insured, and death in January 1980 would result in a lump-sum benefit of $255 and monthly benefits payable to the family of 90 percent of the worker's average earnings in the last three years. Since Social Security benefits are tax free, this benefit would exceed the worker's average take-home pay.

The amount of this benefit, payable in future years, would vary depending upon many factors. It would increase as the Consumer Price Index increased. It would reduce as each child reached age 18 and would terminate altogether when both children reached age 18 (except that a benefit would continue until age 22 for each child who remained a full-time student). Benefits would resume to the spouse at age 65 (or as early as age 60 if a reduced benefit is elected). The monthly benefits payable to any of these beneficiaries would be reduced by $1.00 for every $2.00 of earnings *by that beneficiary* in excess of the "earnings limitation" (in 1980, $3,720 for beneficiaries under age 65 and $5,000 for beneficiaries aged 65 and older). Finally, the remarriage of the surviving spouse or the marriage of a child beneficiary would normally terminate benefits for that beneficiary.

The survivors benefits in this example are substantial and are worth about $175,000 at the death of the worker. In other words, on the average, it would take approximately $175,000 invested at interest to provide these survivors benefits. Most of the surviving family's needs in this example are well satisfied by Social Security in the early years following the worker's death. Once the children have reached maturity, there will be a period when the spouse will have no income (from about age 40 or 45 until age 65). At age 65 benefits to the spouse would resume at about 50 percent of the worker's average earnings in the last three years (adjusted for changes in the Consumer Price Index occurring since then). Supplemental income for the spouse during this period before age 65, as well as after age 65, may be necessary since Social Security benefits alone will not be adequate to maintain the earlier standard of living.

This particular example was chosen to illustrate a situation in which Social Security almost "does it all." Other situations require substantial provision for supplemental benefits through private saving and private insurance, either group or individual. Most workers with above average income need supplemental benefits unless their family's living standard is to suffer in the event of their death. The examples in Table 20.2 illustrate that the initial replacement ratio ranges from 13 percent to 101 percent, depending upon the circumstances of the worker and his or her family; for persons with higher earnings than illustrated, the replacement ratio can be even lower than 13 percent. Obviously, the amount of survivors benefits payable under Social Security can vary widely and is not easy to determine; however, a basic understanding of such benefits and their payment provisions is essential in determining an appropriate level of supplemental coverage.

Many employees are covered under group life insurance plans sponsored by their employers (partially paid for by the employee in some cases). Some people obtain group life insurance benefits through membership in unions or professional organizations, purchase of "credit insurance," and so forth. Many persons buy individual life insurance to supplement their other benefits or to cover specific obligations such as home mortgage loans. Life insurance benefits are normally described by their face amount, such as $10,000 or $50,000, but in most cases a variety of payment methods is available in the event of death. In determining your supplemental insurance needs, it will be helpful to determine the monthly income that can be provided by these insurance policies. This can be added to the monthly income paid by Social Security to indicate any gaps that should be filled to protect your family adequately. Remember that Social Security benefits and most life insurance benefits are tax free and that family expenses are usually lower after the death of a breadwinner.

When deciding how much supplemental life insurance protection and personal savings should be provided, several key decisions must be made regarding the surviving family's lifestyle. Would a spouse who was not working in paid employment begin working? Would the family's house or other major possessions be kept? How long are the children likely to need support, and what financial arrangements will be necessary for their education? Once these and other personal decisions are worked out within the family, attention can be turned to evaluating the overall financial needs that would result from a breadwinner's death, the level of benefits payable by Social Security, employee benefit plans, etc., and the need for any supplemental benefit protection. The effect of future inflation must also be considered. What might seem like an adequate benefit in the first two or three years could prove to be inadequate in later years.

Just as in making contingency plans for sickness and disability, in planning for the possibility of death you must absorb an array of facts and figures to decide what financial alternatives should be devised. Your responsibility in making such plans is more awesome, of course, since you will not be around to modify any arrangements that need adjusting.

Retirement

Retirement is somewhat different from the events just discussed—sickness, disability, and death—which result in extraordinary expenses or loss of income. Barring premature death, everyone will experience old age and for most of us there will come a time when retirement must be considered, and probably will be necessary for one reason or another. Knowing that we must one day retire, however, does not make it any easier to plan for and make the necessary financial arrangements. A person who reaches age 65, a common retirement age at the present time, can expect to live another fifteen to twenty years, on the average, and perhaps as long as thirty-five years or more. This uncertainty itself makes planning for retirement difficult.

Social Security, as originally enacted, was designed solely to replace a portion of the income that was lost because of old age. Social Security has expanded over the years and now provides a wide variety of benefits in the event of a worker's retirement; for example, benefits may be paid to:

a retired worker aged 62 or over;

the spouse aged 62 or over of a retired worker, if the retired worker is also receiving benefits;

the wife of a retired worker who is receiving benefits, if the
wife is under age 65 and caring for an eligible child;
a divorced spouse aged 62 or over, who was married to the
insured worker for at least ten years, if the insured
worker is receiving benefits; or
an eligible child.

Table 20.3 illustrates the benefits payable upon the retirement of a worker at different retirement ages and in different family situations. The examples reflect the actuarial reduction of benefits for retirement before age 65 and the effect of the "delayed retirement credit" for retirement after age 65. Benefits are shown as a percentage of average earnings in the last three years before retirement, hence are referred to as replacement ratios. Benefits are assumed to commence in January 1980; examples for later years would show slightly less variation for different ages at retirement.

As indicated in Table 20.3 there is an extremely wide varia-

Table 20.3

Ratio of Initial Social Security Retirement Benefits to Average Earnings Prior to Retirement for Illustrative Workers

Earnings Level of Worker[b]	Replacement Ratio[a] for Worker Retiring at...		
	Age 62	Age 65	Age 70
(1)	(2)	(3)	(4)
	Single Worker		
Minimum	51%	71%	79%
Average	39	55	63
Maximum	28	39	44
Twice Maximum	14	20	22
	Worker and Spouse		
Minimum	74%	106%	116%
Average	57	83	94
Maximum	40	59	65
Twice Maximum	20	29	32

[a]Replacement ratio equals the retirement benefits payable in the first year divided by the average of the last three years of earnings prior to retirement. In each example, the worker is assumed to attain the indicated age in January 1980.
[b]"Minimum" denotes earnings equal to the minimum wage in each year. "Average" means earnings in each year equal to the average wages of all covered employees. "Maximum" and "Twice Maximum" refer to the level of the maximum contribution and benefit base under Social Security.

tion in the replacement ratios, depending upon the age at retirement, earnings level, and family status. The replacement ratios shown range from 116 percent for a low wage earner who retires late to 14 percent for a high wage earner who retires early. The replacement ratio would be even lower for persons with higher earnings. The replacement ratio that is necessary to permit suitable retirement depends upon a variety of factors including preretirement earnings level, family status, and postretirement standard of living. Also, Social Security benefits are tax free, income taxes are lower for persons over age 65, Social Security taxes stop when earned income stops, expenses associated with employment cease, personal savings after retirement may be lower, medical costs for the elderly are usually higher, and so forth.

If one's preretirement standard of living is to be maintained, retirement benefits of some 60 to 85 percent of average preretirement earnings are probably necessary—depending upon the factors mentioned above. Furthermore, these benefits must be adjusted periodically to reflect changes in the cost of living. Social Security benefits satisfy these criteria reasonably well for workers with average earnings or less, provided they retire at age 65 or later. Even for these workers, there is some need for supplementation through private saving or a job-related retirement plan. This need, however, is relatively small compared with that of the above-average wage earner for whom substantial supplementation is needed if preretirement living standards are to be maintained.

Supplemental retirement income is available from several sources. The majority of full-time permanent employees in private employment are covered by a pension or profit-sharing plan sponsored by their employer. Most public employees are covered by employer-sponsored retirement systems. Many self-employed persons have so-called "Keogh" or "HR 10" retirement programs. An increasing number of people are establishing Individual Retirement Accounts. Many people have cash value life insurance, as well as endowment and retirement income insurance policies that are earmarked for retirement purposes. Finally, personal saving (investments, equity in a home, etc.) is accumulated for general purposes but may be used eventually for support in retirement years.

Just as in analyzing the needs discussed earlier, it is quite difficult to compare your retirement needs with the various sources of income that will be available and thus to determine what level of supplementation is required. In studying your needs it is well to keep in mind that Social Security and other benefits may be less than they appear, as indicated by the following examples.

A wife may appear to be protected by Social Security by reason of her marriage to a person in Social Security covered employment. An untimely divorce (particularly before ten years of marriage) would normally terminate this financial protection. The payment of Social Security benefits is subject to the earnings limitation discussed earlier; and if you or your dependents or survivors work in order to supplement Social Security benefits, it may result in a reduction or complete loss of such benefits. A retirement income that is adequate for a couple may be reduced upon the death of one of the members (as is the case with Social Security), leaving the survivor with an inadequate income. Retirement benefits that are not adjusted for inflation (unlike Social Security which is so adjusted) may be adequate at their inception but inadequate just a few years later because óf continuing inflation.

If you receive a pension under a government pension plan as a result of being an employee of a federal, state, or local government (this includes policemen, firemen, and public school teachers) and you were not under Social Security in such employment, you may not receive Social Security benefits you thought you would receive. This is because Social Security benefits payable to you as a dependent or survivor will be reduced by any benefits under such a government pension plan, thus reducing or completely eliminating your Social Security benefits. This provision was enacted in 1977 and does not apply to:

> anyone entitled to Social Security benefits before December 1977; or
>
> women (or men who can prove dependency on their wives) who are eligible to receive a government pension any time between December 1977 and November 1982.

The net result of an analysis of Social Security retirement benefit protection is that most persons need some supplemental protection, and workers with above average earnings need substantial additional benefits unless a significant reduction is made in their preretirement standard of living. Even workers with average earnings or less need to make provision for supplemental retirement benefits if they desire to retire earlier than the standard set by Social Security.

Conclusion

In the event of the sickness, disability, death, or retirement of any member of your family, the family's financial situation will change—sometimes drastically. None of these events can be predicted with certainty. The only certainty is that at least one such event will occur, probably at a time it is least expected.

It is tempting to assume that one's financial needs in time of crisis will be met by Social Security or some other governmental program or by a job-related fringe benefit program. This is a dangerous assumption and is not one that can be relied upon.

To protect your family from financial stress you must compare what you need with what you have—much easier to say than to do. If you provide the principal financial support for your family, define your needs and those of your family if you should become sick, disabled, die, or retire. Do the same for other family members who provide financial support. Also define the needs that will arise if a member of your family becomes sick or disabled.

Then analyze all the programs that will provide benefits in any of these events: Social Security and other government programs, job-related fringe benefit plans, personal insurance and saving, and so forth. A surprising number of unmet needs will be revealed. In some cases there may be duplications in benefit protection. You can then set about to fill the gaps in protection and eliminate the duplications.

You can get help in making this analysis and taking corrective action; but in the end, you must get heavily involved and do much of the work yourself. Perhaps this is as it should be. Your family financial situation is a unique and personal matter, and you cannot expect a stranger to have the same level of interest as you.

21
How to
Take Advantage
of Social Security

The government has a thorough method of collecting Social Security taxes. Even without any initiative on your part, the government will almost certainly find you and collect the taxes you owe.

Getting your benefits is another matter. The government does not take the initiative in locating you, determining your eligibility, and then paying any benefits to which you may be entitled. It is up to *you* to take the first step and apply for the benefits. Before you can do this, of course, you must know enough about Social Security to apply for the right benefits at the right time.

Know Your Social Security Benefits

The first step then to take full advantage of Social Security is to obtain all the benefits to which you and your family are entitled. To do this you must learn as much as possible about the benefits: the various events in which benefits may be payable (old age, disability, illness, or death); the eligibility requirements you must meet; the events that may terminate the payment of benefits; and the basis for calculating benefits (so you can take the steps necessary to maximize benefits).

As a bare minimum you should know when to ask your local Social Security office whether you are eligible for benefits. A recent Social Security publication suggests that you get in touch with a Social Security office if:

> you are unable to work because of an illness or injury that is expected to last a year or longer;
> you are 62 or older and plan to retire;
> you are within two or three months of 65, even if you don't plan to retire; or
> someone in your family dies.

Many other events can affect the type and level of benefits to which you and your family may be entitled. These events include marriage, divorce, bearing of children, a child's reaching age 18 (22 if in college), disability of family members, job change, moving from the United States and its possessions, and your parents' becoming dependent upon you. Learn as much as possible about Social Security benefits, and when in doubt, ask questions of your local Social Security office.

Eliminate Gaps and Duplications

There is another reason that becoming familiar with the benefits provided by Social Security will enable you to take full advantage of it. On the one hand, you can more easily avoid costly and wasteful duplication of benefit protection; and on the other hand, you can more easily fill the gaps in benefit protection which, unfilled, could leave you or your family in serious financial trouble. By way of illustration, consider the following examples.

If you should die, in some cases Social Security would pay monthly benefits to your surviving spouse and children. In addition, you may be eligible for death benefits under a group life insurance program provided by your employer. Under some circumstances the total death benefit protection thus provided may be adequate to meet the needs of your spouse and children, yet you may be buying added life insurance on a personal basis—insurance which you cannot easily afford and which you do not really need. Under other circumstances the death benefits provided by Social Security and employer group life insurance may be less than adequate and you may need additional personal life insurance to protect your family adequately.

The same principle applies to all the contingencies against which you must protect yourself and your family: old age, disability, illness, and death. Disability protection is often found to be inadequate. Old-age retirement protection is frequently less than desirable. The starting point to eliminate these gaps and duplications in benefit protection is to be thoroughly familiar with benefits provided under Social Security and employer-sponsored fringe benefit plans.

Under ideal circumstances, you will be able to tailor your personal security plans so as to eliminate the gaps and duplications in benefit protection. In some situations, however, this will not be possible because of the particular combination of benefits provided under Social Security and employer-sponsored plans. To correct any such inconsistencies will require the cooperation of both employer and employees in making appropriate modifications in the employer-sponsored benefit plans.

Ways to Increase Your Benefits

There are numerous ways to get the most benefits from Social Security for your tax dollar. In some cases the local Social Security office will help you. Most of the time it will be up to you, however, to take at least the first steps. Here are some examples of how to maximize your Social Security benefits.

Satisfy Minimum Eligibility Requirements

As indicated in Chapter 3, you must satisfy a variety of requirements to be eligible for benefits. These can include having paid Social Security taxes for a minimum number of quarters, satisfying certain marital status requirements, keeping earned income within specified limits once benefits commence, filing a timely application for benefits, and so forth. In some cases you may almost, but not quite, meet all these requirements. With a relatively small effort you may be able to satisfy the minimum eligibility requirements and obtain extremely valuable benefits.

A classic example of this is the person whose principal career employment is not covered by Social Security—for example, most employees of the federal government and some employees of state and local governments and nonprofit organizations. Such persons can work in covered employment on a part-time basis during their careers and qualify for Social Security benefits worth many times their Social Security taxes.

Another example is the woman who worked in employment covered by Social Security but left her job to rear a family prior to becoming permanently entitled to retirement benefits. Just a few more months in covered employment, even on a part-time basis, may be enough to qualify her for significant benefits.

To qualify for disability benefits, you must have a recent attachment to the work force, hence you cannot leave covered employment and be permanently eligible for benefits. Generally speaking, five years' continuous absence from covered employment will cause a loss in the right to disability benefits. These rights can be maintained, however, by working part time every few months in covered employment.

Verify Your Earnings Record

The government (Internal Revenue Service) collects taxes on your earnings that are subject to Social Security tax. The Social Security Administration keeps a record of these earnings and uses it to determine whether you are eligible for benefits and the amount of such benefits. Obviously, if the records are wrong, your benefits will be wrong. Mistakes do happen and you should do everything possible to make certain that the government's records of your earnings are correct.

Each year you should review carefully the Form W-2 Wage and Tax Statement supplied by your employer and determine that Social Security taxes have been paid on the correct amount of earnings. The items on the form that relate to Social Security are entitled "total FICA wages" and "FICA tax withheld." FICA is the acronym for Federal Insurance Contributions Act, a less than obvious reference to Social Security.

This annual review of your Form W-2 is only a beginning step to check your records and does not ensure that the government's records are correct. To verify this, you can file a form with the Social Security Administration (Form OAR-7004) and request a statement of your Social Security earnings. You will then receive a statement showing the amount of earnings on which Social Security taxes have been paid in each of the past three years, as well as the total for your lifetime. It is important that you request this earnings statement and verify your records at least every three years so that any errors can be corrected. In general, an earnings record can be corrected at any time up to three years, three months, and fifteen days after the year in which earnings were received. After that it is still possible—though more difficult—to have a mistake corrected.

Someday, perhaps, the government will take the initiative in confirming the amount of earnings on which you have paid Social Security taxes (as recommended in Chapter 9). Until then, you are on your own.

Do Not Overlook Military Service

If you were on active military duty at any time from September 16, 1940 through December 31, 1956, you may be eligible for special wage credits of $160 for each month of service. These wage credits do not appear on your Social Security earnings record maintained by the government. It will be up to you or your survivors to notify Social Security about this service at the time application for benefits is made. The Social Security representative will then ask for a record of service if this will result in higher benefits. It would be particularly easy for survivors to overlook this military service and thus be deprived of benefits to which they are entitled.

There is yet another item regarding military service that does not appear on the government's records of Social Security earnings. For each quarter in which you have active duty pay after 1956 and before 1968, you are to receive additional earnings credits of $300. Although these free credits do not appear on your earnings statement, they are supposed to be considered in figuring monthly benefits. Similar earnings credits are provided for military service in 1968 and later, but these amounts are shown directly on your earnings record. At the time your benefit is determined you should verify that you have in fact received all such earnings credits.

Apply for Benefits Even If Not Retiring

You should consider applying for benefits at age 65 even if you do not actually quit working until later. There are several reasons this may yield unexpected benefits.

The earnings test (described in Chapter 12) permits you to have a limited amount of earnings without losing any Social Security benefits. This exempt amount of earnings is a flat dollar amount regardless of your level of benefits or preretirement earnings. Accordingly, low wage earners may be able to continue working beyond age 65 in the same job for the same pay *and* collect full Social Security retirement benefits.

For example, consider a low wage earner reaching age 65 in 1980 who earns $5,000 per year and is entitled to the "special minimum benefit" of $252.80 per month. Such a worker could continue working and receive full wages *and* Social Security benefits. Higher wage earners who continue to work beyond age 65 would not fare as well and would lose some or all of their Social Security benefits because of earnings above $5,000; however, you should consider applying for benefits regardless of your earnings level, particularly if you have family members entitled to benefits on your earnings record, because of the possibility of receiving unexpected benefits.

If you plan to retire during the early part of the year, you should apply for benefits earlier than you actually stop working, even if you are a high wage earner. For example, if you were aged 65 at the beginning of 1980 and quit working March 1, 1980, you could have had total earnings of $5,000 in January and February and still collected full Social Security benefits for January and February (because of the exempt earnings amount in 1980 of $5,000). Social Security benefits for these two months could be as much as $1,716 for a retired person with an eligible spouse. These are tax-free benefits which could be overlooked easily.

You are eligible for Medicare benefits at age 65, even if you have not retired and are not receiving monthly cash retirement benefits. You are also eligible for Medicare after you have received Social Security disability benefits for twenty-four months or if you have chronic kidney disease requiring dialysis or a kidney transplant. But this valuable Medicare coverage is not automatic; you must apply for it.

Get the Most from Medicare

Medicare has two parts: Part A (Hospital Insurance) helps pay for inpatient hospital care and for certain follow-up care after leaving the hospital; Part B (Supplementary Medical Insurance) helps pay for doctors' services, outpatient hospital services, and many other medical items and services not covered by Part A.

If you are aged 65 or older and are entitled to Social Security (or Railroad Retirement) benefits—even though you may not be receiving them—you are eligible for Part A of Medicare. You need not pay any specific additional contributions or taxes since Part A is financed by Social Security taxes paid by active workers.

Part B of Medicare is another matter. It is optional and requires premium payments of $9.60 per month after July 1, 1980 (subject to increase in the future as the cost of medical care increases). These premiums finance only about 30 percent of the cost of Part B. The balance is financed from general revenue; that is, general taxes paid by everyone, whether or not they participate in Social Security or receive Part B benefits. By the year 2000 it is estimated that individual premiums will pay for only 10 percent of the cost of Part B, with general revenue paying for the remaining 90 percent.

Since Part B provides needed medical benefits and since an individual pays directly for less than 30 percent of the cost, you should have some very good reasons if you elect not to be covered. When you become covered by Part A, you will be covered automatically by Part B and the monthly premium will be deducted from your regular Social Security or Railroad Retirement checks unless you advise Social Security that you do not want Part B coverage.

If you have not been a regular participant in Social Security (or the Railroad Retirement system) and thus are not eligible automatically for Part A benefits, you can elect to be covered by Part A by paying a premium of $78 per month after July 1, 1980, subject to increase in the future as the cost of hospital care increases. To make this election, you must be a resident of the U.S. and a citizen or an alien lawfully admitted for permanent residence who has resided in the U.S. continuously for five years. This election may be made during the month you reach age 65 or during the three months before or after that month. If you do not enroll at this time, you may enroll later during the "general enrollment period" from January 1 through March 31 of each year. If you are not eligible automatically for Part A of Medicare and you do *not* elect to be covered thereunder, you should have some very good reasons. The cost may appear to be high, but it is consistent with the average cost of benefits. Furthermore, the cost is a bargain if your health is worse than average. If you elect to be covered by Part A, you must also elect to be covered by Part B. You can enroll in Part B without enrolling in Part A, but this would not be a wise decision except for a person assured of alternative hospital insurance for his or her remaining lifetime.

If your spouse is older than you, there may be some advantage to filing an application for retirement benefits when you reach age 62, even if you do not actually receive benefits until a later time when you stop working. This establishes your "entitlement" to retirement benefits and thus affords Medicare protection for your spouse after he or she attains age 65. The provision of Medicare protection for your spouse could be valuable should hospital insurance coverage provided by your employer terminate or reduce significantly upon a spouse's attainment of age 65.

Medicare does not pay for hospital and medical care outside the United States, except in Canada for U.S. residents living nearby and in a few other limited cases. Accordingly, if you depend normally upon Medicare and you plan to travel abroad, you should make alternative arrangements for temporary health insurance.

Consider Effect of Marriage on Benefits

Many Social Security benefits are paid as a result of a person's being a wife, husband, widow, or widower. The state of marriage has an important bearing on whether benefits become payable and whether they continue to be payable. This should be duly considered when decisions are made about whether and when to marry, remarry, divorce, and, perhaps, whom to marry. Even though eligibility for Social Security benefits may not affect these basic decisions about marriage, it should certainly be taken into account in arranging personal financial affairs.

Significant gaps in income security protection usually occur when changes are made in marital status. Chapter 22 gives examples of some of the many ways in which benefit protection can be affected by such changes in status.

Maximize Survivors Benefits

Benefits paid to your widow or widower and children may require supplementation if their standard of living is to be maintained. Yet, if one or more of your survivors earns more than a nominal amount, it may result in the forfeiture of Social Security benefits, thus requiring even further supplementation (because of the "earnings test" described in Chapter 12 and mentioned elsewhere). One way to prevent your surviving spouse from having to work while caring for young children (and then losing Social Security benefits as a result of such work) is to buy an appropriate amount of life insurance. Life insurance benefits payable after your death will not reduce Social Security benefits and, for the most part, are not taxable.

Maximize Educational Benefits

The child of a retired or disabled worker is entitled to a benefit of as much as $286 per month (early in 1980). The child of a deceased worker is entitled to a benefit of as much as $429 per month (early in 1980). Payment of these benefits normally stops at age 18; but if the child is a full-time student, payment continues until age 22 (until the end of the semester or quarter the child reaches age 22 provided an undergraduate degree has not yet been received).

The earnings test described in Chapter 12 applies to student beneficiaries. Accordingly, to avoid the loss of student benefits it may be preferable for a student to borrow (rather than earn) a portion of the additional funds needed to continue in school. Appropriate life insurance benefits provided by a deceased parent would permit the continued education of a student without the necessity of work that may result in loss of Social Security benefits.

Be Persistent in Applying for Disability Benefits

If you are denied Social Security disability benefits but believe your claim to be legitimate, you would be well-advised to consider appealing and, perhaps, using an attorney to help you pursue your claim.

The number of hearings requested by Social Security claimants after being denied benefits has grown at a substantial rate in recent years. Currently, about two-thirds of all disability claims are denied initially. More than half of all appeals are reversed, and the chances of winning an appeal seem to be greater if an attorney is involved.

Control Timing of Earnings

Prior to 1978, benefits could be paid for any month you earned one-twelfth or less of the annual exempt amount and performed no substantial work in your own business. Accordingly, there was a tendency for persons who could do so to concentrate their earnings in certain periods and keep income low in as many months as possible. This technique was blocked by imposing an "annual measure" of earnings instead of a "monthly measure."

Nevertheless, it is still advantageous to control the receipt of earnings so as to minimize the effect of the earnings test and reduce the forfeiture of Social Security benefits. This is because the monthly measure is still used during the first year benefits are paid; earnings after attainment of age 72 (age 70 after 1981) are not considered in applying the earnings test; and earnings can be shifted from one year to another (instead of from one month to another as in the past). Self-employed persons sometimes facilitate this shifting of income by carrying out their business activities in a corporate form rather than a proprietorship.

Maximize Purchasing Power of Pension

After you have done everything possible to receive the maximum benefit available, the next logical step is to reside in a locale where the dollar has maximum purchasing power. Some areas of the United States have markedly lower costs of living than others, particularly in the South and Midwest. In the past twenty years the number of Social Security beneficiaries living abroad has tripled. According to the latest count, there are more than 300,000 beneficiaries residing in 130 foreign countries and receiving approximately $800 million per year in benefits.

There are some restrictions on the payment of benefits to those living abroad, particularly to aliens. The restrictions are relatively lenient, however, except for those living in the following countries that are currently on the U.S. Treasury Department's restricted list: Albania, Cambodia, Cuba, North Korea, Vietnam, East Germany, and the Russian zone of Berlin. Aliens who qualify for Social Security benefits can often retire to their homeland and enjoy a comfortable and less expensive life among old friends and family. Despite the vicissitudes of the dollar in recent years, it is still a sought-after currency in many countries. It is sometimes converted into a local currency at a rate more favorable than the official tourist rate and it is sometimes spendable in hard-currency shops that sell popular Western goods.

There are many considerations in deciding whether to retire abroad, not the least of which is the availability and cost of hospital and medical care. As already mentioned, Medicare generally does not provide benefits outside the United States. This disadvantage may or may not be compensated for by lower cost hospital and medical care in the country being considered.

There may be another advantage in living abroad as a result of conditions relating to the continued payment of benefits while working. If you live in the United States, because of the "earnings test" your earnings in excess of the exempt amount will result in a forfeiture of part or all of your Social Security benefits. If you live abroad and have foreign earnings (that are not covered under the U.S. Social Security program), the "earnings test" is different. It is not based upon the amount of your *earnings* but upon the amount of *time* employed. If you are employed on seven or more days during a month in a foreign country, the benefit for that month is completely withheld; otherwise, you receive the entire benefit. Accordingly, you might be able to maximize benefits by concentrating your work during selected days or months during the year. As once observed by a noted authority on the subject, thorough administration of such a provision is difficult and depends to a considerable extent on the good conscience of the individuals involved.

In the final analysis the selection of a place to live in retirement is a personal decision in which economic factors are only part of a multitude of considerations. It would be imprudent, however, not to take these economic factors into account.

Benefits That May Be Overlooked

A host of unique benefits are provided under the Social Security program. It is not feasible to list every conceivable situation that will result in benefit payments; however, the following examples will alert you to some of the types of benefits frequently overlooked.

Benefits Payable to Children

A child may be entitled to monthly benefits in the event of the retirement, death, or disability of one of his parents who is covered by Social Security. The child must be unmarried and:

less than 18 years old;

between 18 and 22 years old and a full-time student; or

18 years old or older with a severe physical or mental disability that began before age 22.

It is not necessary that a child be living with or receiving support from a parent in order to receive benefits based upon the parent's earnings record. Furthermore, a child can receive benefits based upon a stepparent's earnings record if the child lives with the stepparent *or* receives half his support from the stepparent.

Consider, for example, a child living with his father and stepmother, both of whom are covered by Social Security. Assume also that the child's natural mother is covered by Social Security. If any one of the three parents should retire, die, or become disabled, the child could be eligible for a benefit. It would be easy to overlook the availability of a child's benefits based upon the earnings record of a natural mother or father with whom the child does not reside.

A child may be able to receive benefits based on one parent's Social Security account even though the other parent is working and furnishing his support. An example would be when the child is entitled to benefits because of the death of his mother who was a covered worker. The fact that the child's father was supporting him would not matter.

A child may be eligible for benefits based on a grandparent's earnings record. The grandparent must have provided at least half the child's support; the child's parents must be dead or disabled; and the child must have begun to live with the grandparents prior to age 18.

Disability After Early Retirement

If you begin receiving Social Security retirement benefits before age 65, they will be reduced somewhat to offset the expectation that they will be paid over a longer period than if they had commenced at age 65. If you become disabled (seriously enough to meet disability benefit requirements) after benefits commence but prior to age 65, you should ask Social Security to switch your benefits from age-retirement to disability benefits. Disability benefits will be greater than the reduced age-retirement benefits you were receiving, since the early-retirement reduction will be eliminated with respect to the period between disability and age 65.

The net result will be larger monthly benefits for the remainder of your life and, in some cases, larger benefits for your widow or widower after your death. The total value of this increase in benefits could be as high as $15,000. It would be easy to overlook this opportunity for increased benefits since the disability would not be related to a cessation of work.

If family benefits are payable, however, the question of whether to apply for disability benefits becomes more difficult. This arises because maximum family disability benefits are generally lower than maximum family retirement benefits. As is true in all cases of actual benefit eligibility, it is advisable to consult your local Social Security office.

Retroactive Disability Benefits Paid After Death

It is possible for a person to become disabled and die without ever filing for disability benefits, even though all eligibility requirements have been met. In such cases it may be possible to establish retroactive eligibility for disability benefits and thus receive such benefits for as much as twelve months. Although an application can be filed within three months after the death of a disabled person, it should be filed as early as possible to prevent possible loss of benefits.

Earnings While Disabled

The rules governing work by disabled persons receiving Social Security benefits are surprisingly liberal, purportedly in an attempt to encourage rehabilitation.

A disability beneficiary is allowed unlimited earnings for as much as nine months of trial work without losing any disability benefits. (Disabled widows and widowers receiving benefits on the basis of a spouse's earnings record are not eligible for this nine-month trial period.) Even after it has been determined that disability ceased, full benefits are paid for that month and for the next two months.

Furthermore, a person who is disabled and receiving Social Security benefits can generally have earnings of up to $300.00 per month indefinitely without losing any benefits. This was the limit in effect in 1980; it will probably be increased in the future. Social Security sometimes reviews disabled persons' earnings in *covered employment* to determine whether they are disqualified from receiving further disability benefits. It is more difficult, if not impossible, for Social Security to discover any earnings in *noncovered employment.*

Benefits for Divorced Wives

Divorced wives (including surviving divorced wives) are entitled to certain Social Security benefits based on their former husband's earnings record provided the marriage lasted for ten years. This ten-year requirement was effective for benefits payable for months after December 1978. For benefits payable earlier, it was required that the marriage last twenty years. Accordingly, there may be many divorced wives married between ten and twenty years who became eligible for benefits in January 1979 but who are not aware of it.

Until recently, a divorced woman was not eligible for benefits based on her former husband's earnings record unless he contributed to her support after the divorce. This support requirement was eliminated in 1972; therefore, a woman denied benefits because of this support requirement may now be eligible for benefits.

Benefits for Widows and Widowers

As the result of a recent change in the law, remarriage of a surviving spouse after age 60 will not reduce the amount of widow's or widower's benefits with respect to benefits for months after December 1978. Accordingly, many widows and widowers who married after age 60 but prior to December 31, 1978 first became eligible for benefits in January 1979. For the most part, these benefits are being paid automatically; however, there may be some widows and widowers who are not aware of their eligibility.

A widow who remarries before age 60 may receive benefits on a deceased husband's earnings if she is not married when she applies for benefits. A widower, however, who remarried before age 60 cannot get such benefits even if the subsequent marriage has terminated (except in certain cases where the new wife is a beneficiary).

A widower with an entitled child in his care can receive benefits payable based on the earnings record of his deceased wife. The law does not read this way but it has been so administered since a successful challenge in the courts in 1975 (Weinberger v. Wiesenfeld).

An aged divorced husband can receive benefits payable based on the earnings record of his wife. The law does not read this way, but it has been so administered since a successful challenge in the courts in 1977 (Oliver v. Califano).

Several other changes have been made recently in the law or the way it is administered with respect to males, married as well as divorced; for example, the finding in 1977 that a man does not have to be financially dependent on his wife in order to receive husband's or widower's benefits based on his wife's earnings record. It is likely that these changes made some males eligible for benefits of which they are still unaware.

Benefits for Persons Aged 72 or Over

A person who reached age 72 before 1969 (in some cases, 1972) may be eligible for small monthly benefits even if the normal requirements for insured status have not been met. As in the case of all benefits, the local Social Security office should be consulted first to determine whether benefits are payable. Since this is a unique benefit, however, you should make a special effort to ensure that your case receives proper consideration.

Ways to Decrease Your Taxes

There are not many ways to decrease your Social Security taxes; however, they do exist. They usually involve a reduction in earnings on which Social Security taxes are paid, hence a reduction in benefits. Careful study is necessary, therefore, to determine whether the reduction in taxes is offset by the reduction in benefits (perhaps considering both employer and employee taxes).

Refund of Excessive Tax Payments

In each calendar year there is a maximum amount of earnings on which you must pay Social Security taxes. In 1980 this maximum was $25,900, and in 1981 it is scheduled to be $29,700. It will increase each year thereafter as the nation's average wages increase.

If you work for more than one employer in a calendar year and if your total wages exceed this maximum taxable amount, you will probably pay more Social Security tax than is required. This is because each employer determines the maximum taxable wages without regard to earnings from other employers.

Assume, for example, that you earned $40,000 in 1980: $30,000 from employer A and $10,000 from employer B. Employer A would have withheld taxes on the first $25,900 of the $30,000 of earnings; and employer B would have withheld taxes on the entire $10,000 of earnings. Thus, you would have paid Social Security taxes on $35,900 of earnings. Your total taxes would have been $2,200.67, or $613.00 more than you were required to pay.

If you are aware that you have overpaid your taxes you can get a refund. One of the lines on Form 1040 of the U.S. Individual Income Tax Return is entitled "Excess FICA and

RRTA tax withheld (two or more employers)." You can enter any excess Social Security tax payment on this line and it will be applied toward any federal income taxes that are due, and refunded to the extent not needed to pay such taxes.

In this example, your two employers also would have paid $2,200.67 in Social Security Taxes, or $613.00 more than if you had received all your earnings from just one employer. No refund of these "excess" taxes will be made, however, with respect to the employers' taxes. An exception to this treatment of taxes paid by multiple employers was made by the 1977 Social Security Amendments; namely, two or more financially related employers are not required to pay more in Social Security taxes for any given employee than if the employee were on the payroll of a single employer. This requires compliance with several technicalities that are relatively simple.

Incorrectly Collected Taxes

In some cases an employer may deduct Social Security taxes from an employee's wages and determine later that such taxes were not in fact payable. For example, domestic workers must receive cash pay of $50 or more in a calendar quarter before Social Security taxes are payable; and agricultural employees must receive cash pay of $150 or more in a calendar year (or meet certain other employment tests). If an employer begins withholding before these tests are satisfied and later finds out that the employee does not meet the test, the employer must repay the Social Security taxes deducted or, if the employer cannot locate the employee, send the incorrectly collected taxes to the Internal Revenue Service. Under these circumstances an employee would be well-advised to verify that the correct Social Security taxes have in fact been collected.

Method of Payment of Social Security Taxes

Social Security taxes are normally paid by employees as well as employers. It is possible, however, for the employer to make these employee tax payments from its own funds on behalf of the employee and reduce the employee's gross earnings by the amount of such tax payments. The tax payments must be included in the employee's income for federal tax purposes; however, the tax payments are not counted as wages for Social Security tax purposes. In this way an employer can reduce the wages that are taxable for Social Security purposes (with respect to employees whose wages after being reduced by Social Security taxes are less than the maximum taxable earnings base), and thus reduce both employee and employer Social Security taxes payable with respect to such employee. Total Social Security taxes for such employees can thus be reduced by an amount equivalent to about 0.88 percent of payroll in 1981. The percentage saving will rise in the future as the Social Security tax rate increases.

This procedure will, of course, reduce future Social Security benefits to the extent that an employee's average earnings—on which such benefits are based—are reduced. The procedure of reducing the wages subject to Social Security tax also reduces the wages subject to unemployment insurance tax, resulting in additional saving in taxes. Furthermore, the reduction in cash earnings brought about by this procedure may result in a reduction in other fringe benefits (and the costs thereof) that are related to cash earnings—for example, group life insurance and disability benefits. Finally, the personal income taxes paid by an employee may be reduced slightly (by the amount of personal income tax on the reduction in Social Security taxes payable on behalf of the employee).

The option for the employer to pay the employee Social Security tax and thus reduce certain taxes was available for *all* employees until the enactment of the Omnibus Reconciliation Act of 1980. This act eliminated the tax-saving effect of the option for all employment except domestic service in a private home and agricultural labor—effective in 1981 for private sector employees and in 1984 for public sector employees (provided the public sector practice was in effect on October 1, 1980).

Method of Payment of Unemployment Insurance Taxes

In three states (Alaska, Alabama, and New Jersey), employees must pay taxes to help finance a state-administered unemployment insurance program which provides partial income replacement for a limited period to persons who become unemployed. The employer can make these employee tax payments from its own funds on behalf of the employee, and reduce the employee's gross earnings by the amount of such tax payments (not necessarily directly and immediately). The employee's income for federal income tax purposes will not change (since unemployment insurance tax payments made by the employer on behalf of the employee are taxable); however, the tax payments are not counted as wages for Social Security tax purposes. In this way an employer can reduce the wages that are taxable for Social Security purposes (with respect to employees who earn less than the maximum taxable earnings base), and thus reduce Social Security taxes payable by the employee and the employer. This procedure will, of course, reduce future Social Security benefits to the extent that average earnings—on which such benefits are based—are reduced.

If the unemployment insurance tax is levied on total cash income (not including the unemployment insurance tax payments made by the employer on behalf of the employee), this procedure would reduce the total unemployment insurance taxes paid by both employer and employee. In some cases it would also reduce unemployment insurance benefit protection that is related only to the cash income.

Until enactment of the Omnibus Reconciliation Act of 1980 the tax advantages of the optional payment of unemployment insurance taxes was available for all employment. Effective in 1981 for the private sector and in 1984 for the public sector (provided the practice was in effect on October 1, 1980), the option is available only for employment in domestic service in a private home and in agricultural labor.

Taxes on Sick Pay

Most employers and employees pay Social Security taxes on all their wages, even though some of these "wages" may be legally exempt from such taxes (and, in some cases, exempt from federal unemployment insurance taxes). This overpayment is done for convenience in some cases; but, in others, it is probably out of ignorance of the law.

Payments made to an employee under a sick-pay plan (which

meets certain requirements) are not subject to Social Security taxes. There is no exemption, however, for payments for unused sick leave since such payments are not made "on account of sickness or accident disability." Taxes that have been paid in error can be recovered for up to four years in the past (Internal Revenue Code, Section 3121 (a)(4)). A decision to recover or not to recover past overpayment of taxes can mean thousands of dollars to an employer and its employees. Any recovery of past tax overpayment attributable to withholding from employee earnings is, of course, refundable to the employee. It is possible that such amounts would be considered owed by the employer to the employee, even if they are not recovered by the employer, since the payment of Social Security taxes on qualified sick pay is a mistake, though perhaps well-intentioned.

This reduction in taxes, including any retroactive recovery, would affect only employees whose earnings (excluding sick pay) were less than the maximum taxable earnings base for the year under consideration. Since a reduction in taxes results from a reduction in earnings on which taxes are payable, future Social Security benefits would be reduced also.

Taxes on Stand-by Pay

Once you reach age 62 any pay you receive for periods in which you perform no work is not considered earnings subject to Social Security tax (except for vacation and certain sick-leave pay). This could include stand-by pay, subject-to-call pay, idle-time pay, and the like.

Convert Taxable Earnings Into Nontaxable Earnings

There are numerous ways to convert earnings that normally would be subjected to Social Security tax into forms of income that are not considered subject to such tax. The validity of some but not all of these conversions is questionable.

One method that is reportedly used by small groups of individuals who are in business together is as follows: The individuals incorporate as a small business corporation and then arrange to receive dividends but little or no salary. Dividends are not subjected to Social Security tax, hence Social Security taxes *and benefits* are reduced.

It is ironic that at the same time some people are trying to keep their income from being subjected to Social Security tax, others are trying to make their nontaxable income subject to Social Security tax so they will be eligible for additional benefits.

Opt Out of Social Security

Of course, the ultimate way to decrease taxes is to opt out of Social Security altogether. Generally speaking, the only persons eligible to opt out of Social Security are employees of state and local governments and nonprofit organizations, and members of certain religious groups. Less than fifteen percent of the work force is eligible to do this, and even then such an option can be exercised normally only by an entire group of employees and not by an individual.

Chapters 17 and 18 contain more details about groups for whom participation in Social Security is optional and the many considerations involved in making a decision to participate or not participate. Even though withdrawal from Social Security is a way to save Social Security taxes and thus may be of advantage to some persons, it is not necessarily the best way for most persons to take advantage of Social Security.

Domestic Workers

Failure to pay Social Security taxes on work performed by domestic workers is *not* a good way to decrease taxes. Domestic workers and casual workers, as well as their employers, may be less inclined than those in a more formal employer-employee relationship to follow the cumbersome administrative procedures and pay all the Social Security taxes required by law. This may be due in part to a misunderstanding of their taxpaying obligations, but also to a lack of appreciation of the value of Social Security benefits.

It is easy to depreciate Social Security benefits when the taxes fall due, but these benefits will be quite valuable at the time of old age, disability, illness, or death. The most prudent course, especially for workers with a casual attachment to the labor force, is to qualify for the maximum possible benefits afforded by Social Security. An employer who deprives employees and their dependents of needed benefits by failure to carry out an obligation to pay Social Security taxes may be taking unwarranted legal risks. This is entirely apart from the moral obligation of the employer to the employee to afford this needed protection.

Conclusion

There are several things you can do to take maximum advantage of Social Security. Learn as much as possible about the benefits provided by Social Security so that you can supplement those benefits appropriately with your own personal arrangements for financial security. There are ways to decrease Social Security taxes as well as to increase benefits. Extreme care should be taken in arranging a decrease in taxes, however, since this usually results in a decrease in benefits. Apply promptly for any Social Security benefits to which you may be entitled since, in general, benefits cannot be paid retroactively for more than six months (twelve months for certain disability benefits). Periodically verify your earnings record maintained by the Social Security Administration to be sure your record is accurate. Notify the Social Security office of any changes in your personal situation and that of your family members. The benefit provisions are complicated and are ever changing; thus you cannot be certain about your eligibility for benefits. If the answers you get from Social Security do not seem reasonable, double-check them. More and more mistakes are being made as Social Security becomes increasingly complicated and every precaution should be taken to prevent you and your family from being an innocent victim of an innocent mistake.

22
Social Security as a Determinant of Behavior

Most people think of Social Security as a program that collects taxes from the active working population and provides benefits in the event of old age, disability, illness, or death. This is certainly true, but it may be useful to look at Social Security from another point of view that may be of even greater importance in the long run.

Social Security is in effect a complex system of rewards and penalties for various kinds of social and economic behavior among its participants. As such, it is an important determinant of the behavior of the individual participants; thus it will ultimately shape the habits of the nation as a whole. Here are some examples of how Social Security affects our behavior.

Normal Retirement Age

We usually think of age 65 as the "normal retirement age." If we retire before age 65 it is called "early retirement." If we retire after age 65 it is called "late retirement."

Why is age 65 the normal retirement age instead of 66, or 67, or 70, or 60? It is because the planners of Social Security back in the 1930s thought this was a good compromise between the high cost of paying full benefits at age 60 and the limited usefulness of a retirement age of 70 for combatting unemployment. Since

269

then, Social Security has been changed to permit retirement benefits to commence as early as age 62, but on a reduced basis. Age 65 remains the normal retirement age, the earliest age at which unreduced benefits are payable.

Most private and many public employee pension plans have followed the Social Security practice of normal retirement at age 65. This is partly for convenience and consistency but also because the Internal Revenue Service regulation of private pension plans is related to the standards set by Social Security.

Social Security, then, started it all and has effectively defined the retirement age pattern for the nation. After forty-five years of being told that normal retirement is at age 65, most people have begun to believe it. In fact, many people believe that it is their inalienable right to retire at age 65 and that it is absurd to suggest they should work longer, even if they are in good health.

Whether or Not to Work

Decisions about whether or not to work depend largely upon a person's financial situation, state of emotional and physical health, and the availability of work the person considers suitable. Social Security plays an important role in this decision by virtue of the benefits it provides or does not provide. Furthermore, the existence of Social Security has influenced significantly the birth and growth of the private pension movement. Social Security, directly and indirectly, has thus spawned an entirely new way of thinking about work and retirement.

The influence of Social Security on our acceptance of age 65 as the normal retirement age has already been noted. Through its various provisions concerning the payment of benefits, Social Security also influences early and late retirement practices. Social Security pays full benefits at the "normal retirement age" of 65. Benefits may commence as early as age 62, in which event they are "actuarially reduced" to offset their expected payment over a longer period of time; however, the method of calculating benefits favors retirement at age 62, and the worker receives greater total value in relation to Social Security taxes paid by retiring at age 62. The commencement of benefits may be deferred until after age 65, in which event benefits will be increased to reflect partially, not fully, the shorter remaining lifetime during which they will be paid. The worker thus receives relatively less value if benefits commence after age 65.

Chapter 12 discusses in some detail the retirement test, or earnings test. If the worker begins to receive benefits but also continues in paid employment, his Social Security benefits are reduced if his earnings exceed certain "exempt amounts." These exempt amounts are lowest under age 65, next lowest between ages 65 and 72, and are highest after age 72 when there is no limit on earnings. The provisions of the current law would seem to encourage a person to retire at age 62, to engage in limited paid employment until age 65, to increase the level of his activity in paid employment from age 65 to 72, and then to work in full-time paid employment after age 72—an apparent irrational set of provisions. (After 1981 references in this paragraph to age 72 should read age 70.)

Spouses and children who receive benefits based on the work record of a retired worker, or because of the death or disability of a worker, are also subject to the earnings test. Accordingly, they may lose part or all of their benefits if their earnings exceed the exempt amount. In cases where the maximum family benefit is in effect, however, a family member could earn more than the exempt amount and lose part of his or her own benefit without causing a reduction in the total amount received by the family. This is because the reduction in family benefits as a result of excess earnings is made before the maximum family benefit is determined.

The influences exerted by Social Security on the decision of whether or not to work are subtle and are different for each type of beneficiary. Unfortunately, many of the beneficiaries, particularly the worker's family members, are not aware of the effect of their working on the receipt of benefits early enough to make informed decisions about related financial matters.

Whether to Marry or Remarry

Many benefits are paid under Social Security to wives, husbands, widows, and widowers. Of course the payment of such benefits presupposes that marriage has taken place. Even though common-law marriages are recognized, this is frequently an ambiguous situation. Just living together will not necessarily create an entitlement to these benefits—benefits which may be quite important in the event of death, disability, or illness, particularly if dependent children are involved. The failure to formalize a de facto marriage could result in substantial financial hardship.

If you are the widow (nondisabled) of a worker covered by Social Security, your eligibility for widow's benefits will cease if you remarry prior to age 60 (except if you marry a person who is entitled to a widower's, father's, parent's or disabled child's benefit, or if you are receiving a mother's benefit and you marry another Social Security beneficiary). Remarriage at age 60 or later does not affect a widow's benefit.

If you are receiving benefits as a result of being a dependent parent of a worker covered by Social Security, your benefits will cease if you remarry after the worker's death (except if you marry a person who is entitled to a widow's, widower's, mother's, father's, divorced wife's, parent's, or disabled child's benefit).

If you are receiving benefits as a result of being a divorced widow of a worker covered by Social Security, your benefits will cease if you remarry at any age (unless you marry a person who is entitled to a widower's, father's, parent's, or disabled child's benefit).

If you are receiving benefits as a result of being a divorced wife of a worker covered by Social Security, your benefits will cease if you remarry someone other than the worker; however, your benefits will not be terminated if you marry an individual entitled to widower's, father's, or parent's monthly benefits, or an individual aged 18 or over who is entitled to childhood disability benefits.

Some children receive benefits because one of their parents is receiving retirement benefits (as a result of disability or having attained age 62), or because one or both of their parents have died. To continue receiving these benefits, such a child must be *unmarried* and:

> under age 18;
> under age 22, if a full-time student; or
> any age, if disabled before age 22.

In any of these circumstances, marriage could result in a substantial loss of benefits.

Whom to Marry

Some people marry to attain financial security. If this is your objective, all other factors being equal, it may be preferable to marry someone who will work in employment covered by Social Security. This excludes about 10 percent of the nation's workers at any given time: some nonprofit organization employees, some governmental employees, some members of religious orders, and so forth.

If you are a divorced wife who was married at least ten years to a man who will become entitled to Social Security benefits, you may eventually be entitled to benefits yourself based upon his work record. You will retain this benefit if you remarry someone receiving Social Security benefits as a widower, father, parent, or disabled child. You will lose this benefit if you marry anyone else.

If you are a disabled person aged 18 or over and are receiving benefits as a result of being a child of a worker covered by Social Security, your benefits will cease if you marry (except if you marry another disabled child aged 18 or over who is receiving child's benefits, or if you marry a person entitled to old-age, widow's, widower's, mother's, father's, parent's, disability, or divorced wife's benefits).

These comments about whether and whom to marry, taking into account the Social Security benefits that may be gained or lost, may appear to be somewhat overdrawn. There is, perhaps, an element of satire in the exposition in the sense it is "used for the purpose of exposing folly." Consider, however, Chart 22.A, which is a copy of page 322 of the following government publication: *Social Security Handbook*, U.S. Department of Health, Education, and Welfare, Social Security Administration, HEW Publication No. (SSA) 77-10135, July 1978.

Whether (or When) to Divorce

A divorce at any time will result in a potential loss of future benefits. A divorce *prior* to ten years of marriage can result in a *total loss* of benefits a person may have become eligible to

Chart 22.A

1856. The Effect of One Beneficiary's Marriage to Another Beneficiary is Summarized in the Following Chart:

Male beneficiary	Retirement insurance benefits	Disability insurance benefits	Divorced wife	Child under 18 and child 18 or over in school	Disabled child 18 or over	Widow under 60	Widow 60 or over	Surviving divorced wife	Mother	Parent
Retirement insurance beneficiary	C	C	CT¹	CT	C	CT	C½*	CT	C	CT
Disability insurance beneficiary	C	C	CT¹	CT	C²	CT	C½*	CT	C²	CT
Child under 18 and child 18 or over in school	TC	TC	T	T	T	T	TC½*	T	T	T
Disabled child 18 or over	C	C	C²	T	C²	C²	C³	C²	C²	C²
Widower under 60	TC	TC	C	T	C	C	C	C	C	C
Widower 60 or over	C½*	C½*	C	C½T*	C	C	C	C	C	C
Father	C	C	C	T	C	C	C	C	C	C
Parent	TC	TC	C	T	C	C	C	C	C	C

"T" means Termination; "C" means Continuation of benefit; the arrow indicates the beneficiary affected.

*½ means that, effective with the month of marriage, the benefit of the widow or widower, while not terminated, is reduced to 50 percent of the deceased worker's primary insurance amount. This reduction is effective for months prior to 1979. As of January 1979, there is no reduction because of the remarriage of a widow(er) age 60 or over.

¹The divorced wife's benefits end unless the retirement insurance or disability insurance beneficiary is the insured worker on whose earnings record her benefit is based.

²If the male's benefits terminate for any reason other than his death or his entitlement to retirement insurance benefits, female's benefits will also terminate. However, termination of a female disability or childhood disability benefit will not terminate any benefit which her husband is receiving on another earnings record.

³If, subsequent to the marriage, the male's childhood disability benefit terminates for a reason other than death or entitlement to retirement insurance benefits, the widow's benefit is reduced to 50 percent of her former husband's primary insurance amount for benefits payable before 1979. Beginning January 1979, there is

receive based on the other person's coverage by Social Security. A divorce *after* ten years of marriage will result in a *partial loss* of such benefits. From the standpoint of receiving Social Security benefits, it is obviously preferable to divorce after ten years and one month of marriage rather than after nine years and eleven months. The difference in a few days could amount to a loss of thousands of dollars.

Consider, for example, a divorced wife aged 30 with one child aged one month, whose former husband died in January 1980 leaving her with maximum Social Security benefits. The actuarial value of these benefits at the time of the former husband's death would be as follows (the actual dollar amount payable over the years would be more than four times these amounts):

Divorced Mother's benefits	$ 72,000
Divorced Widow's benefits	33,000
Child's benefits	85,000
Total	$190,000

This example assumes that the divorce occurred after at least ten years of marriage. If the divorce had occurred just prior to ten years of marriage, no divorced widow's benefits would have been payable and $33,000 worth of benefits would have been lost, probably unwittingly. The divorced mother's benefits would still be payable but would usually terminate upon remarriage. The child's benefits, worth about $85,000 and payable in any event, would be controlled by whichever party is given custody of the child.

Generally speaking, a divorced wife of a marriage that endured at least ten years will receive the same benefits as if the divorce had not occurred. There are, however, at least three exceptions:

The wife of a person entitled to disability or retirement benefits will receive monthly benefits if she is caring for a child entitled to benefits if under age 18 or disabled, even if the wife is less than age 62. A divorced wife in these circumstances will receive no such benefit.

A widow who remarries prior to age 60 loses any benefits to which she is entitled on her husband's earnings record; remarriage after age 60 does not result in such loss of benefits. A surviving divorced wife loses such benefits if she remarries at any age, even after age 60.

The wife's benefits may be reduced if the total family benefits would otherwise exceed the family maximum. A divorced wife's benefits are not subject to such a reduction.

Therefore, the benefits payable to a divorced wife may be equal to, less than, or greater than, the benefits payable if the divorce had not occurred, depending upon the circumstances. Even though a divorced wife may be entitled to the same benefits as if divorce had not occurred, these benefits can be forfeited completely in the event of her remarriage; and the amount of Social Security benefits resulting from the remarriage may be equal to, greater than, or less than, the benefits forfeited.

A divorce frequently has significant financial consequences as a result of lost Social Security benefits. Oftentimes, these consequences are not fully recognized until it is too late to prevent the loss (sometimes they are never recognized), in large part because the myriad of benefits provided by Social Security is not widely appreciated.

Whether to Recover from Disability

Social Security pays disability benefits to persons who are so severely disabled, mentally or physically, that they cannot perform any substantial gainful work. Needless to say it is not always possible to determine conclusively whether a person is disabled. Subjectivity is sometimes involved, not only on the part of the administrator who is assessing the disability but also on the part of the potential beneficiary.

I shall ignore the question of whether a potential beneficiary feigns disability just to collect benefits. Undoubtedly some do, but most people are not inclined to go to such lengths and are not aware of the relatively generous benefit levels, so let us assume most disabilities are determined fairly at their inception. Once benefits commence, however, there may not be sufficient incentive to recover.

Consider the following example: A married couple, both aged 35, with two children under age 18. Each adult earns the same as the average person covered by Social Security: that is, $11,479 in 1979 for combined gross earnings of $22,958 per year. The annual net take-home pay after federal, state, and Social Security taxes is $17,734 (based on the standard deduction and an average of representative state tax rates). Assume that one of the spouses qualifies for disability benefits early in 1980 of $9,581 per year payable monthly (for the disabled spouse and the children). The disability benefit is not taxable of course. The net take-home pay after federal, state, and Social Security taxes is now $19,490. This is $1,756 per year more than when both parents worked. After disability benefits have been paid for two years the disabled spouse also receives Medicare, free of charge except for a nominal premium for Supplementary Medical Insurance ($9.60 per month in July 1980). Furthermore, the disabled spouse is not subject to the earnings test applied to retired persons; and under rules followed by Social Security, a disabled person can earn about $300 per month without jeopardizing the disability status. Finally, the disability benefits are automatically and fully adjusted for changes in the Consumer Price Index—which may be more than can be said of the working spouse's earnings.

Some attempt is made by Social Security to rehabilitate disabled workers. For such an attempt to be successful in the example given, however, the rehabilitation effort would have to be Herculean, the disabled person would need an overwhelming desire to reenter paid employment, and both the man and wife would need to perceive Social Security as a fair program and not one that they should try to take advantage of.

Social Security was amended in 1980 (PL 96-265) to reduce disability benefits somewhat for persons first becoming eligible on July 1, 1980 and later. The change was not great enough, however, to have a material effect on the incentive to recover from disability.

Which Employer to Select

Social Security has the potential to influence our selection of employers in many ways. If it does not, frequently it is because of our failure to appreciate how much variation exists in the employee benefit plans provided in various jobs and how this may affect our future security.

Suppose you are a public school teacher in a state that provides Social Security coverage for its teachers. Suppose further that you would like to move to another state and continue teaching, and you believe that Social Security provides appropriate benefits for you because of your circumstances at this time (and there are many valid reasons this can be true). There are twelve states you may not want to consider any further because their teachers are not covered by Social Security. Alternatively, perhaps you would like to leave the teaching field and get a job in state or local government. There are six states that do not provide their public employees with Social Security. Perhaps you are considering a job with the federal government in the new Department of Education. If so, remember that civilian employees of the federal government do not participate in Social Security. True, federal employees have their own benefit plans, but these may not provide adequate benefits for short periods of service and you may not plan to make a career with the federal government.

On the other hand, you may not now be in a job that is covered by Social Security, but you may want such a job at some point in your career so you can obtain at least some of the benefits Social Security provides. For example, you may be a career employee with the federal government who plans to retire from government service at age 55 but work in other employment until age 65. In this event, you would probably choose your next job to be one that is covered by Social Security.

In some cases a person may want to spend the last few years of his career in a job *not* covered by Social Security, particularly if covered by Social Security during the first part of his career. The reason is that such employment frequently provides larger retirement benefits than employment covered by Social Security. Accordingly, the total benefit at retirement may be larger than if work continued in jobs covered by Social Security.

Each year thousands of employment decisions are made that reflect, or should reflect, factors similar to those mentioned.

To Save or Not to Save

The existence of Social Security discourages individuals and their employers from saving for their eventual retirement needs. Whether this affects the total saving habits of the nation is debatable; however, it seems reasonable to assume that it does.

Imagine that your employer does not provide a pension plan and that there is no Social Security program. Under these conditions would you save any of your current earnings for a time when you may not be able to work because of poor health or old age? Any prudent person past middle age would almost certainly answer yes. On the other hand, if you participate in Social Security do you make less provision for your retirement than if you were not covered by Social Security? Again, the only reasonable answer is yes.

If you are covered by Social Security and your employer also provides a pension plan, are the benefits lower under this employer plan than they would be if you were not covered by Social Security? Once again, the most common answer is yes.

Accordingly, it seems clear that the existence of Social Security results in individuals' and employers' making less provision for retirement than if there were no Social Security. And this means less saving by individuals and employers for retirement. This reduced saving by individuals and employers is not offset by increased saving under Social Security since Social Security is operated on a pay-as-you-go basis and does not generate saving.

Since the existence of Social Security results in less saving for retirement purposes, it is logical to assume that total national saving for all purposes is reduced. This has not been, and probably cannot be, proven conclusively. Furthermore, if there is no capital shortage in the nation, it may not matter whether total national saving is reduced. However, if there is a capital shortage in the nation, now or in the future, the negative influence exerted by Social Security on saving may be very important.

Whether to Feel Responsible for Oneself and One's Family

Social Security is changing our attitudes about our responsibility for saving and providing for our own future needs and those of our extended family. Part of this change in attitude is justified by the facts about how Social Security is now satisfying some of our financial needs. Another part of this change in attitude is not justified by the facts, rather it is based upon confusion about what Social Security is all about.

The average individual does not know what to expect from Social Security. Should he expect it to meet all of his needs (and those of his dependents) in the event of old age, disability, death, or sickness? Or should he expect it to be merely a floor of protection in meeting these needs, a floor upon which he and his employer should build through supplemental private saving and insurance and some form of retirement program? Apart from his expectations, what type and level of benefits does Social Security actually provide in meeting these various needs? Most people don't know. Under a system as complex as the present Social Security program, it is doubtful that a clear delineation of such responsibility will ever be possible—*a situation almost certain to result in people's expecting more and thus eventually receiving more from the government (that is, from the active working taxpayers).*

A number of factors, not the least of which is the general misunderstanding about the role of Social Security, have caused more and more people to believe that their economic needs in time of adversity should and will be met by someone else, namely the government. This change in attitude about responsibility for self is frightening. Its consequence has been and will continue to be a decline in individual initiative and self-reliance and thus a decline in the productivity of the nation as a whole.

Conclusion

Our Social Security program plays an important role in satisfying the population's economic security needs. While satisfying these needs, Social Security exerts strong influences, both good and bad, on the social and economic behavior of the nation's citizens. We must recognize that the design of Social Security is not only a reflection of our nation's existing social and economic structure, it is an important determinant of that structure in the future.

The nation must decide the extent to which it wants its citizens to have freedom of choice and the extent to which it wants to regulate their activities. It can then design an appropriate public policy as to the optimum roles to be played by the three natural sources of retirement income: government, employers and trade unions, and individuals. By properly designing and implementing such a policy, the nation can ensure that its citizens' basic economic security needs are met by methods that are consistent with the social and economic environment in which the nation will flourish, not wane. The challenge of finding and implementing the optimum mix that is the most favorable to this given end is considerably greater than merely satisfying the population's economic security needs during the next few years.

23
The Great American Retirement Dream

Many Americans believe that if they work until about age 60 or 65 they will then be able to live the balance of their lives in carefree and leisurely retirement, occupying themselves with hobbies, sports, and travel—activities for which they had neither the time nor the money in their earlier years. They believe this will be possible because of some combination of Social Security benefits, employer-paid pension benefits, and private savings in one form or another (a paid-for house, personal life insurance and annuities, etc.).

Not everyone really believes that this period of carefree and leisurely retirement will actually occur; however, most people want it to happen, hope that it will happen, and after a few years of nourishing such wants and hopes begin to believe that it *should* happen—that they are *entitled* to a leisurely retirement after having worked a lifetime in a job they consider difficult, or frustrating, or boring, or unsatisfying in some way. Indeed, this Great American Retirement Dream serves as a kind of opiate in making life more tolerable in the face of a sometimes onerous job, not to mention the everyday difficulties of living.

The Great American Retirement Dream has failed to materialize for most people in the past. Those who live to the "normal retirement" age of 60 or 65 are frequently disappointed because of the ill health of themselves or their immediate family, the loss of friends and relatives, or their inability to disengage from work-related activities and substitute new activities. In addition to these problems, most people experience significant financial difficulties. In an inflation-plagued economy, fixed pension benefits lose their purchasing power, and the cost of maintaining a "paid-for house" escalates unduly as real estate taxes and other costs increase; increased sickness in old age and skyrocketing medical costs combine to produce extremely high health care costs; personal savings do not prove to be as significant as planned, dissipated perhaps by unexpected health care expenses or high education costs for children; Social Security benefits and employer-provided pension benefits prove to be less than hoped for.

Just as the Great American Retirement Dream has failed to materialize in the past, it will probably fail in the future. It is not a goal that can be achieved for the majority of the population. It is not affordable, at least at a price the nation will be willing to pay. It is not a healthful concept, particularly if there is so little chance it can be achieved. It is a sad commentary on our way of life that anyone would spend most of his or her adult years looking forward to retirement.

The nation's concept of work, education, leisure, and retirement must be revised. It must be presumed that an individual will engage in gainful employment suitable to his physical and mental condition until well beyond age 60 or 65 and possibly until the end of his life. A trend toward later retirement may be a natural development as health and life expectancy improve and as the growth in the work force slows because of the low fertility rates now being experienced and expected to continue in the future. For this trend to be consummated, however, significant changes will be required in existing social and economic arrangements. Jobs must be structured to be more meaningful and satisfying to the individual. Persons must undergo training and retraining to enable them to have not just second careers, but third and fourth careers. In some instances jobs must be designed to fit the capabilities of the human resources available. For older persons as well as disabled persons, less strenuous jobs and part-time employment must be made available. Significant advances will be required in our ability to match persons with jobs. Sometimes this complete utilization of an individual can be achieved with one employer, but in some cases it will involve many different employers and may require geographical relocation as well. Attitudes must change to make these new concepts possible.

These changes must begin to take place during the next ten years, and they must be well underway by the turn of the century when the children of the post-World War II baby boom begin to reach their forties and fifties. Bringing about these changes will be a slow process that will require the cooperation of many institutions, not just Social Security.

The first step in the process is the recent action by Congress prohibiting an employer from imposing mandatory retirement at an age lower than age 70 (with certain exceptions). This action was coincidental and was just another step in the direction of eliminating job discrimination altogether. Nevertheless, it fits in well with the need for a more complete utilization of the nation's human resources. As time goes by and the health of the elderly continues to improve, further increases in the mandatory retirement age will probably be adopted. In fact, mandatory retirement may one day be eliminated (as it has been already for federal civilian employees).

The next step is to revise the Social Security program so that it is consistent with a policy of more complete utilization of the nation's human resources. It is sometimes said that the Social Security program has no particular influence on the nation's retirement policy since it does not specify the age at which a person can retire and it does not impose a mandatory retirement age. Nevertheless, the Social Security program effectively dictates the retirement policy of the nation.

It does this in part through the manifold and complicated conditions under which benefits are payable. Full benefits are payable at age 65, the "normal retirement age" selected somewhat arbitrarily in the 1930s by the program's designers. Benefits may commence as early as age 62, in which event they are "actuarially reduced" to offset their expected payment over a longer period of time; however, the method of calculating benefits under the present law favors retirement at age 62, since the worker receives greater total value by retiring at age 62. The commencement of benefits may be deferred until after age 65 in which event benefits will be increased to reflect partially, but not fully, the shorter remaining lifetime during which they will be paid. The worker thus receives less value if benefits commence after age 65.

If the worker continues in paid employment, his Social Security benefits are reduced if his earnings exceed certain levels. These levels of "permitted earnings" are lowest between ages 62 and 65, next lowest between ages 65 and 72, and are highest after age 72 when there is no limit on earnings.[1]

The Social Security program's influence on other retirement systems and thus on the nation's employment practices is pervasive. Private and public employee pension plans must as a practical matter follow the retirement patterns fostered by Social Security. Internal Revenue Service regulation of private pension plans is related to the standards set by Social Security. Practices followed by Social Security in determining eligibility for disability benefits influence the practices of private pension plans and private insurers.

Although the Social Security program is influencing the retirement policy of the nation through these many complicated provisions, it is rather difficult first to determine and then to state in a concise way exactly what that retirement policy is. The provisions of the current law would seem to encourage a person to retire at age 62, to engage in limited paid employment until age 65, to increase the level of his activity in paid employment from age 65 to 72, and then to work in full-time paid employment after age 72.[1]

Of more significance, however, the mere existence of the Social Security program sets a standard, and thus creates an expectation that fosters a presumption of entitlement, for retirement in a person's early to mid-sixties, regardless of the condition of his health and his ability to continue as a productive and useful member of society.

This retirement policy, which is inherent in the Social Security progam and which effectively sets the nation's retirement policy, should be reviewed carefully to determine whether it is in fact the retirement policy that is appropriate for the nation at this time as well as in the future. Moreover, and more importantly, careful attention should be given to the question of the extent to which the Social Security program should set the retirement policy for the nation and the extent to which such policy should be determined otherwise. The nation's retirement policy must vary from time to time depending upon a variety of factors, not the least of which is the fluctuating birth rate which causes shifts in the proportions of the population that are aged and young—the principal reason for the substantial projected Social Security cost increase beginning about thirty years from now. The present Social Security program may not be flexible enough to accommodate a variable retirement policy. In this connection it should be noted that one important reason for adopting Social Security in the first place was to alleviate the hardships of the widespread unemployment that prevailed in the 1930s. Much of the present design of the program is thus attributable to conditions that existed forty-five years ago.

Finally, work must begin on training and retraining individuals to meet existing job opportunities, as well as designing and redesigning jobs so they can be performed by available human resources. More sophisticated ways must be developed to appropriately match individuals and jobs.

The nation should provide an environment in which the capabilities of each individual can be utilized effectively, an environment that fosters meaningful activity, not empty idleness. Both the incentive and the opportunity should exist to enable every individual to work and produce throughout his lifetime in a series of endeavors compatible with his changing physical and mental abilities. Governmental policies should be directed toward these goals and not toward the removal from the active work force of able-bodied persons who must then be supported by the remaining active workers.

It will not be easy for the nation to move in this direction of full utilization of its human resources. The alternative will be continued high unemployment and underemployment, an ever-increasing pool of idle "disabled persons" and "aged persons," and a total cost to society that will become increasingly unbearable and that will eventually become destructive.

24
What Is the Outlook for Social Security?

The public is frequently given official assurance that the Social Security program is in sound financial condition during the foreseeable future and that there is nothing much to be concerned about. Such statements overlook the dramatic effect on costs of the growth in the aged population relative to the active working population shortly after the turn of the century. They also ignore the financial condition of the Hospital Insurance program which is financed by a portion of the Social Security payroll tax. Projections of future costs prepared by Social Security actuaries—contained in unpublished as well as published studies—indicate that the tax rate for the Old-Age, Survivors, Disability, and Hospital Insurance programs will at least double within the working lifetime of today's young workers: that is, it will rise from 6.13 percent in 1980 to about 8 percent by the year 2000 and 12 percent by the year 2025. The maximum wages to which these tax rates apply are also scheduled to increase: from $25,900 in 1980 to $29,700 in 1981, rising thereafter in proportion to increases in national average wages. Of course these are just the employee taxes; the employer pays a matching tax. The tax rate for self-employed persons is projected to rise from 8.10 percent in 1980 to about 11 percent in the year 2000 and 16 percent by the year 2025.

These projections assume that the Social Security law is not changed (except to increase tax rates enough to pay benefits), that present financing practices are followed, and that current patterns of retirement continue. Such assumptions will probably not materialize, particularly in view of the large projected tax increases as well as the increase that will occur in the average age of the population if the present relatively low birth rates continue. As has been highly publicized in recent years, this aging of the population will result eventually in only two workers paying taxes for every one person receiving benefits— in contrast to the present situation of three workers for every beneficiary.

What Changes Lie Ahead?

What kinds of change can be expected in the present law and in the behavior of the population covered by that law because of these projected rising costs, the aging of the population, and various other factors? The following seven points seem to be reasonable expectations for the future. They may or may not be desirable, depending upon your point of view.

First, taxpayers must become accustomed to paying higher taxes for Social Security benefits unless benefits are reduced substantially from current levels. It is just not possible to pay for the current Social Security program with the taxes now being collected or even those scheduled in the current law.

Second, it seems unlikely that the payroll tax will continue to be the primary source of tax revenue for the program. Taxpayers are increasingly asking what benefits they receive for their Social Security tax payments. As it becomes more evident that the relationship between taxes and benefits is tenuous for any given individual (that is, the program gives more emphasis to social adequacy than to individual equity), there will be increased resistance to payroll tax rate increases. This will probably result in the use of some form of nonpayroll tax (such as general revenue or a value-added tax) for at least one-third of Social Security expenditures sometime before the turn of the century. It seems unlikely that present Social Security payroll tax rates will be reduced significantly; the new form of taxation will represent additional taxes.

Third, all state and local government employees and federal civil servants will eventually become participants in the Social Security program. Perhaps participation will be made compulsory for such employees. Alternatively, if and when nonpayroll taxes are used to a significant degree to finance Social Security, these employees may insist on being covered by Social Security in an attempt to obtain their money's worth from their general taxes. Also, as the real costs of existing public employee retirement systems become more evident, there may be an inclination to reduce benefits under such systems and integrate them with the Social Security program. Full participation by all state and local employees and federal civil servants would permit a reduction in the average tax rate paid by employees and employers of less than one-half percent each.

Fourth, beginning about twenty-five to thirty-five years from now, employees will be working longer and retiring at higher ages. This will be a natural development as health and life expectancy improve, and as the growth in the work force slows because of the low fertility rates. For this to be feasible, present socioeconomic arrangements must be revised to make it easier for persons to continue working until advanced ages, perhaps in less strenuous jobs or part-time employment. This development could lessen the financial problems of the Social Security program during the next century since a later effective retirement age, other things being equal, is tantamount to a reduction in benefits. The cost effect of later retirement, however, could well be offset by increased longevity. Also, further liberalizations in the retirement test or further increases in the delayed retirement credit would negate any cost savings resulting from later retirement.

Fifth, social and economic changes in the nation will result in substantial revision of the program. The changing role of the family unit and of women; changing patterns in the incidence of work, education, and leisure throughout a person's lifetime; lengthening life expectancy and improved health in old age; and increased (or reduced) need to work in order to maintain the desired standard of living—all of these changes and more will require that significant revisions be made in the benefit structure if the evolving economic security needs are to be satisfied appropriately. The net effect of all these changes will not necessarily be an increase in costs.

Sixth, if the nation experiences sustained inflation at relatively high levels, it is likely that the portion of an individual's economic security needs that are met by the private sector will decrease over time; the needs must somehow be met; and the federal government (probably through an expanded Social Security program) will be left as the only entity with the audacity to make unqualified promises to pay benefits seventy-five to one hundred years in the future based upon indeterminable cost-of-living increases. Obviously, the cost of an expanded Social Security program would be correspondingly higher.

Seventh, the Medicare program as well as the nation's entire health care system will be changed beyond recognition during the next twenty-five years. This will be the inevitable result of diverse attempts to make more adequate health care available to society at large, but at the same time prevent total health care costs from continuing to rise as a percentage of the Gross National Product. Early in 1977, the management of Medicare and Medicaid, the nation's two largest health care programs, was consolidated under the newly formed Health Care Financing Administration. These two programs will be reshaped in various ways and will probably evolve into a comprehensive national health insurance program.

These seven areas in which Social Security and the behavior of the nation's citizens can be expected to change are stated only in general terms. The exact nature of the changes will depend upon a variety of future events: demographic shifts in the population (affected, in turn, by birth rates, health care developments, and immigration), the nation's economic health, inflation, conditions throughout the world over which we may have little control, and so on. Moreover, public understanding or misunderstanding will play a much more critical role in determining the shape of Social Security in the future than it has in the past—when the payroll tax was relatively low and when the taxpayer was in a less questioning frame of mind. It is obviously preferable for changes to arise from a clearheaded appraisal on the basis of an understanding of our present system rather than from a frenzied cry for change on the basis of misunderstanding and frustration.

Even though a variety of future events—some of which we cannot control—will influence the Social Security of the future, it would be a mistake to be fatalistic. It is still up to us to shape Social Security so that it is appropriate for tomorrow's environment—so that it provides a system of benefits consistent with our needs and our ability to pay for them.

The outlook for Social Security, then, is whatever we desire—and have the courage to achieve.

25
Can Social Security Be Abolished or Changed Drastically?

More and more often questions are being asked such as, "Can't the Social Security program be abolished?" or, "Isn't there some alternative to Social Security?" or, "Wouldn't I be better off if I quit Social Security and invested my tax payments in the stock market?" These questions are usually prompted by concern over the seemingly endless rise in Social Security taxes, dissatisfaction with the benefits a particular individual expects to receive in relation to his tax payments, misunderstanding about how the program actually works, general antipathy for any large governmental program, fear that the present Social Security program is going bankrupt and will be unable to make good on its promises, and so on.

What are the facts? Are there any real alternatives to the present Social Security program?

Without question the present program can be revised and it should be revised—slightly now and significantly later. There are certain practical limits, however, concerning the extent to which changes can be made as well as the speed with which they can be implemented. Complete termination of the Social Security program, as suggested by some, is out of the question.

Some form of national social insurance is absolutely necessary. There is virtually no alternative in a nation that is so large and diverse and that is based on an industrial economy and a highly mobile and dynamic society. The days of the static, agrarian society, built around an extended family with all its attendant mores, are over. In any society it is inevitable that there will be persons unable to work and care for themselves because of conditions virtually beyond their control. In an orderly society, provision must be made in an organized manner for some minimum level of support for such persons. Some form of social insurance must fill this role in modern industrial society.

The present Social Security program, supplemented by an array of welfare programs, is an important element in providing this minimum level of support. To the extent it fills this role, the Social Security program cannot be terminated. It can be revised, consolidated with other components of the total welfare system, or called by another name; but it must continue to exist in one form or another.

The present Social Security program, however, provides not only this *minimum level of support* but also, in some instances, a much higher level of support. The portion of the Social Security program that provides these "supplemental" or "discretionary" benefits is not necessarily essential to the well-being of the nation. Social Security may or may not be the best vehicle by which to provide these "supplemental" benefits depending in part upon:

the freedom of choice desired by the people in providing for their discretionary needs;

the practical alternative means that are available to provide for such needs; and

the differing effect on the economy of these alternative means.

In any event, the portion of the Social Security program that provides for discretionary needs is certainly amenable to study and revision.

In considering any revision in Social Security, an extremely important factor is the long-term promises, express or implied, that have been made to millions of Americans who have paid Social Security taxes in the past. In 1981, monthly cash benefits of approximately $140 billion will be paid to 35 million people—retired and disabled workers and their dependents, widows and orphans, and dependent parents. One of every seven Americans is receiving a monthly Social Security benefit check. Millions of people who are just a few years from retirement have built their plans around the present Social Security program. Furthermore, over 100 million people have worked and paid Social Security taxes in the past and have some expectation of future benefits.

But that does not mean Social Security cannot be changed. It can be changed, and it can be changed significantly. We are often too quick to say that Social Security is so large and complex and that it has been in existence so long that it will be difficult, if not impossible, to make substantial revisions.

Consider the following important statistics—numbers not called to our attention by those who insist that Social Security should not and cannot have major revisions. The post-World War II generation, approximately 135 million persons under age 35, now (in mid-1981) comprises 65 percent of the total population that is less than age 65. In other words, at least 65 percent of the population that is not yet retired is still young enough to adjust to any retirement policy they decide is appropriate for them. These young persons will begin reaching their sixties just twenty-five years from now in the year 2006. It is today that a general framework should be constructed regarding the retirement of this generation—the type and level of benefits to be provided, the source of benefits, the approximate age at which benefits will commence, and so on. In making these choices we need not be influenced unduly by decisions made in the past for different generations of people living under different circumstances. The only reverence we owe these past decisions is to fulfill the promises made to date to our older population.

It is entirely reasonable, therefore, that we give serious consideration to a completely new type of social insurance system for the relatively young segment of our population, even if we continue the present system for the older segment of the population. Significant change is possible if we really want such change.

Remember this astonishing statistic: 65 percent of the present population that is not yet retired is less than age 35. This youthful population of 135 million persons has had more influence on our way of life than any group of youngsters in modern history. Are they not entitled also to decide the ground rules that will apply to their retirement, provided only that they not disturb the promises already made to our older population?

Part Four
The Freedom Plan

Presumably, the reader of the first three parts of this book will have concluded that Social Security should be changed— or, at least, that pressures are building that will indeed cause it to be changed, like it or not. Assuming this is true, it is important to do whatever is necessary to ensure that any change be conceived and implemented on as rational a basis as possible.

Part Four offers suggestions for a new Social Security program—the Freedom Plan—intended to satisfy the essential income security needs of our nation's citizens within an environment that affords maximum freedom of choice.

26
Social Insurance in Perspective

A particular system of social insurance is good or bad only in relation to the yardstick by which it is measured. Most people have a set of standards by which they judge Social Security, although the standards are not usually stated explicitly. Unfortunately, this set of standards is not always consistent, either internally or with standards used to judge other aspects of our social and economic life. In thinking about any revised system of Social Security, it is well to consider for a moment the nature of social insurance and the standards we wish to govern our behavior. Of course, even among persons with consistent and well-articulated sets of standards, there will not always be agreement as to which set of standards should apply.

The Meaning of Government Sponsorship

Many of us have fallen into a bad habit of referring to "government sponsored" programs, "governmental responsibility," and having the "government pay" for things. Sometimes we behave as if the "government" not only *should* be ready to help us in time of financial need, but that the "government" *owes* us something—a retirement benefit, support for our dependents if we die, and so forth. When something in our lives goes wrong, the first place many people look for help is to the government.

301

Who is this "government" we keep looking to for help? Where does it get its money? We all know the answer: the government is simply a system we have established and a group of people we have hired or elected to carry out our wishes. Bureaucrats and politicians do not have any money to give us except what we ourselves have paid in taxes. When we demand a benefit from the government, we are demanding it from our friends and neighbors.

There is a basic truth of economics that people frequently overlook and that some people never even knew existed: Before the government can give one dollar to anyone, it must confiscate that dollar from some other person who has earned it. And to earn a dollar a person must produce something.

If the government sets up a program to give someone food stamps worth $100, the government must do two things:

Find someone who is willing and able to perform work for which he or she will earn $100; and

Convince such working person that he or she should give the government (by paying taxes) this $100 (plus governmental administrative expenses).

This reasoning is equally true whether we are considering food stamps, or disability benefits, or retirement benefits, or any other "income transfer" program the government uses to redistribute the production of America's workers.

It cannot be emphasized strongly enough that casual references to "governmental responsibility" or having the "government pay" for all or part of Social Security are extremely misleading. Stripped to its essentials, a governmental program like Social Security is just an agreement among the people of the nation that one segment of the population will receive certain benefits and that another segment of the population will pay for such benefits (with a certain amount of overlapping). The government may administer and enforce compliance with a program but, in the final analysis, any governmental program is paid for by and is for the benefit of the people of the nation. The government is simply the intermediary that carries out the wishes of the people.

Who Should Assume Responsibility?

Assume, for the moment, that you live in a typical small community of 25,000 people. Most of the people work and support themselves in a variety of jobs. A few are retired, others are in school, some are unemployed from time to time. A few are rich, some are poor, and most are somewhere in between.

What if your family doctor came around one day and announced he was only aged 62 and still in good health, but he was tired of working; he wanted you and the rest of the townspeople to take up a collection and pay him a monthly pension so he could spend full time fishing and hunting. It is doubtful that you and the other citizens of the community would feel any obligation to honor this request. Would it be any different if it were the butcher or the baker? Probably not, if they were in good health and capable of working.

What if the cashier at the bank died leaving behind a wife and two young children? Would the community have an obligation to support the survivors? Would it matter if the local life insurance agent had tried in vain to get the cashier to use part of his earnings to buy life insurance to protect his family, and the cashier had said, "Let them fend for themselves after I'm gone; I'd rather spend my money for a new motorcycle"?

What if a young fireman became totally and permanently disabled while fighting a fire that threatened to destroy the town? What if the town librarian reached age 70, was unable to work any longer, and had lost all his or her savings in a stock market recession? Would the community have an obligation to support these individuals? If so, what level of support should be provided?

Questions such as these deserve much thought, and they are not always easy to answer. Social Security, however, answers all these questions and many more. It defines the circumstances in which benefits will be paid, the amount of the benefits, and who will pay the taxes required to provide the benefits. It does all this on an impersonal basis not only for people in your community but also for people throughout the land. It is so impersonal, in fact, that we sometimes forget who pays for the benefits.

This Part Four of the book, The Freedom Plan, presumes that Social Security no longer answers all these questions the way the majority of the public would like them answered. In designing new answers, of course, we need a set of standards to follow. Proposals for the revision of Social Security as presented in Part Four are based upon the following set of principles (previously mentioned in Chapter 11):

An individual should have freedom of choice to the fullest
extent possible consistent with the interest of the
nation as a whole.

An individual should be afforded maximum opportunity
and incentive to develop and utilize his abilities
throughout his lifetime.

A government (federal, state, or local) should provide those
benefits, and only those benefits, that an individual
cannot provide for himself. In meeting this responsibility, the government should become involved to the
least extent possible, consistent with the interest of
the nation as a whole.

What are the economic security risks that an individual
cannot reasonably be expected to protect himself against—risks
that call for governmental intervention in the form of requiring
active workers to give up part of their production for the benefit
of those in need? There are several such risks:

Unbridled inflation at a time when the worker does not
have the protection normally afforded an active wage
earner: that is, during a time when the worker is
unable to be in the active work force because of old age
or disability;

Abnormally long life spans that are unpredictable and that
result from breakthroughs in health care; and

Misfortune, financial or health related, not reasonably
controllable by the individual.

Were it not for these three risks, an individual could—in
theory at least—make adequate provision for virtually every
mishap that might befall him or his family. Sometimes this
could be done by acting alone, but sometimes it would require
joining with a group of individuals to utilize some form of
voluntary pooling or risk-sharing arrangement. The techniques
involved are simply:

Analyzing the risks that one must be protected against (old
age, disability, death, or illness); and

Setting aside from current earnings an amount sufficient to
provide for these risks. In some cases these savings can
be accumulated on an individual basis; in others they
must be applied to purchase some form of insurance or
annuity.

The risk of unemployment is not discussed here. Unemployment can be the result of an individual's inadequacy or choice, or an employer's financial hardship, or a society's failure to provide training or retraining necessary to equip persons for the types of employment that exist from time to time. The risk of unemployment is not covered by Social Security as it is defined and discussed in this book; thus it is not discussed as part of a suggested revision in Social Security. It is believed, however, that the proposed revision in Social Security would create an environment in which future unemployment would be reduced.

Deficiencies of Present Social Security

The main deficiencies of our present Social Security program may be summarized as follows:

It is so complex that most people will never know what benefits to expect and will never know how much responsibility to assume for themselves and their families. This will lead to the individual's looking blindly to the government, hat in hand, for whatever benefits Big Brother is dispensing at the time and pressing for ever more benefits from the government cornucopia. The inevitable result will be erosion of initiative, individuality, and self-respect, as well as the loss of any sense of control over a vital aspect of our lives. Unfortunately, this process has already begun.

It trespasses upon almost every aspect of our personal lives by imposing an unnecessary straightjacket of behavioral standards: when to retire, how much to earn between ages 62 and 72, when to divorce, whether to remarry (as well as when and to whom), and so on (Chapter 22). It destroys the flexibility needed for us to manage our lives as we see fit.

It is, in effect, a rigid mechanism for dividing the population into two groups: those who work and produce goods and services, and those who are inactive but still share in such production. The particular division fostered by Social Security may have been appropriate in the past, but it will not be appropriate for tomorrow. For example, the early sixties will not be a proper age to divide the active from the inactive population as the baby boom of yesterday becomes the senior boom of tomorrow. A flexible system is needed that will permit this division of the population into active and inactive groups to adjust itself voluntarily in response to changing proportions of old and young, improved health at older ages, longer lifetimes, more women in the paid work force, and so on.

It discourages personal saving, including private pension plans, retards the capital formation necessary for a strong economy, and thus reduces the growth in national productivity that would improve the standard of living for all—active and retired alike.

It is structured to reward life patterns (for example, male breadwinner and female homemaker, and lifelong marriages) that are becoming much less representative of modern life. It is not flexible enough to accommodate the changing role of the family unit; and, in particular, of women as they move toward independence and equality. The roles of men and women will continue to evolve and will never again be as stereotyped as they once were.

It combines the elements of individual equity and social adequacy (welfare, as it is now usually called) and effectively hides any connection between the taxes an individual pays and the benefits he receives. Yet, all the while the public has been told there *is* such a connection between taxes and benefits (through the rhetoric of "contributions" paid to a "trust fund" under an "insurance" program to acquire an "earned right" to specified benefits). Indeed, the public's belief that they were buying their own benefits with their own contributions was an important element in the extraordinary public acceptance of Social Security until the mid-1970s—when they began to find out that was not the way it worked. A clear understanding of how the taxes are used and a belief that the program is fair and equitable are essential when taxes are at today's levels.

A Plan for Tomorrow

Chapters 27 through 30 present an outline of a revised Social Security program intended to overcome the deficiencies of the present Social Security program and to be consistent, insofar as practicable, with the principles listed in this chapter. The suggested plan has limitations since it is difficult to formulate a perfect program to accommodate a heterogeneous society such as exists in the United States. The best way to accommodate these diverse needs, of course, is to minimize government-dictated standards and maximize individual freedom of choice. The purpose of the following chapters is to outline a revised Social Security program in sufficient detail to demonstrate its feasibility. Refinements and more complete details concerning the transition from the present system to the revised system can be designed easily if the overall plan is considered desirable by enough of the population.

The proposed plan would be considerably different from the present one. It would provide a basic floor of protection for all citizens against fundamental economic need. It would provide additional benefits through a voluntary component. There would be a clear separation between benefits that are related directly to the individual's tax payments and those that are not. It would thus be perceived (by most people) as more equitable and fair. It would be easier to understand and administer. It would afford greater freedom of choice to the participant in the type and level of benefits provided. It would permit a more natural and flexible separation of the population into the active and inactive segments. It would accommodate the changing roles of women, as well as men, however they may evolve in the future. It would result in increased private saving and would facilitate the capital formation needed to restore and sustain a strong economy. Finally, it would encourage and reward individual initiative and self-sufficiency and would improve our standard of living, materially and spiritually. In short, the proposed new Social Security program would be based on less governmentalism and more individualism and would thus be called the Freedom Plan.

The proposed effective date of the Freedom Plan is July 4, 1984. The significance of July 4, Independence Day, is obvious.

George Orwell, in his satirical novel entitled *1984,* predicted that we would be completely engulfed by Big Brother by 1984. With a little luck and a lot of hard work we can thwart that prediction.

27
Provision
for Old Age

Most of life's events for which we must make future provision usually come as a surprise: death, disability, illness. Even if the events are certain, their timing is seldom predictable. This is not true for what we frequently refer to as old age, since the majority of adults will experience it for at least a few years. Consider a group of people aged 40 to 45, an age by which most people are aware that old age is a real possibility for them. Approximately 80 percent of this group will live until at least age 65, 70 percent will live until at least age 70, and 60 percent will live until at least age 75.

Old age can be anticipated and financial plans can be made accordingly. It would not be necessary for the government to be involved in any way in our retirement planning except for the contingencies already cited—inflation, extraordinary life spans, and misfortune outside the control of an individual in financial planning for old age.

It is proposed that Social Security continue unchanged until July 4, 1984; and that for everyone aged 45 and over on July 4, 1984, Social Security continue unchanged for the balance of their lifetime with regard to the payment of old-age retirement benefits, including related dependents' benefits.

It is proposed that everyone who is less than age 45 on July 4, 1984, participate in the new Freedom Plan. The Freedom Plan would thus apply to 168 million people, or 79 percent of the population less than age 65 as of July 4, 1984. The old Social Security program would continue to apply to 46 million people, or 21 percent of such population; and, of course, it would continue to apply to some 28 million people aged 65 or older, as well as their dependents, most of whom would already be receiving Social Security benefits.

The Freedom Plan, insofar as the provision of retirement benefits is concerned, would consist of three parts:

A mandatory Senior Citizen Benefit program;

A Freedom Bond program of optional retirement savings bonds; and

A Cost-of-Living Supplement for Private Pension Plans.

Senior Citizen Benefits

The proposed system of Senior Citizen Benefits would protect the individual against risks that he cannot reasonably be expected to bear: unbridled inflation at a time when he does not have the protection normally afforded an active wage earner, and breakthroughs in health care that may result in abnormally long life spans. It would also provide a genuine floor of protection against financial adversity in old age—whether caused by misfortune or poor planning.

At age 70, a monthly benefit of a uniform amount would be payable to each resident citizen of the country regardless of his previous employment, earnings history, marital status, financial need, or any other factor. The benefit would be payable to men and women alike, regardless of whether they had worked in paid employment. Residency for at least twenty-five years during the period from age 35 to age 70 could be required. The benefit would be payable for the individual's remaining lifetime.

Citizenship is relatively easy to attain and is not an onerous requirement to impose on someone who is going to derive thousands of dollars from the tax payments of the nation's working population. An applicant for citizenship must have lived in the U.S. for at least five years, must not have been a member of the Communist Party within the last ten years, and must not have been in jail more than 180 days. He or she must know basic U.S. history and civics and have a grasp of "simple" English, a standard that is very loosely interpreted.

Since the amount of the benefit would be the same for everyone, its purpose would not be to sustain varying preretirement standards of living, but rather to provide a minimum level of support. Benefits would be set at approximately the subsistence level so that every aged person could live without fear of deprivation of life's necessities, even if the vicissitudes of life should leave him with no other resources. (This presumes, of course, the existence of an appropriate health care program for the aged.) The amount of the benefit could be related to the average earnings of all workers, the average national industrial wage, or, perhaps, the minimum wage. If substantial differences continue to exist in the cost of living in various regions of the country, perhaps the amount of the benefit would vary with the geographical area of residence during retirement.

An appropriate benefit level for 1980 would probably be in the range of $225 to $275 per month. For purposes of discussion and the cost projections presented in Chapter 30, it has been assumed the Senior Citizen Benefit would be $250 per month in 1980, and an equivalent amount relative to average wages of the nation's workers in later years. By way of comparison, the following statistics for April 1980 may be of interest:

Social Security average benefit in current-payment status

Retired worker	$295.51
Aged widows and widowers	267.69

Supplemental Security Income maximum federal payment

Individual	$208.20
Couple	312.30

Aid to families with dependent children (AFDC) average family benefit $270.92

A few words of explanation may help interpret the significance of the $250 Senior Citizen Benefit relative to the benefit levels under various existing programs. For purposes of this comparison, it is assumed that the Senior Citizen Benefit program is in effect now; however, the payment of retirement benefits under the program would not actually begin until some twenty-five years hence.

Although the average monthly Social Security benefit for retired workers was $295.51 in April 1980, it does not follow that all retired workers would suffer a benefit decrease if the Senior Citizen Benefit program were in effect and they were receiving only $250. Approximately one-third of the retired workers were receiving *less* than $250 in April 1980, hence they would receive higher benefits under the Senior Citizen Benefit program; on the other hand, two-thirds of the retired workers would receive lower benefits under the program. Aged widows and widowers would be similarly affected. Benefits would be higher under the Senior Citizen Benefit program for the vast majority of dependent spouses of retired workers.

Generally speaking, it is the lower wage earners who receive the lower benefits under Social Security. It seems fair to conclude, therefore, that the Senior Citizen Benefit program would provide increased monthly retirement benefits for approximately one-third of the population—the segment with the lowest earnings. It would provide lower benefits for approximately two-thirds of the population—the segment most capable of providing supplemental benefits for its own retirement (especially, as a result of the lower future taxes that would be made possible by enactment of the Freedom Plan).

The amount of the Senior Citizen Benefit would be adjusted for changes in the average wage or other index to which it was originally related. Accordingly, all persons aged 70 or over would be receiving the same monthly benefit in any given year, regardless of when they reached age 70.

The benefit would not be subject to federal income tax—for several reasons. First, income tax is normally imposed on earnings resulting from the production of goods and services but not on transfer payments, which themselves are derived from taxes. Second, taxing the benefit would be equivalent to paying a smaller Senior Citizen Benefit to some individuals than to others and would be contrary to the intention of providing a uniform minimum benefit for every elderly person. Finally, a benefit payable in old age would offer questionable security if it were subject to taxation at rates to be determined at the whim of some future Congress.

The benefit would be financed on a "current-cost" basis: that is, taxes would be collected each year in the amount estimated to be necessary to pay benefits for that year. The tax used to provide these benefits would be some form of general revenue, as distinguished from the payroll tax currently used to finance Social Security. The essential features of the tax, whatever form it may take, are:

> That it be clearly identified so that any change in benefit levels is made with a full understanding of the cost implications;
> That it be spread among the population in a way that is not only "fair" but that is generally *perceived* as fair; and
> That it be assessed and allocated in such a way that "deficit spending" is not involved—in other words, so that we do not borrow from future production to support the current aged population. By operating this system of benefits on a current-cost basis, we would already be deferring the liability as long as is justified. Further deferral would be irresponsible.

The selection of age 70 for commencement of benefits is somewhat arbitrary, but it can be judged against the following benchmarks. Based on projected improvements in mortality, a 70-year-old person early in the twenty-first century would have a remaining life expectancy exceeding that of a 65-year-old person in the 1930s—when Social Security adopted 65 as the retirement age.[1] If the retirement age during the second quarter of the twenty-first century were about age 72, the ratio of active workers to the retired population would be about the same then as it is now.[2] Allowing for future productivity gains (increases in the productive capacity of the nation's work force), an age somewhat less than 72 may be appropriate. Whatever age is selected, it should take into account several factors, most of which are interrelated:

> The age beyond which it is presumed the majority of the population is unable to work enough to support itself completely;
> The general health of the elderly and their longevity;
> The prevailing birth rates and the growth in the size of the young work force;
> The general economic health of the nation, including national productive capacity; and

The nature of available work opportunities, particularly for the older population.

All of these factors, as well as several others, are determinants of the size of the active working population that is needed to produce the goods and services required to sustain the nation's total population. On balance, it seems likely that if the active working population is maintained at the requisite size, there will be a natural increase in the retirement age prevailing in the early part of the twenty-first century.

If it is appropriate for the Senior Citizen Benefit to commence at age 70 for persons reaching that age about thirty years from now, a different age—probably higher—may be appropriate for future generations reaching age 70 later in the twenty-first century. This benefit age would be subject to adjustment from time to time depending upon the circumstances. Any increase in the benefit age would be determined well in advance so as not to disrupt retirement planning. For example, by the time a group of persons reaches its forties, the benefit age should be fixed and not subject to change except under extremely unusual circumstances. Demographic projections of the relative sizes of the working and the aged populations—an important determinant of a logical benefit age—can be made with relative certainty with respect to the remaining lifetime for those who have reached their mid-forties. Most of the other factors having a bearing on the selection of a benefit age should also be determinable twenty-five or thirty years before a person's retirement.

The time of old age is different for each individual and, to a large extent, is determined by our attitudes. It is not necessary—it is not even appropriate—to have a government-imposed standard telling us when we have reached old age and when we can no longer work effectively. The establishment of the Freedom Plan with age 70 as the benefit age for the Senior Citizen Benefit does not imply that everyone should work until age 70; and it does not imply that the elderly should live out their lives on the relatively low Senior Citizen Benefit. Rather, it implies that no one has the right to demand support from one's fellow citizens except from age 70 onward and except at the subsistence level—and even this concession is made necessary only by the practicalities of life in an uncertain future environment.

If an individual chooses to retire earlier than age 70, it would be as a result of advance saving by himself or his employer. If an individual chooses to have a higher income after age 70 than the Senior Citizen Benefit, it would be as a result of advance saving by himself or his employer or a decision to work, perhaps part-time, beyond age 70. Complete freedom of choice would be afforded each person in this matter of whether to save more and retire earlier, or save less and retire later. Essential financial security would be assured for every resident beyond age 70, but no government benefits (that is, no support from fellow taxpayers) would be provided for a healthy individual before attainment of age 70, and it would clearly be the responsibility of the individual to care for himself before that time.

The cost of the system would be borne primarily by the active working population. This is a logical obligation for the relatively young, active working population to assume. Anyone who attains age 70 after having spent the majority of his adult lifetime in the United States can be presumed to have borne his share of developing the country and supporting the aged while he was actively employed. True, there will be some who reach age 70 without having contributed enough to the nation's development—at least from an economic standpoint—to warrant support in old age. There are humane considerations, however, and these same people will probably not have provided financially for their old age and will have to be supported by the active workers in any event. By holding these benefits to a minimum standard, unfair burdens on the producing taxpayer can probably be kept acceptably low.

Some would say this Senior Citizen Benefit should not be paid to those who have sufficient income without it. Why not? It is these same persons who have paid the bulk of the taxes that make the benefit possible in the first place. Paying retirement benefits only to those who need them can have several offensive characteristics: it requires too much delving by the government into the private affairs of an individual; it discourages people from striving for self-sufficiency since the reward is loss of benefits; it encourages people to hide assets since an appearance of poverty will entitle them to "government benefits." There is certainly a place in welfare planning for benefits based upon "needs" and "means," but not in the provision of basic minimum benefits for the elderly.

Payment of the Senior Citizen Benefit to all citizens, men and women alike, would go a long way toward alleviating the present special financial problems of women—an increasing proportion of the elderly population. Benefits would be paid regardless of marital status, previous attachment to the paid labor force, and other conditions imposed by the present system that have caused it to be criticized as "unfair." The vast majority of today's younger women, all of whom would be participants in the Freedom Plan, will have had an opportunity to be in the paid work force and acquire retirement benefits that are supplemental to the Senior Citizen Benefit.

The many advantages of this simplified system of Senior Citizen Benefits are significant, not the least of which is the clear separation of governmental and nongovernmental responsibility for providing for an individual's economic security at advanced ages. Under a system as complex as the present Social Security program, it is doubtful that a clear delineation of such responsibility will ever be possible—a situation almost certain to result in people's expecting more, and thus eventually receiving more, from the government (that is, the active working taxpayers), with a consequent decline in individual self-reliance and productivity of the nation as a whole.

Freedom Bond Program

The Senior Citizen Benefit is intended to provide a minimum standard of living from age 70 onward for persons who are less than age 45 on July 4, 1984, and will thus reach age 70 in the year 2009 and later. This is *not* a government-imposed standard that says everyone *must* work until age 70 or that everyone *must* have only a minimum standard of living. A person can retire whenever he pleases on any standard of living his thrift or good fortune will support.

The general social and economic environment makes it much easier to provide for retirement today than in the past. When Social Security was enacted forty-five years ago, the existing conditions included:

> relatively few reliable institutional channels through which an individual could invest and save for the future;
>
> an almost completely undeveloped system of private pensions and other employee benefits; and

family units that tended to be larger, with a male bread-winner and a female homemaker.

The changes that have occurred in all these areas make it much easier to provide for retirement today than in the 1930s. But a new problem has arisen: INFLATION. Continued high inflation over a long period of years makes it virtually impossible for the average individual to save for retirement.

A large proportion of the nation's employees participate in formal pension plans, usually sponsored by their employer. These private pensions, together with the Senior Citizen Benefit, often will meet a person's retirement needs adequately. In most cases, however, supplemental individual savings will be desirable, and in some cases essential.

If we believe it is healthful for individuals to take responsibility for themselves and save for their retirement, and if we believe continued high inflation is a possibility, there seems to be no alternative to getting the government involved—not to pay for anything, but to provide a mechanism by which the active working population can preserve the value of any savings that individuals accumulate for retirement.

It is proposed that the government offer retirement savings bonds—designated as Freedom Bonds—under the following general conditions to provide a supplemental mechanism for an individual to save for retirement:

The Bonds would be sold after July 4, 1984, to any resident citizen between ages 45 and 70 provided he or she was less than age 45 on July 4, 1984.

The maximum amount of Bonds an individual could purchase in any year would be 10 percent of his taxable earnings in the prior year; but any eligible individual could purchase a specified minimum amount of Bonds regardless of earnings (approximately equal to 10 percent of average earnings of the nation's employees for the prior year).

Each year the value of Bonds purchased in a prior year would be adjusted to reflect changes in the relative purchasing power that had occurred between the purchase date and the current valuation date. No interest would be payable on the Bonds, however.

No federal, state, or local taxes would be payable on the Bonds, including any increase in nominal value, when they are redeemed. The Bonds would have been purchased with funds that had already been subjected to tax.

The Bonds would be redeemed for their current value upon the individual's death. They would be redeemable, at the option of the individual, upon his bona fide disability or anytime after his attainment of age 60.

The Bonds could be redeemed in a lump sum or in a series of instalments, at the option of the individual or his survivors. If taken in instalments, the unredeemed Bonds would continue to be indexed to reflect changes in purchasing power until fully redeemed.

The rationale for these Freedom Bonds is largely self-evident; however, the following comments may add perspective.

The purpose of indexing the Bonds would be to preserve their purchasing power—no more and no less. Accordingly, the indexing factor could be based upon changes in average wages, a specially constructed cost-of-living measure, or some other element.

No interest is provided and no taxes are involved. The Bonds are not intended to be an attractive investment, but merely a hedge against inflation. During times of high inflation, purchase of the Bonds would be particularly attractive; during periods of no inflation or low inflation, alternative investments would be preferred.

The funds for adjusting the value of the Bonds would come from general revenue. This indexing procedure would not remove the nation's incentive to eliminate inflation since the population would be protecting itself against inflation by paying increased taxes as necessary.

The Bonds could be purchased only after age 45 and only in limited amounts. The purpose of the Bonds is to offer a safe and inflation-proof vehicle to accumulate a reasonable supplemental retirement income during the latter half of one's working life. The Bonds would not be available to persons aged 45 and over on July 4, 1984, since they would be continuing in the existing Social Security system and accruing benefits that are indexed to changes in average wages and prices. Perhaps an exception could be made in certain situations—such as for persons not participating in an employer-sponsored retirement plan. Special consideration could also be given to persons aged 45 and over on July 4, 1984, not participating in Social Security.

An individual who purchased Freedom Bonds worth 10 percent of his earnings every year from age 45 to age 70 would accumulate enough to provide a lifetime retirement benefit from age 70 onward of 20 to 30 percent of his average preretirement earnings (depending upon the individual's earnings pattern and sex).

The Bonds would be available to persons even though they were not in paid employment. This provision is intended primarily for spouses not working in paid employment but would include other situations also. This opportunity for individual saving together with the Senior Citizen Benefit seems to be appropriate provision for persons not working in paid employment. Of course, a spouse not in paid employment would not normally have any funds to save except funds provided by the other spouse. This proposal assumes a voluntary agreement as to sharing income between two spouses, which is preferable to some of the arbitrary, government-imposed "earnings-sharing" proposals recently advocated by some study groups.

It is proposed that the Bonds be redeemable only in the event of death, disability, and after age 60. It may be advisable to provide for their redemption also in the case of carefully defined emergencies, including long-term unemployment. The basic purpose of the Freedom Bonds, however, is to provide for retirement. Other vehicles are available to serve as ordinary savings accounts.

The purpose of the issuance of the Bonds is not to compete with private investment opportunities or to raise additional funds for the government to spend. To prevent this latter possibility, appropriate restrictions should be adopted to control the government's use of the proceeds from the Bond sales, perhaps by requiring that such proceeds be used only to refinance existing national debt. (Issuance of the Bonds would thus not *increase* the national debt.) This would make some of the funds currently invested in government securities available for private investment and thus facilitate the increased capital formation needed to revitalize the economy.

Cost-of-Living Supplement for Private Pension Plans

Ideally, the proposed Senior Citizen Benefit system and the Freedom Bond program would be the extent of government involvement in retirement planning. The majority of the nation's workers are covered by a retirement program sponsored by their employer or groups of employers. Many such programs have resulted from collective bargaining. These retirement programs are referred to here as private pension plans (to distinguish them from the federal Social Security system), but the term also includes pension plans covering employees of federal, state, and local governments. The diversity of such pension plans reflects the diversity of the circumstances of employees in various occupations; on the whole, the private pension system is well suited to the goals of maximum individual freedom of choice and minimum governmental interference.

Once again, however, the spectre of inflation rises to impede the smooth functioning of our financial institutions and suggests the need for some form of governmental intervention. As inflation erodes the purchasing power of private pensions, they are sometimes adjusted upward. It is unusual, however, for a private pension to be adjusted fully to reflect changes in the cost of living; and it is almost never that a full adjustment is guaranteed for the remaining lifetime of the pensioner.

Pensions represent promises to pay benefits for twenty-five years or more after an employee retires and leaves the employer's payroll. It is unrealistic for the average employer to attempt to assume the risk of substantial inflation that may occur many years after an employee leaves its payroll and, perhaps, many years after the employer ceases to exist. This would require the provision of retirement benefits adjusted fully for indeterminable cost-of-living changes in the distant future. Such benefits cannot be funded in advance because the extent of the liability cannot be determined in advance. Furthermore, such benefits cannot be provided by an employer *on a guaranteed basis* as the benefits become payable, since there can be no assurance the employer will still be in business and also be able to afford such a benefit twenty-five years or more after an employee retires.

It should not be surprising, therefore, that very few

employers do in fact assume the risk of adjusting retirement benefits for substantial inflation at the present time; furthermore, it appears unlikely that they will be able to do so in the future. The only notable exceptions are the retirement systems covering most federal employees, and the retirement systems of a limited number of public employers—situations where perpetual existence of the employer is presumed. This limitation of the private pension system's ability to cope with rampant inflation is not a reason to scrap the entire system. Relatively limited governmental intervention would seem to make much more sense.

It is proposed that the government provide cost-of-living supplements for all private pension plans in accordance with the following general guidelines:

> Private pension plans, including those of federal, state, and local governments, would be covered provided they met federal standards for approved plans (Internal Revenue Service requirements for "qualified" plans, for example).

> Monthly pension benefits payable for life would be covered, but only with regard to benefits payable after age 70.

> Every year, benefits payable to persons aged 70 or older would be supplemented by the amount necessary to sustain the purchasing power in the prior year in accordance with a cost-of-living index constructed especially for the elderly.

> The cost of these supplemental benefits would be paid from general revenue, that is, primarily by the active working taxpayers.

It may be worthwhile to remind ourselves that these supplemental benefits do not represent a "government subsidy" since the government does not pay the cost of anything. The government is simply formulating a standard with which the majority of the population presumably would agree (namely, the protection of the elderly population against the ravages of inflation with respect to certain monthly retirement benefits) and then providing a mechanism by which the active working taxpayer can support that standard.

This cost-of-living supplemental benefit program would need

careful study to ensure a rational formulation, but there is no need to phase it in gradually (except to mitigate the cost impact); it could be made effective as of July 4, 1984, when major changes in Social Security are proposed to take effect. Perhaps this type of cost-of-living supplement could apply to Individual Retirement Accounts and other forms of monthly retirement income as well as to private qualified pension plans.

Conclusion

Under the proposed Freedom Plan, an individual would retain principal responsibility for himself until age 70; after age 70 he would have responsibility for himself beyond the minimum standard of living provided by the Senior Citizen Benefit. He would be able to retire anytime before age 70, or enjoy any standard of living after age 70, permitted by his private saving or job-related retirement benefits. The Freedom Bond program would offer a reliable method of private saving for retirement in time of inflation.

Employer-provided retirement plans would still entail a substantial commitment, particularly if benefits are related to final average earnings. On the other hand, the most unmanageable of the retirement burdens of an employer—inflation after a worker has reached age 70—would be shifted to society as a whole, the only logical place for it. Of course, another portion of the retirement burden would be shifted from the individual and the employer to society as a whole through the Senior Citizen Benefit program and the "inflation-proofing" aspect of the Freedom Bond program (as well as through the Medicare program described in Chapter 28).

To the extent that individuals remain in the work force until higher ages than at present, both the individual and the employer must assume increased responsibilities: retraining of individuals, redesigning of jobs, finding more sophisticated methods of matching individuals and jobs, and doing whatever else is necessary to develop and utilize an individual's skills and talents during a longer proportion of his healthy lifetime.

All things considered, the proposed Freedom Plan seems a reasonable way to allocate the cost of retirement and to employ effectively the nation's most neglected asset—our human resources.

28
Provision for Illness

Illness is a certainty for most of us sometime during our life. Although we may not be able to predict when it will occur, we can make advance provision for the financial loss caused by illness—either by personal saving or the purchase of health insurance. It would not be necessary for the government to be involved in any way in our planning for illness were it not for the contingencies of inflation, extraordinary life spans, and misfortune in financial planning. These contingencies make some form of governmental intervention advisable for most of the aged population.

It is proposed that Social Security continue unchanged with regard to the provision of Medicare benefits (Hospital Insurance and Supplementary Medical Insurance benefits) until July 4, 1984; and that for everyone aged 45 and over on July 4, 1984, as well as for their dependents, Medicare continue unchanged for the balance of their lifetimes.

It is proposed that everyone who is less than age 45 on July 4, 1984, participate in a revised Medicare program with these characteristics:

Benefits, including "deductibles" and "coinsurance," provided under the present Medicare program (Hospital Insurance and Supplementary Medical Insurance) would continue substantially unchanged.

All resident citizens aged 70 and over would be eligible for Medicare benefits for the balance of their lifetimes.

Residency for at least twenty-five years during the period from age 35 to age 70 could be required—to be consistent with eligibility requirements for Senior Citizen Benefits.

Benefits would be provided for persons eligible for monthly cash disability benefits under the Freedom Plan during the same period that such disability benefits were payable.

Benefits would be financed on a current-cost basis from earmarked general revenue. The payroll tax currently used to finance the HI program and the monthly premiums used to finance a portion of the cost of the SMI program would be discontinued.

Benefits would continue to be nontaxable: that is, excluded from income in computing federal, state, and local income taxes.

Although no particular changes are proposed in Medicare benefits at the time of the general restructuring of Social Security on July 4, 1984, the benefit design is certainly not perfect and should be revised. Revision could begin almost immediately and continue through the years as health care practices change. On the one hand, the "deductible" and "coinsurance" features as well as the reimbursement provisions should be revised to make it mutually advantageous to the patient and the providers of health care services that costs be controlled and services not be overutilized. The net result of such changes would probably be an increase in the cost to the patient for relatively minor illnesses. On the other hand, the cost to the patient for major illnesses should be reduced by having Medicare assume an increased proportion of the cost of expensive, extended illnesses.

Medicare benefits and administrative procedures should be revised from time to time to provide an appropriate level of health care for the elderly. This will probably always require a compromise between the level of health care that is technologically possible and financially feasible.

This statement about compromise in determining health care levels should give pause for concern. The continued existence of Medicare, or any similar program, over a long period will have far-reaching effects on our lives. Under a program such as

Medicare, a governmental agency (in accordance with laws enacted by Congress) effectively defines the particular health care services that will be provided by determining whether they will be paid for by the program: the number of days in a hospital, the number of days in a skilled nursing facility, the type and level of services by hospitals and physicians that will be deemed reasonable, and so on. In theory an individual can buy any health care services desired even if they are not provided by Medicare. In practice, however, the availability of such services will be greatly influenced by the norms of Medicare.

It is not an overstatement to say that a program like Medicare places the power over our life and death in the hands of government. Witness this example: Since Medicare began providing treatment for persons with chronic kidney disease requiring dialysis or kidney transplant, regardless of their age, the health of such persons has undoubtedly improved and many are alive who would otherwise have died. Is there any reason that persons with kidney ailments should be favored over persons with hypertension, cancer, or emotional problems? Who should make such decisions and on what basis?

Medical technology already exists that would make us healthier, extend our lives, and prolong our lives in the event of a lingering final illness; however, this technology is not used uniformly throughout the population because of its high cost. It appears that medical technology will continue to advance more rapidly than our ability or willingness to pay for it. Therefore, important choices and decisions lie ahead concerning the level of health care it is feasible to provide the nation as a whole as well as any particular individual. The larger the role played by the government in providing health care services, the larger will be the role of the government in influencing the type and level of health care available to us all. Because of its important role in administering Medicare and Medicaid, the government cannot avoid being a powerful determinant of the health and longevity of the elderly population. It must be borne in mind as these decisions are being made that the purpose of Medicare should be to provide a basic level of health care to the entire population aged 70 and over regardless of an individual's financial resources. The purpose is not to inhibit continued advances in medical technology, or to set maximum standards of health care for the elderly, or to prevent an individual from utilizing alternative forms of health care—at his own expense.

The rationale for financing Medicare from some form of general revenue is the same as that applied to the financing of Senior Citizen Benefits. The Medicare benefit is not something "bought and paid for" by an individual's own contributions or premiums; it is a program of minimum health care for every aged resident citizen regardless of prior employment, marital status, financial need, or any other factor. Accordingly, the cost of Medicare should be spread over the entire active working population to the extent possible.

There is a danger in using general revenue unless it is "earmarked" in some way to ensure that the taxes needed to provide benefits are actually collected. Otherwise, there may be a temptation to borrow the necessary funds and thus shift the cost to subsequent generations. By operating Medicare on a current-cost basis, we would already be deferring the liability as long as is justified. Further deferral would be irresponsible.

Persons can arrange for health care services prior to reaching age 70 in a variety of ways: personal saving, purchase of health insurance, utilization of job-related insurance and health benefits, and so on. It is only at advanced ages after a person has left the mainstream of employment that governmental intervention may be necessary to ensure the provision of adequate health care. This is true largely because future health care costs are indeterminable—partly as a result of possible inflation and partly as a result of rapidly changing, and increasingly costly, medical technology.

Because of poor planning or genuine misfortune, some individuals under age 70 will not have adequate health care services, and other taxpayers will have to pay for such services through some form of welfare program such as Medicaid. In order to care for the truly needy, however, it is not necessary to impose on the whole of society a complex and arbitrary set of health benefits—and taxes to pay for such benefits.

29
Provision for Death and Disability

Many of us will be disabled and unable to work sometime during our life. Some of us will be severely disabled for long periods. All of us will die. Death and disability arouse our compassion and tend to lure us into advocating government benefits for widows and orphans. But remember that "government benefits" is a euphemism for "benefits provided by other taxpayers," and that we are attempting to outline here a program of benefits that emphasizes freedom of choice and self-sufficiency—a program that calls for governmental intervention only in those instances when an individual cannot reasonably be expected to provide for himself and his family.

Provision for Death

It is proposed that Social Security continue unchanged until July 4, 1984; and that for everyone aged 45 and over on July 4, 1984, as well as their dependents, Social Security continue unchanged for the balance of their lifetimes insofar as the payment of death benefits is concerned, including both lump-sum and monthly survivors benefits. Also, everyone receiving survivors benefits on July 4, 1984, regardless of age, would continue to receive such benefits as if Social Security were unchanged. Additional transition provisions may be advisable to avoid discontinuity in some cases.

It is proposed that everyone who is less than age 45 on July 4, 1984, participate in the Freedom Plan. No death benefits would be paid under the Freedom Plan except in connection with the optional Freedom Bond program outlined in Chapter 27.

Provision for Disability

It is proposed that Social Security continue unchanged until July 4, 1984; and that for everyone aged 45 and over on July 4, 1984, as well as their dependents, Social Security continue unchanged for the balance of their lifetimes insofar as the payment of disability benefits is concerned. Also, everyone receiving disability benefits on July 4, 1984, regardless of age, would continue to receive such benefits as if Social Security were unchanged. Additional transition provisions may be necessary because of the nature of the disability risk.

It is proposed that everyone who is less than age 45 on July 4, 1984, participate in the Freedom Plan, which would have these characteristics with regard to the provision of disability benefits:

Benefits would be payable only to persons who were totally and permanently disabled, and who had been so disabled for twelve full months.

Benefits would be payable to any adult resident citizen of the country who satisfied minimum requirements of recent attachment to the paid work force. A minimum period of residency could be required if considered necessary to avoid abuse.

Benefits would be payable only to persons who agreed to participate in a qualified rehabilitation and retraining program. Substantially more emphasis would be placed on such a program than is the case with the present Social Security system.

Monthly benefits equal to the then current Senior Citizen Benefit, including adjustments to reflect changes in the cost of living, would be payable for as long as the individual remained disabled.

Medicare benefits would be provided during the same period that monthly cash disability benefits were payable.

Benefits would be financed by some form of general revenue, earmarked in such a way as to prevent deficit
financing.

Benefits would be nontaxable: that is, excluded from
income in computing federal, state, and local income
taxes.

There is no need for excessive government-imposed standards concerning the financial arrangements to be made upon a
person's death or disability. An individual can anticipate the
needs of his family and estate in the event of his death. He can
anticipate the needs of his family and himself in the event of his
disability. He can provide in advance for most of these needs by
personal saving (including participation in the Freedom Bond
program), by purchasing appropriate life insurance and disability insurance, by making arrangements with family members or
friends, and so forth. The nation's insurance companies have
adequate facilities to provide a wide range of death and disability benefits consistent with affording each individual maximum
freedom of choice.

Because of poor planning or genuine misfortune, some individuals will die without having made appropriate financial
arrangements for their survivors and some will become disabled
without having provided for themselves and their family
members. In an orderly society, the other taxpayers must
provide financial support in these unfortunate situations.
Accordingly, some form of welfare program must be continued
as a supplement to the Freedom Plan. "But help for a few
hardship cases hardly justifies putting the whole population in
a straightjacket," as so aptly stated by Milton and Rose Friedman in their book *Free to Choose: A Personal Statement.*[1]

30
Cost and Financing of Proposed Social Insurance Program

The proposed social insurance program consists of the Freedom Plan for the younger part of the population and continuation of the present Social Security program for the older part of the population. Since this proposed program covers the entire population while the existing Social Security program covers only about 90 percent of the working population and an even smaller percentage of the nonworking population, it is difficult to compare the cost of the two programs. Chart 30.A makes this comparison by illustrating the projected expenditures for benefits and administration during the next seventy-five years:

>For the present Social Security program as if it remained unchanged.

>For the revised social insurance program but with respect to the same limited population covered by the present Social Security program.

Projected expenditures are shown as a percentage of the taxable payroll of the population for whom benefit expenditures are shown and are based on the same intermediate assumptions used throughout the book.

331

Projected expenditures for the present Social Security program are the same as those shown in Chart 4.A and include expenditures for the OASDI, HI, and SMI programs combined. They rise from a current level of approximately 13 percent of taxable payroll to about 27 percent of taxable payroll in the middle of the twenty-first century.

Projections for the proposed social insurance program include expenditures for the mandatory part of the new program, including Senior Citizen Benefits and Medicare and disability benefits. The projected expenditures do not include the optional Freedom Bond program for discretionary retirement saving or the Cost-of-Living Supplement for Private Pension Plans, an entirely new program not related to the existing Social Security and thus not relevant to any cost comparison. Expenditures for the proposed program increase slowly for the next thirty-five years and then increase more rapidly for the following twenty years as the children of the post-World War II baby boom reach their seventies. Expenditures then level off during the middle of the twenty-first century in the range of 19 to 20 percent of taxable payroll, approximately 50 percent higher than present expenditures of 13 percent of taxable payroll.

Chart 30.A indicates with a broken line which part of the expenditures is for persons aged 45 and over and which part is for persons under age 45 on July 4, 1984, the date of introduction of the proposed new system. Not surprisingly, virtually all of the cost during the next twenty years is attributable to the group of persons aged 45 and over—the group for whom the present Social Security would continue unchanged. The cost for the large group of persons under age 45 on the date of change would increase steadily until leveling off in the middle of the twenty-first century after all these persons have begun to receive retirement benefits.

Chart 30.A is a striking illustration of the long-term nature of promises made under a social insurance system and the significance of an accrued liability. The bulk of the accrued liability of some $6 trillion under the present Social Security program as of January 1, 1979 (discussed in more detail in Chapter 7) represents promises made to persons aged 45 and older. The proposed social insurance system would honor these promises

Chart 30.A

Projected Expenditures for Benefits and Administration of Existing Social Security Program and Proposed Social Insurance Program, Expressed as a Percentage of Effective Taxable Payroll[a]

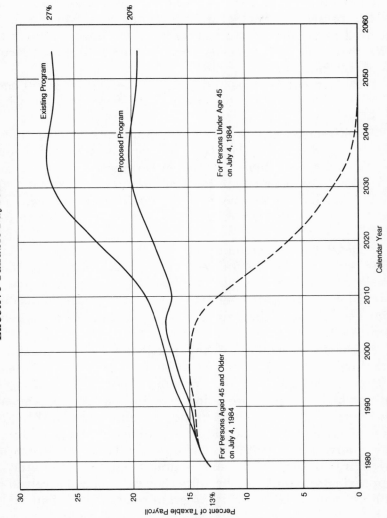

[a]Projections are based on the intermediate demographic and economic assumptions described in the Appendix. Expenditures are for the same limited population covered by the present Social Security program.

completely; hence, it would take a very long time and a substantial amount of money to discharge this liability.

Although adoption of the proposed program would not result in an immediate reduction in expenditures, it would eliminate the rapid increase in cost that would begin around the year 2006 if the present Social Security program were continued. The revised social insurance program has the following characteristics that make it less costly than the present Social Security program for future generations:

> Retirement benefits and Medicare benefits begin at age 70 (instead of age 65, or even earlier for retirement benefits).

> Retirement benefits are basic minimum benefits that are the same for everyone (instead of increased amounts for individuals with higher earnings).

> Disability benefits are basic minimum benefits that are the same for everyone; and benefits are not paid until disability has lasted twelve months (instead of five months).

> Death benefits are not provided.

The revised social insurance program has one feature that is *more* costly than the present Social Security program: the provision of Medicare benefits after twelve months of disability (instead of approximately twenty-nine months as presently provided).

From the viewpoint of any particular individual and his employer, the lower future cost of the revised program compared with the present program may be partially offset by the higher cost of providing benefits that are supplemental to the mandatory social insurance benefits: that is, the higher cost of saving for the individual's retirement, and providing for his family in the event of death or disability. If people continue to retire in their early sixties and to arrange privately for approximately the same benefits they would have received had the present Social Security program remained unchanged, the total cost of benefits—publicly and privately provided—would be about the same as if the present Social Security program had continued. There is no way to provide the same benefits for less money—and that is not the purpose of the proposed revision in Social Security.

The purpose of the revised program is to reduce government involvement in employee benefit planning—to reduce government-imposed standards and give the individual more freedom of choice in deciding what benefits are to be provided and how they are to be financed. The difference between the expenditures shown in Chart 30.A for the existing program and the revised program represents the amount by which the revised program would shift responsibility for providing employee benefits away from a government-imposed program. The purpose of the revised program is not to set standards as to the age at which people should retire, the amount of the benefits on which they should retire, or any other aspect of employee benefits. The revised program leaves this responsibility for setting standards to the individual and provides the vehicles— where they do not already exist—by which such standards can be realized.

How would the cost of the revised program be paid? As indicated in earlier chapters, persons aged 45 and over on July 4, 1984, would continue to pay the same Social Security taxes as if the program had not changed. So would their employers and so would self-employed persons. These taxes would finance only a small portion of their benefits and the balance would be financed by general revenue paid by the entire working population, including of course this group of persons aged 45 and over. Since the revised program would pay benefits to everyone, not just to approximately 90 percent of the working population as in the present program, it would be more costly in some respects. On the other hand, the total cost of various welfare programs would be reduced since the need for welfare benefits would be lessened. For example, the cost of public assistance to survivors would probably increase, but this would be more than offset by a decline in the cost of Supplemental Security Income.

A rough estimate has been prepared of the expenditures for benefits and administration during the next seventy-five years under the revised social insurance program (excluding the optional Freedom Bond program and the Cost-of-Living Supplement for Private Pension Plans). These expenditures are shown in Chart 30.B as a percentage of the Gross National Product and thus represent the proportion of goods and

Chart 30.B

Projected Expenditures for Benefits and Administration of Proposed Social Insurance Program
Expressed as a Percentage of Gross National Product—Proportion Financed by
Payroll Taxes and by General Revenue[a]

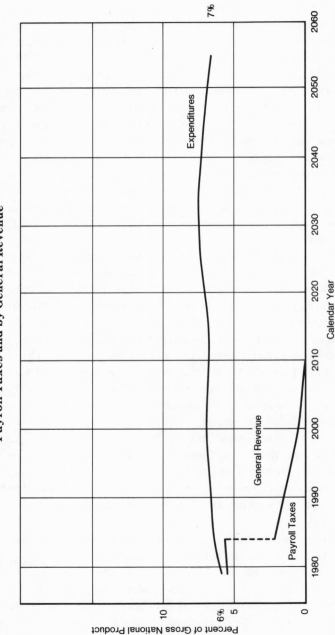

[a]Expenditures and total taxes are assumed to be equal. Projections are based on the intermediate demographic and economic assumptions described in the Appendix.

services that must be allocated to the new social insurance program. Projections are based on the same intermediate assumptions used throughout the book. The practice used earlier in the book of relating expenditures to the taxable payroll of those participating in the system is not used since the new system covers the entire population, and benefits and supporting taxes are not related to an individual's earnings. Payroll taxes show a marked decline in mid-1984 when persons under age 45 stop paying payroll taxes. A corresponding increase in general revenue must occur at that time since total taxes under the revised program will not become significantly lower than under the present program until some twenty years hence. Although expenditures for the revised social insurance program illustrated in Chart 30.A increase significantly as a percentage of taxable payroll, the expenditures illustrated in Chart 30.B, expressed as a percentage of Gross National Product, increase by a relatively smaller amount and remain in the range of 6 to 7 percent of Gross National Product throughout the projection period. This is because taxable payroll is a steadily decreasing percentage of the Gross National Product according to the assumptions used in making the projections.

Chart 30.C depicts the approximate expenditures for the proposed social insurance program based upon three alternative sets of demographic and economic assumptions described in the Appendix and employed in projections shown in earlier parts of the book. Projected expenditures are for the entire population and are shown as a percentage of the Gross National Product. Expenditures are shown for the present Social Security program from 1979 through July 4, 1984 to give a point of reference for the later expenditures under the proposed social insurance program. The projected expenditures shown in Chart 30.C are very rough estimates; the most significant conclusion to be drawn from them is that the nation can probably afford the proposed social insurance program based upon any reasonable assumptions about the future. Indeed, the nation must provide these benefits—regardless of the cost—since the proposed social insurance program calls only for minimum benefits and only for benefits an individual cannot reasonably be expected to provide for himself.

Chart 30.C

Comparison of Projected Expenditures for Benefits and Administration of Proposed Social Insurance Program Based upon Alternative Assumptions, Expressed as a Percentage of Gross National Product[a]

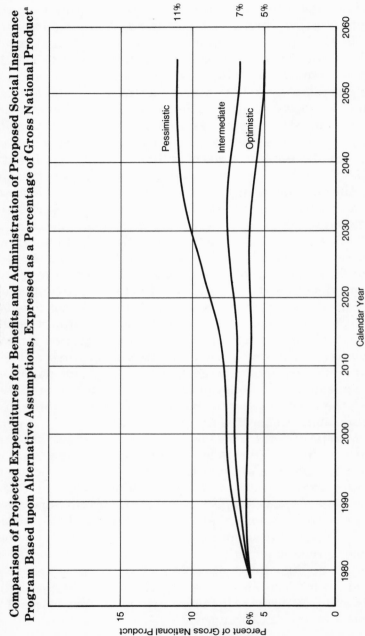

[a]Projections are based on the alternative sets of demographic and economic assumptions described in the Appendix.

This observation brings to mind a very important and basic distinction between the existing and proposed social insurance programs. The proposed program calls only for minimum benefits that are necessary in an orderly, humane society; hence, the benefits must be provided, regardless of the cost. The present program, on the other hand, calls for minimum benefits *and discretionary benefits that are not essential to an orderly, humane society.* Advocates of the present program would have us believe that all these benefits are essential and must be provided regardless of the cost. Accordingly, these advocates seem to be comfortable in ignoring the large future costs of such benefits. There appears to be no other rationale to explain this indifference by otherwise intelligent and responsible people to the probable high future benefit costs of the present social insurance program.

This basic distinction between the existing and proposed social insurance programs is also important in defining a rationale for financing. The use of general revenue, which inevitably obscures future costs, is not appropriate to finance the existing program to the extent that such program provides nonessential benefits. General revenue is appropriate, however, to finance the essential benefits provided under the existing program, just as it is appropriate to finance the mandatory part of the proposed program since it provides only essential benefits. This interrelationship between the method of financing and the level of benefits is a subtle yet quite important factor in the design of a social insurance program.

The proposed social insurance program assumes that the proceeds of the sale of Freedom Bonds would not be used to finance other portions of the revised program, and would not be used to permit additional government spending and thus increase the national debt. Instead the Freedom Bonds would refinance existing national debt; hence, Freedom Bondholders would gradually hold more of the national debt and others would hold correspondingly less, thus freeing private saving for use in developing the economy. In a sense, this procedure amounts to operating the optional Freedom Bond portion of the new Freedom Plan on an advance-funded basis. This level of advance funding appears to be feasible since it would be instituted gradually as persons attaining age 45 become eligible

to buy Freedom Bonds. Nevertheless, overall economic considerations may indicate such advance funding is not desirable,
and that part or all of the proceeds of the sale of Freedom
Bonds should be used to pay benefits under other parts of the
revised program. To the extent this practice is followed, the
amount of general revenue required for the revised program
would be less, and the existing unfunded accrued liability would
not be reduced. Instead, as Freedom Bonds were issued, the
unfunded accrued liability would be formally recognized as it
shifted to the Freedom Bondholder population.

Important questions of equity, or fairness, can be raised
about the old and new social insurance programs and how they
are financed—in the past as well as the future. The following
observations may lend perspective to these questions. There are
no simple criteria for equity that would be commonly agreed
upon by the various sectors of the population affected (Chapter
11 discusses some of the many considerations). Even if the
principles of equity could be agreed upon, it would be possible
to achieve only very rough equity in the future—particularly if
an attempt were made to balance the procedures of the past
with the proposals for the future and obtain some predeter-
mined standard of equity for the combined past and future. A
further difficulty is that participants in Social Security have
believed all along that certain principles of equity existed in the
past—but they did not.

I would consider the proposed social insurance program,
including the suggested financing arrangements, to be as fair as
is practicable under the circumstances. Of course, there is
considerable latitude in designing the exact method by which
general revenue is assessed to finance the revised program, the
details of which would be the final determinant of equity.

The cost of the proposed social insurance program presented
in this chapter is only a rough approximation intended to
demonstrate the feasibility of such a revision. No estimates
have been made of the cost effect of the revised social insurance
program on the various welfare programs, although the net
effect would be a reduction in welfare costs. Neither have cost
estimates been prepared for the Cost-of-Living Supplement for
Private Pension Plans or the adjustment to maintain the

purchasing power of the Freedom Bonds. Of course, if there is no inflation there is no cost for these two programs.

If the general approach outlined here is considered desirable by enough of the population to warrant further study, these and other cost estimates can be prepared and refinements can be developed in all the major areas of recommended change including appropriate methods of implementation.

31
Conclusion

Social Security, one of the largest single government programs in history, touches the lives of virtually everyone in the nation. Until the mid-1970s Social Security was regarded widely as the most successful government program ever enacted.

But this is not the current mood of the citizens. There is growing uneasiness and frustration about Social Security—among those who receive the benefits as well as those who pay the taxes—and it appears likely that this discontent is building to a demand for significant change.

Unfortunately, public perception of Social Security has been allowed to grow so far apart from reality that an objective appraisal of the present system by the public is difficult. The first step, then, toward rationally conceived change is increased public understanding of the present system. The second step is to obtain general agreement on a set of principles to form the underlying basis for a new Social Security. These principles may well be unique to America; ideally they will reflect the social and economic environment we desire for tomorrow, not just the environment that exists today.

Part Four of this book presents a conceptual framework for a substantial revision in Social Security that is intended to:

preserve the rights and expectations of the 35 million persons already receiving Social Security benefits and of the 46 million persons within twenty years of their anticipated retirement; and

permit the 168 million people who are under age 45 (almost 80 percent of the population not yet retired) the freedom to manage their own financial affairs as they see fit, but at the same time provide for their essential income security needs.

Designing and implementing a revised Social Security program may be a difficult task. But it will be no more difficult than trying to live with a program that is becoming so unpopular that its continued financial support by the working population is in serious doubt. Besides, the difficulty of the task of revising Social Security makes it no less essential to the well-being of the nation and its citizens.

We have an extraordinary opportunity to give today's youth and the youth of generations to come a matchless legacy—a social and economic environment of opportunity that will encourage and reward initiative and creativity, not one that will stifle. An appropriately designed Social Security program— such as the proposed Freedom Plan—is an essential part of this environment.

The Congress and the President, given the support of a substantial body of public opinion, can take this opportunity to restore to Americans the Freedom of Choice on which this country was founded and has prospered—and, we can hope, will continue to prosper. Such a grand opportunity may not pass this way again.

Appendix

Summary of Principal Actuarial Assumptions Used in Cost Projections

Throughout the book, reference has been made to actuarial estimates of the future financial operations of the Social Security program. The purpose of these actuarial projections is not to predict the future, since that is obviously impossible, but rather to analyze how the Social Security program would operate in the future under particular economic and demographic conditions. Because the actual future circumstances could develop in many different ways, it is only prudent to evaluate the program under a variety of different assumed conditions, any of which could be reasonably expected to occur (from today's point of view). Proper use of such projections will facilitate the design and understanding of the Social Security program, as well as help ensure that the program will be able to meet its financial obligations—and thus serve its purpose—in future years.

The official government cost projections for the Social Security program (OASDI and Medicare) are based upon assumptions and methodology explained in detail in the annual reports of the Board of Trustees of the OASI, DI, HI, and SMI trust

347

funds. The same economic and demographic assumptions employed in the 1979 annual reports were used for the financial projections contained in this book. Additional assumptions had to be made, however, in instances when the annual reports did not encompass the same period as the projections in the book. In particular, assumptions had to be made about hospital costs after the year 2000 and medical costs after the mid-1980s. In both instances it was assumed that costs would increase ultimately at about the same rate as the increase in average earnings of the nation's workers; present rates of increase were assumed to grade into these ultimate rates by about the year 1995 for medical costs and about the year 2000 for hospital costs.

Three different sets of economic and demographic assumptions were used, characterized as "optimistic," "intermediate," and "pessimistic." These characterizations refer to the effect of a given assumption on Social Security costs, not to the social desirability of a particular trend. For example, an assumption of longer life expectancy is called "pessimistic" since benefits would be paid over a longer period, thereby raising the costs. The alternative sets of assumptions were designed to illustrate a broad range within which one might reasonably expect the actual future experience to fall. Given the past volatility of such factors as inflation, hospital costs, and birth rates, however, there can be no assurance that future experience will fall within the range so defined.

The alternative sets of assumptions are summarized in Tables A.1 and A.2. It was assumed that the retirement-age patterns in the future would be substantially the same as those being experienced currently, with relatively little variation among the three alternatives. Assumptions were also made concerning variables such as migration levels, insured status, disability termination rates, marital status, administrative expenses, the timing pattern of fertility, and many others. The actual future development of all these factors will undoubtedly exhibit fluctuations and considerable variation. Since such cycles and abrupt changes cannot be foretold, the ultimate long-range values of the assumptions shown in Tables A.1 and A.2 are designed to represent the average trend levels that would result if the fluctuations were smoothed out. For the first few years of the projection period, however, an attempt was made to forecast cyclical behavior in the economic factors.

Appendix Table A.1

Selected Economic Assumptions under Optimistic, Intermediate, and Pessimistic Alternatives, Calendar Years 1979–2055

				Percentage Increase in Average Annual . . .			
Calendar Year	*Real GNP*[a]	*Wages in Covered Employ- ment*	*Consumer Price Index*	*In- patient Hospital Costs*[b]	*Real Wage Differ- ential*[c]	*Average Annual Interest Rate*[d]	*Average Annual Unem- ployment Rate*
(1)	(2)	(3)	(4)	(5)	(6)	(7)	(8)
1960–64	4.0	3.4	1.3	—	2.1	3.7	5.7
1965–69	4.3	5.4	3.4	15.1	1.9	5.2	3.8
1970–74	2.5	6.3	6.1	13.7	0.2	6.7	5.4
1975	−1.3	6.5	9.1	18.7	−2.5	7.4	8.5
1976	5.7	8.4	5.8	15.7	2.5	7.1	7.7
1977	4.9	6.9	6.5	13.7	0.4	7.1	7.0
1978	3.9	8.5	7.6	12.7	0.9	8.2	6.0
Alternative I (Optimistic)							
1979	3.7	8.3	9.3	12.6	−1.0	9.1	6.0
1980	2.3	8.6	7.3	13.1	1.3	8.6	6.2
1981	4.4	8.7	6.5	13.9	2.2	8.5	5.7
1982	4.9	7.9	5.2	13.4	2.7	7.8	4.9
1983	5.0	5.8	4.0	12.2	1.8	7.0	4.2
1984	3.9	4.9	3.1	9.9	1.8	6.1	4.0
1985	3.6	5.0	3.0	9.0	2.0	6.1	4.0
1986	3.9	5.1	3.0	8.8	2.1	6.1	4.0
1987	3.9	5.4	3.0	8.8	2.4	6.1	4.0
1988	4.0	5.5	3.0	8.6	2.5	6.1	4.0
1989	3.8	5.5	3.0	6.9	2.5	6.1	4.0
1990	3.8	5.5	3.0	6.7	2.5	6.1	4.0
1995	3.1	5.4	3.0	5.7	2.4	6.1	4.0
2000 and later	3.1[e]	5.25	3.0	5.7[f]	2.25	6.1	4.0
Alternative II (Intermediate)							
1979	3.7	8.3	9.4	12.6	−1.1	9.1	6.0
1980	2.0	8.0	7.4	13.1	.6	8.8	6.2
1981	4.0	9.1	6.6	14.1	2.5	8.4	6.0
1982	4.7	7.4	5.5	14.0	1.9	7.6	5.3
1983	3.6	6.0	4.5	12.8	1.5	6.9	5.0

Appendix Table A.1 (continued)

Calendar Year	Real GNP[a]	Wages in Covered Employment	Consumer Price Index	In-patient Hospital Costs[b]	Real Wage Differ-ential[c]	Average Annual Interest Rate[d]	Average Annual Unem-ployment Rate
			Percentage Increase in Average Annual...				
(1)	(2)	(3)	(4)	(5)	(6)	(7)	(8)
1984	3.0	5.4	4.0	11.3	1.4	6.6	5.0
1985	3.1	5.3	4.0	11.3	1.3	6.6	5.0
1986	3.2	5.4	4.0	11.3	1.4	6.6	5.0
1987	3.3	5.7	4.0	11.3	1.7	6.6	5.0
1988	3.3	6.0	4.0	11.4	2.0	6.6	5.0
1989	3.2	6.0	4.0	10.5	2.0	6.6	5.0
1990	3.2	6.0	4.0	10.4	2.0	6.6	5.0
1995	2.9	5.9	4.0	9.3	1.9	6.6	5.0
2000 and later	2.9[e]	5.75	4.0	9.2[f]	1.75	6.6	5.0
Alternative III (Pessimistic)							
1979	2.3	9.2	10.3	12.6	−1.1	9.1	6.3
1980	−1.1	8.7	8.9	13.1	− .2	9.0	8.2
1981	5.4	9.2	7.3	15.5	1.9	8.5	7.4
1982	4.1	7.7	6.3	15.5	1.4	8.1	6.9
1983	4.0	7.2	6.0	15.7	1.2	8.1	6.4
1984	3.7	7.1	6.0	15.6	1.1	8.1	6.0
1985	2.9	7.2	6.0	15.2	1.2	8.1	6.0
1986	2.9	7.1	6.0	15.3	1.1	8.1	6.0
1987	2.9	7.3	6.0	15.1	1.3	8.1	6.0
1988	2.9	7.5	6.0	15.1	1.5	8.1	6.0
1989	2.8	7.5	6.0	14.2	1.5	8.1	6.0
1990	2.8	7.5	6.0	14.1	1.5	8.1	6.0
1995	2.7	7.4	6.0	13.0	1.4	8.1	6.0
2000 and later	2.7[e]	7.25	6.0	12.6[f]	1.25	8.1	6.0

[a]The total output of goods and services in the Nation expressed in constant dollars.

[b]Includes hospital costs for all patients, not just HI beneficiaries. Data unavailable for years 1960–64.

[c]The difference between the percentage increase in average annual wages in covered employment and the percentage increase in the average annual CPI.

[d]The average of the interest rates determined in each of the 12 months of the year for special public-debt obligations issuable to the trust funds.

[e]This value is for the year 2000. The value for the year 2055 is 3.3, 2.4, and 0.8 for alternatives I, II, and III, respectively.

[f]Value is for 2000. Subsequent unit hospital cost increases are assumed to equal the annual increases in average wages in covered employment.

Appendix Table A.2

Selected Demographic Assumptions under Optimistic, Intermediate, and Pessimistic Alternatives, Calendar Years 1979–2055

Calendar Year	Total Fertility Rate[a]	Age-adjusted Mortality Rate[b]		Adjusted Gross Disability Incidence Rate[c]	
		Male	Female	Male	Female
(1)	(2)	(3)	(4)	(5)	(6)
1970	2,434	10.96	8.05	5.06	3.54
1971	2,249	10.66	8.06	5.92	4.10
1972	1,997	10.77	7.94	6.35	4.50
1973	1,865	10.66	7.85	6.72	4.93
1974	1,827	10.26	7.54	7.03	5.64
1975	1,771	9.88	7.17	7.76	6.06
1976	1,719	9.73	7.07	7.23	5.51
1977	1,784	9.53	6.89	7.41	5.46
1978	1,757	9.35	6.72	5.97	4.25
Alternative I (Optimistic)					
1979	1,831	9.45	6.80	5.79	4.12
1980	1,871	9.36	6.72	5.85	4.17
1981	1,911	9.32	6.68	5.92	4.22
1982	1,952	9.28	6.64	6.02	4.29
1983	1,992	9.25	6.60	6.12	4.37
1984	2,033	9.21	6.56	6.23	4.46
1985	2,074	9.17	6.52	6.34	4.55
1990	2,292	9.04	6.39	6.62	4.78
1995	2,443	8.92	6.26	6.68	4.84
2000	2,493	8.80	6.13	6.69	4.86
2005 & later	2,500	8.69[d]	6.01[d]	6.69	4.86
Alternative II (Intermediate)					
1979	1,793	9.18	6.55	5.87	4.19
1980	1,809	9.02	6.38	5.97	4.25
1981	1,824	8.85	6.22	6.09	4.34
1982	1,839	8.82	6.18	6.25	4.46
1983	1,855	8.78	6.15	6.42	4.57
1984	1,870	8.75	6.11	6.61	4.72
1985	1,887	8.72	6.08	6.79	4.86
1990	2,036	8.55	5.92	7.25	5.22
1995	2,075	8.39	5.76	7.34	5.32
2000	2,100	8.23	5.60	7.36	5.35
2005 & later	2,100	8.08[d]	5.45[d]	7.36	5.35
Alternative III (Pessimistic)					
1979	1,737	8.92	6.30	5.95	4.25
1980	1,715	8.67	6.07	6.09	4.34

Appendix Table A.2 (continued)

Calendar Year	Total Fertility Rate[a]	Age-adjusted Mortality Rate[b]		Adjusted Gross Disability Incidence Rate[c]	
		Male	Female	Male	Female
(1)	(2)	(3)	(4)	(5)	(6)
1981	1,693	8.57	5.97	6.26	4.46
1982	1,671	8.46	5.86	6.48	4.66
1983	1,649	8.36	5.76	6.71	4.78
1984	1,627	8.26	5.67	6.99	4.98
1985	1,606	8.16	5.57	7.23	5.16
1990	1,544	7.85	5.26	7.87	5.66
1995	1,524	7.58	4.97	8.01	5.79
2000	1,509	7.34	4.72	8.03	5.83
2005 & later	1,500	7.12[d]	4.48[d]	8.03	5.83

[a]The number of children that would be born to 1,000 women in their lifetimes if they were to experience the observed age-specific birth rates and were to survive the entire child-bearing period. Ultimate rates are reached in 2005.

[b]The annual number of deaths per 1,000 persons in the enumerated population as of April 1, 1970. Improvement is projected to continue throughout the projection period.

[c]The number of awards per 1,000 persons exposed to disability, adjusted for changes from the 1978 age distribution.

[d]This value is for the year 2005. Mortality rates are assumed to continue declining throughout the remainder of the projection period.

Note: Figures shown in Tables A.1 and A.2 for 1978 and earlier represent actual experience as estimated at the time the 1979 Trustees Reports were prepared. Certain of these figures have since been slightly revised based on more accurate data.

Notes

Chapter 1

1. The dollar amounts in this paragraph relate to all the benefits usually thought of as Social Security: Old-Age and Survivors Insurance, Disability Insurance, and Medicare (Hospital Insurance and Supplementary Medical Insurance).

2. There is no employer tax paid on behalf of self-employed persons; however, self-employed persons pay higher tax rates than employed persons.

3. These and other figures throughout the book are based upon the 1979 Trustees Reports (intermediate assumptions) unless noted otherwise. More recent projections based upon the 1980 Trustees Reports (intermediate assumptions) indicate the maximum Social Security tax in 1990 will be $5,118 for an employee ($10,236 for employee and employer combined) and $7,192 for a self-employed person.

Chapter 2

1. *Social Security Handbook,* U.S. Department of Health, Education, and Welfare, Social Security Administration, HEW Publication No. (SSA) 77-10135, July 1978.

2. Ibid., p. 2.

3. In addition to these noncovered employees, there are approximately 530,000 active railroad employees who are not included in Social Security but who are covered by their own railroad retirement system. For all practical purposes, however,

these railroad employees may be considered to be covered by Social Security. They generally receive benefits at least equal to those provided by Social Security as a result of the transfer of wage credits between the systems for employees with less than ten years of service and as a result of the financial interchange provisions applicable to all railroad employees.

4. "The Desirability and Feasibility of Social Security Coverage for Employees of Federal, State, and Local Governments and Private, Nonprofit Organizations," Report of the Universal Social Security Coverage Study Group, March 1980.

5. This figure includes the resident population of the fifty states and the District of Columbia, American Armed Forces and certain civilians overseas, and the residents of Puerto Rico, Guam, American Samoa, the Virgin Islands, and the Canal Zone. These groups comprise the total population eligible to participate in the Social Security program.

6. Robert M. Gibson and Charles R. Fisher, "Age Differences in Health Care Spending, Fiscal Year 1977," *Social Security Bulletin,* January 1979.

7. Subsequently, in 1980, the functions of the Department of Health, Education, and Welfare were allocated to two new departments: the Department of Education, and the Department of Health and Human Services—the Social Security Administration and the Health Care Financing Administration forming part of the latter.

8. *The Budget of the United States Government, Fiscal Year 1981.*

Chapter 3

1. According to the Omnibus Reconciliation Act of 1980 signed into law on December 5, 1980 (Pub. L. No. 96-499), some of these Medicare provisions will be liberalized as of July 1, 1981: the period within which a beneficiary must be transferred from a hospital to a skilled nursing facility and still qualify for post-hospital extended care will be increased from fourteen days to thirty days; with respect to home health visits, the three-day prior hospital stay will be eliminated under HI, the 100-visit ceiling will be removed under HI and SMI, and the $60 deductible will be eliminated under SMI.

Chapter 4

1. W. R. Williamson and R. J. Myers, "Revised Cost Estimates for Present Title II." Unpublished study, Actuarial Study No. 12, October 1938, Social Security Board, Office of the Actuary.

2. All projections were based upon the Social Security benefit provisions in effect on January 1, 1979. Most of the projections were obtained from the 1979 Trustees Reports or unpublished estimates prepared by the Social Security actuaries in conjunction with the preparation of the Trustees Reports. In cases where particular estimates were not available, the author has prepared his own estimates on the basis of the 1979 Trustees Reports assumptions.

3. As mentioned before, the SMI program is not financed by the Social Security payroll tax; it is financed primarily from general revenue (currently 70 percent) and enrollee premiums (currently 30 percent). By the year 2000, it is expected that general revenue will provide over 90 percent of SMI financing. Since SMI costs are properly included as "Social Security costs," they have been shown as a percentage of taxable payroll in order to have a uniform basis for comparison.

Chapter 5

1. J. Douglas Brown, *The Genesis of Social Security in America,* Industrial Relations Section, Princeton University, Princeton, N.J., 1969, p. 14.

2. Ibid., p. 13.

3. Arthur M. Schlesinger, Jr., *The Age of Roosevelt,* vol. 2, *The Coming of the New Deal* (Houghton-Mifflin, 1959), pp. 308–9.

Chapter 7

1. *1979 Annual Report of the Board of Trustees of the Federal Old-Age and Survivors Insurance and Disability Insurance Trust Funds* (House Document No. 96-101, 96th Congress, 1st Session), 1979.

2. In recent years the OASDI program has been operated on what may be characterized as a current-cost basis, since the

trust fund balances have been relatively low. Should the trust fund balances in fact increase as implied by Chart 7.A, the program would more properly be described as "partially advance-funded," at least for the next fifty years.

3. Based on more recent projections, scheduled OASDI tax income will not exceed expenditures until the mid-1980s; the resulting deficits will be relatively small but will necessitate corrective legislation.

4. This computation, as well as those throughout the chapter, is based on a "real rate of interest" of 2.5 percent. For example, in the case of the intermediate assumptions, the assumed 6.6 percent interest rate is comprised of a "real rate of interest" of 2.5 percent, compounded with an assumed 4.0 percent annual increase in the Consumer Price Index.

5. *1979 Annual Report of the Board of Trustees of the Federal Hospital Insurance Trust Fund* (House Document No. 96-102, 96th Congress, 1st Session), 1979.

6. Joseph A. Applebaum, "Some Effects of Fully Funding OASDI," Actuarial Note No. 97, HEW Publication No. (SSA) 79-11500, September 1979.

Chapter 11

1. Orlo R. Nichols and Richard G. Schreitmueller, "Some Comparisons of the Value of a Worker's Social Security Taxes and Benefits," Actuarial Note No. 95, HEW Publication No. (SSA) 78-11500, April 1978.

2. The calculations were based on standard actuarial mathematics, and attempted to account for each of the appropriate factors that can influence the results. For example, the probabilities that a worker would die before becoming eligible for retirement benefits, or conversely, that he would live far into old age were accounted for. Similarly, the worker's chances of becoming disabled in any given year were included. The changing value of the dollar (inflation) and the "time value of money" (interest), along with changes in average wages were also accounted for.

3. These examples were derived from the study mentioned in Note 1 but do not necessarily conform to specific examples given in the study.

Chapter 13

1. Executive Summary of *Social Security Financing and Benefits; Report of the 1979 Advisory Council on Social Security,* December 7, 1979, p. 12.

2. *Social Security Financing and Benefits; Report of the 1979 Advisory Council on Social Security,* December 7, 1979, p. 353.

Chapter 14

1. Under the new benefit provisions enacted in the 1977 Social Security Amendments, workers retiring in future years will receive somewhat smaller replacement ratios. For workers retiring at age 65, as in these examples, replacement ratios (based on the worker's benefit alone) will level off ultimately at 57 percent for the minimum wage earner, 44 percent for the average wage earner, 30 percent for the worker with maximum earnings, and 15 percent for twice-maximum earners. The corresponding figures for workers with dependent spouses are 86 percent, 66 percent, 45 percent, and 22 percent, respectively.

2. Under the "offset" method of integration, Internal Revenue Service rules allow a plan to define its benefits as a particular amount (calculated the same way for all participants) reduced by no more than $83\frac{1}{3}$ percent of the retiring worker's Primary Insurance Amount under Social Security. Other methods of integration are allowed, provided they produce approximately the same end result.

Chapter 19

1. Persons attaining age 65 in 1982 or later will have their benefits calculated under the new indexed-earnings benefit formula. For these persons, the "delayed retirement credit" is increased from 1 percent annually to 3 percent to help offset the loss of benefits that would otherwise occur because the indexing of earnings is carried out only through age 60. Thus the net gain for retirement later than age 65 is still intended to be only about 1 percent per year.

2. According to the Omnibus Reconciliation Act of 1980 signed into law on December 5, 1980 (Pub. L. No. 96-499), some

of these Medicare provisions will be liberalized as of July 1, 1981: the period within which a beneficiary must be transferred from a hospital to a skilled nursing facility and still qualify for post-hospital extended care will be increased from fourteen days to thirty days; with respect to home health visits, the three-day prior hospital stay will be eliminated under HI, the 100-visit ceiling will be removed under HI and SMI, and the $60 deductible will be eliminated under SMI.

3. Orlo R. Nichols and Richard G. Schreitmueller, "Some Comparisons of the Value of a Worker's Social Security Taxes and Benefits," Actuarial Note No. 95, HEW Publication No. (SSA) 78-11500, April 1978.

4. Based on an unpublished study by the Social Security Administration actuaries.

Chapter 23

1. When the revisions in the earnings test enacted by the Social Security Amendments of 1977 become completely effective after 1981, references in this paragraph to age 72 should read age 70.

Chapter 27

1. In the 1930s the average remaining lifetime of persons aged 65 was about 12 years for males and 13 for females; today it is about 14 years for males and 19 years for females; for persons aged 65 in the year 2025 it is projected to be about 16 years for males and 22 years for females (based on the most recent studies by Social Security actuaries and not allowing for any major breakthroughs in health care). These same studies indicate that for persons aged 70 in the year 2025 the average remaining lifetime will be about 13 years for males and 18 years for females.

2. In mid-1981 there were approximately five persons aged 20 to 65 for every person aged 65 and over. To maintain this same ratio of "active to retired" persons during the first half of the twenty-first century, the normal retirement age of 65 would have to increase to 67 by the year 2000 and continue rising to 72 by the year 2025, after which time it would remain at about 72 for the next twenty-five years.

Chapter 29

1. Milton and Rose Friedman, *Free to Choose: A Personal Statement,* Harcourt Brace and Jovanovich, New York, 1979, p. 115.

Index

Accrued liabilities, 97–103, 332, 340
  for Hospital Insurance, 99–100
  for OASDI, 98–99
  significance of, 102–103
  for Supplementary Medical Insurance, 100–102
  trust funds and, 99, 100, 101
  unfunded vs. funded, 102–104
Actuarial assumptions, 345–350
Actuarial balance, 81
Actuarial deficit, 64, 81–97
  combined, 89–91, 97
  elimination of, 85–86, 89, 97
  for Hospital Insurance, 86–89
  for OASDI, 82–86
  optimistic-pessimistic assumptions continuum, 82
  for Supplementary Medical Insurance, 91, 93–96
  tax rate and, 104
  trust funds and, 84–85, 89
Actuarial projections, 49–56, 81
Actuarial studies, 46–48
Actuarial surplus, 81
Actuary
  definition, 48–49
  organizations, 48
Administration. *See* Social Security Administration

Advance-funding financing, 75–79
  benefits security and, 76–77
  cost allocation with, 77
  future contribution reduction with, 77
  savings incentives and, 78–79
Advisory Council on Social Security, 1979 report, 178
Affirmative action, 150
Age factor
  in disability benefits, 207
  in earnings test, 30–31, 32, 140, 182, 201
  in Freedom Bond Program, 316–319
  in Freedom Plan, 310, 313–315, 331–337
  in mandatory retirement, 285
  in maximizing benefits, 261
  in Medicare benefits, 218
  in Medicare revised program, 323–324
  in retirement, 269–270
  in retirement benefits, 31–32, 201–202, 242, 270–271, 285–286
  sex factor and, 148, 149
Aid to Families with Dependent Children, 23

Alabama, 264
Alaska, 18, 176, 177, 191, 264
Aliens, 257
American Society of Chartered
    Life Underwriters, 228
Average Indexed Monthly
    Earnings, 28–29

Behavior, Social Security as
    determinant of, 269–281
Benefit statement, 111–119
    content, 117–118
    of private pension plan, 112–
    113
Benefits, 4, 20–23, 25–39. *See
    also specific programs*
    adequacy, 227
    amount, 27–30
    appropriateness, 134–137
    automatic increases, 28, 30,
        161–165, 180–181, 210
    cost projections, 46–55
    dual protection, 168–169
    equity, 182–183
    family maximum, 29, 36, 271
    inflation and, 161–165
    maximizing, 249–258
    maximum, 29, 36, 64, 195, 199–
        225
    minimum, 187
    minimum eligibility
        requirements, 249
    nonduplication, 37
    prospectus, 291
    reduction, 28, 181, 182, 270–
        271
    security of, 76–77
    sex factor, 147–152
    short-term participation and,
        187
    supplementation, 4, 248–249
    taxation relation, 6, 61, 74,
        130–132, 168–169, 170, 174,

182–183, 184–185, 199, 222–
    225, 306, 307
    termination, 28, 30
    universal coverage and, 173–
    174
Birth rate, 52–53
Black Lung Benefits, 14
Blindness, 27, 32, 207
Blue Cross-Blue Shield, 230

California, 19, 176, 177, 191, 233
Catastrophic illness, 231
Child benefits, 4, 20, 34, 35, 204
    with disability benefits, 210–
        211, 212
    for grandchild, 35
    with marriage, 272–273
    maximizing, 258–259, 271
    with retirement benefits, 242
    with survivor benefits, 213,
        214, 216, 237
    termination, 30, 35
Citizenship, 310–311
Civil Rights Act (1964), Title
    VII, 150
Civil service retirement plan, 16–
    17, 171–172
Civil service survivor's annuity,
    sex factor, 149
C.L.U. designation, 228
Colorado, 18, 191
Common-law-marriage, 272
Community property, 149
Company-sponsored plan, 228.
    See also Private benefit
    (pension) plans
Connecticut, 19, 191
Consumer Price Index, 28, 30,
    122, 161–165, 180, 201, 207
Contribution and benefit base,
    195, 196, 198
Cost-of-living adjustments, 122,
    165. *See also* Consumer
    Price Index

Cost-of-Living Supplement, 320–322, 332
Costs. *See* Financing; *specific benefit programs*
Coverage, 14–20, 227. *See also* Participation
  optional vs. universal, 167–174
  universal, 19–20, 167–174
    feasibility study, 19–20, 177–178
Criticisms, 6
Current-cost financing, 71–75, 76, 127, 133
  alternatives, 75–79
  public information on, 76
  tax rate comparison, 73–74
Currently insured status, 26

Death
  benefit termination and, 30
  planning for, 236–241
  provision for under Freedom Plan, 327–328, 334
  retroactive disability benefits and, 259–260
Death benefits, 4, 33, 34–36. *See also* Survivor benefits
  lump-sum, 20, 36, 213, 216, 237, 327–328
  supplemental plans, 157
Decision making, 305
Deficit. *See* Actuarial deficit
Demographic variables, 49–56, 123–124, 133, 223–225, 292, 337
Department of Health, Education, and Welfare, 23
Dependent benefits. *See also* Child benefits
  earning limitation and, 31, 139, 141–142, 187

sex factor and, 147
Disability, planning for, 232–236
Disability benefits, 4, 20, 21, 32–33, 181, 229, 232–236
  application for, 208, 255–256
  automatic increases in, 122, 207
  beneficiaries increase and, 41–42
  for children, 35. *See also* Child benefits
  definition, 32
  earnings and, 31, 33, 139–140, 208, 212, 260
  eligibility, 23, 232–233
  employer-provided, 233
  family benefits with, 209–212
  family maximum, 29, 36
  under Freedom Plan, 328–329, 334
  marriage and, 236, 273
  maximizing, 259, 276–277
  maximum, 33, 206–209
  Medicare benefits and, 37
    application for, 252
  minimum, 32–33
  money-saving hints, 208–209
  promises, 122
  quarters of coverage for, 27, 207, 232–233
  reduction, 33
  remarriage and, 212
  replacement ratio, 211–212, 234–235
  restrictions, 208
  retroactive after death, 259–260
  sex factor, 148
  supplemental plans, 157
  supplementary benefits, 208
  survivor benefits and, 209–211, 216, 237
  termination, 30, 33, 208
  for widows (widowers), 34–35

Disability Insurance, 14
  actuarial deficit, 82–86
  costs, 65–66
Disability insured status, 26, 27
Disasters, 55
Discrimination. *See* Sex factor
Dividends, 266
Divorce, 181
  disability benefits and, 212
  maximizing benefits and, 260–
    261, 273, 275–276
  remarriage and, 272, 273
  retirement benefits and, 34,
    206, 242, 244
  sex factor, 146, 147, 151–152
  survivor benefits and, 35, 213,
    237
Domestic workers, 267–268

Earnings
  with disability, 31, 33, 139–
    140, 260
  indexed, 28–29
Earnings—maximum taxable, 5,
    28, 64, 195–199
  increases, 72–73
  prospectus, 289
Earnings—taxable
  costs comparison, 43–47
  projections, 46–55
  nontaxable conversion, 266
  percentage of total, 45
Earnings statement, 115
  verification, 250–251
Earnings test (limitation), 4,
    139–143, 182, 201, 202, 252,
    271. *See also specific benefit
    programs*
  age factor, 30–31, 32, 140, 182,
    201
  annual exempt amount, 140
  benefit reduction and, 28, 30–
    31, 32, 139

concept of, 142–143
  disability benefits and, 31, 33,
    139–140, 208, 212, 260
  earnings receipt control and,
    256
  family benefit and, 206
  income exemptions, 140
  liberalization of, 142–143
  low- vs. high-wage workers
    and, 141
  monthly measure, 141
  residence abroad and, 257
  survivor benefit and, 139, 141–
    142, 216
Economic variables, 49–56, 123–
    124, 337
Educational benefits. *See*
  Student benefits
Eligibility, 20, 25–31. *See also
  specific benefit programs*
Employee contribution, 4–5, 60,
    61, 62. *See also* Social
    Security taxes
Employee Retirement Income
    Security Act (1974), 76–77,
    112
Employer contribution, 4–5, 60,
    61, 62. *See also* Social
    Security taxes
Employment status, 181, 193
  maximizing benefits and, 277–
    278
  retirement policy and, 284–287
Environmental factors, 55
Equal Employment Act (1972),
    150
Equal Pay Act (1963), 150
Expenditures. *See* Financing;
  Social Security
  Administration; specific
  benefit programs

"Fairness" concept, 130–134
  sex factor, 151

Family benefits. *See specific members and benefit programs*

Family status factor, 181

Father's benefit. *See* Mother's (father's) benefit

Federal debt, 59

Federal employees, 16–17, 168– 169, 171–172, 179

Federal Employees Health Benefits Act (1959), 230

Federal taxation, 57–61. *See also specific taxes*

Financial advisor, 228

Financial planning, 228–245

Financing, 14, 41–56, 57–67. *See also* General revenue; Social Security taxes

across-generation, 132–134, 170, 173, 184–185

actuarial projections, 49–56

advance funding, 41–42

beneficiaries increase and, 41– 42

benefit amount increase and, 42–43

cost-benefit analysis, 127–137

current-cost method, 71–75, 76, 127, 133

alternatives, 75–79

deficits, 64

expenditures vs. collections, 74

expenditures–taxable earnings comparison, 43–47

projections, 46–55

with Freedom Plan, 331–341

government employee participation and, 171–173

nonparticipation effect, 179

government role, 302

individual equity and, 130– 132, 151

interfund borrowing, 64

of Medicare revision, 324, 326

multiple benefits and, 42

new programs and, 41–42

nonparticipation factor, 178– 180

optional coverage factor, 178– 180

optional vs. universal participation and, 170–171

with payroll tax vs. general revenue, 66–67

of private pension plans, 76–77

projections, 46–56, 69–79, 121– 126

prospectus, 290, 291–292

rationale, 61–62

of Senior Citizens Benefits, 312–313, 315

Social Security program– alternative programs comparison, 185

Social Security program maturity and, 45–46

tax reallocation and, 63–64

Forecasts, 121–126

actuarial, 49–56, 81

optimistic-pessimistic assumptions continuum, 50– 55

Form OAR-7004, 115, 251

Form W-2 Wage and Tax Statement, 250

"Fortunate eight percent," 195– 225

Fraud, 130

Freedom Bond Program, 316– 319, 332, 339–340

age factor, 316–319

indexing, 317–318

redemption, 318, 319

Freedom of choice, 135, 304, 307

Freedom Plan, 307, 309–326, 327–344

age factor, 310, 313–315, 331– 337

Freedom Plan (*cont.*)
cost, 331–341
Cost-of-Living Supplement,
320–322, 332
death provision, 327–328, 334
disability provision, 328–329,
334
financing, 331–341
Freedom Bond Program, 316–
319, 332, 339–340
general revenue and, 335, 339,
340
illness provision, 323–326, 334
old age provision, 309–322, 334
Senior Citizen Benefit
program, 310–316
Social Security program and,
307, 309–310, 323, 327, 328,
331–332, 334, 335, 337
Fuller, Ida, 133
Fully insured status, 26, 27
Funding. *See* Financing

General revenue, 59–60, 61, 171,
172, 180, 186, 193, 197–198,
290
for Freedom Plan financing,
335, 339, 340
vs. Social Security taxes
financing, 66–67
Supplementary Medical
Insurance contribution, 59–
60, 64–65, 74
Generation factor, 132–134, 170,
173, 184–185, 297–298
Georgia, 177
Government-employee unions,
17
Government employment, 16–19,
278. *See also* Federal
employees; Local
government employees;
State employees

Government pension, 204, 209,
243, 244
benefit statement, 112–113
survivor benefit and, 216
Government responsibility, 135,
301–302
automatic adjustments and,
162–163
vs. individual responsibility,
302–305

Hawaii, 233
Health Care Financing
Administration, 23–24, 292
headquarters, 24
Health insurance
group, 230
employer-provided, 230
Health maintenance
organization, 230
Home health agency visits, 38
Homemaker, 150
Hospital Insurance, 14, 21, 23,
37–38
accrued liability, 99–100
actuarial deficit, 86–89
with OASDI deficit, 89–91,
97
coinsurance, 38
deductible provisions, 38
duration, 38
forecast assumptions, 86, 89–
91
maximum benefits, 218, 219
participation-withdrawal
effect, 179
projections, 125
reimbursement system, 37–38
voluntary participation, 253–
254
unpaid costs, 230–231
Hospital Insurance trust fund,
accrued liability, 100

HR 10 retirement plan, 243
Husband. *See* Spouse benefits

Illinois, 89, 191
Illegitimacy, 149
Illness, Freedom Plan provision
    for, 323–326, 334
Income redistribution, 170, 302
Income tax, 30, 57–58, 181–182
Incorporation, 266
Indexed earnings, 28–29
Individual responsibility, 109–
    110, 135–136, 241, 279–280,
    302–305, 307, 335
Individual Retirement Account,
    243
Inflation, 161–165, 201, 291–292,
    304, 317, 320
    benefits and, 161–165
    payroll taxes and, 163–164
Insurability status factor, 181
Insured status, 26–27, 200
Internal Revenue Service, 23

Kentucky, 19, 191
Keogh plan, 243
Kidney disease, 37, 208, 229

Labor force
    occupational segregation in,
        150
    women in, 146, 150
Legal factor
    in government employee
        participation, 18
    in nonprofit organization
        participation, 19
    in participation, 18, 19, 175–
        176
    in supplemental benefit plans,
        153, 156–159
Legislation, 13–14. *See also*
    specific acts

Liabilities. *See* Accrued
    liabilities
Local government employees,
    17–19, 168–169, 172–173,
    175–179
Louisiana, 18, 19, 176, 177, 191
Life expectancy, 55, 123–124,
    241, 304
Life insurance, 4, 228, 240–241,
    243, 248–249, 255

Maine, 18, 191
Marriage, 4, 151, 181, 224
    disability benefits and, 236,
        273
    maximizing benefits and, 254–
        255, 271–273
Massachusetts, 18, 19, 191
Maximum contribution and
    benefit base, 64, 71. *See also*
    Earnings—maximum
    taxable
Medicaid, 23
Medicare, 14, 21, 23, 28, 37–38,
    181, 229–231
    administration, 23–24
    application for, 220, 252
    beneficiaries increase, 42
    complementary coverage, 221–
        222
    disability benefits and, 208
    exclusions, 218
    financing, 324, 326
    information on benefits, 114
    lifetime reserve, 221
    maximizing benefits, 253–254
    maximum benefits, 218–222
    money-saving hints, 220–222
    prospectus, 292
    revision, 323–326
Military service, 251
Missouri, 191

Monthly cash benefits, 3, 21, 27–30
Mortality, 53
Mother's (father's) benefit, 35–36, 147, 213
Municipal government employees. *See* Local government employees

Nevada, 18, 191
New Jersey, 233, 264
New York, 233
Nonparticipation, 5, 15–19, 167, 168, 178–180, 227
Nonprofit organizations, 19, 173, 175, 176, 191
Nursing facility care, 38

Old-Age, Survivors, and Disability Insurance (OASDI) programs, 20–23. *See also* Disability benefits; Retirement benefits; Survivor benefits
  accrued liabilities, 98–99
  actuarial deficit, 82–86
    with Hospital Insurance deficit, 89–91, 97
  forecast assumptions, 82, 89–91
  participation-withdrawal effect, 179
  projections, 125
Ohio, 18, 19, 191
Old age, provision for, 309–322
Omnibus Reconciliation Act (1980), 265

Parent benefits, 36, 213, 237
  remarriage and, 272
  sex factor, 147–148
Participation, 5, 14–20. *See also* Coverage

advantages, 191–194
employer-employee decision factor, 187–188
legal factor, 175–176
optional, 175, 178–180, 192, 267
vs. universal, 167–174
prospectus, 290–291
quarters of coverage and, 186
short-term, 187
termination notice, 176, 177
voluntary, 18–19, 175
withdrawal, 18–19, 169, 175–189, 193
  irrevocability, 185–186
Part-time work, 4
Payroll taxes. *See* Social Security taxes
Price-wage relations, 163–165
Primary Insurance Amount (PIA), 28, 29, 31–36
Private benefit (pension) plans, 168, 243, 286, 317
  advance funding, 76–77
  benefit security, 76–77
  benefit statement, 112–113
  cost-of-living supplement, 320–322
  employee termination, 112
  financing, 76–77
  integration with Social Security, 17, 153–159
  legal factor, 153, 156–159
  Medicare coverage and, 221–222
  retirement age and, 270
  Social Security program comparison, 180–182, 184–185
  supplementation of Social Security, 153, 155–159
Profit-sharing plans, 243
Public Assistance, 14

Public information, 5–9, 107–110, 113–119, 228, 247–248, 292
  adequacy of, 116–119
  specialized, 115–116
Public Law 96–265, 236
Puerto Rico, 19, 191, 233

Quarters of coverage, 26–27. *See also specific benefit programs*
  participation and, 186

Railroad Retirement Act, 21, 37, 229, 253
Rehabilitation, 33, 208, 277
Remarriage
  disability benefits and, 212
  maximizing benefits and, 271–273
  retirement benefits and, 206
  sex factor, 148, 151
  survivor benefits and, 35–36, 216, 261
Replacement ratio, 154, 157
  for disability benefits, 211–212, 234–235
  for retirement benefits, 154, 205–206, 242–243
  for survivor benefits, 214, 238–239, 240
Residence
  abroad, 4, 221, 254, 256–257
  benefits maximization and, 256–258
Retirement
  age of, 269–270
  encouragement of, 136–137
  expectations, 283–287, 297
  national policy, 286–287
  planning for, 241–245
Retirement benefits, 4, 20, 31–32,

241–245. *See also* Earnings test
  application for, 202–203
    time of, 252
  automatic increases, 122
  beneficiaries increase and, 41–42
  family benefits, 203–206
  family maximum, 29, 36, 205
  under Freedom Plan, 310–322, 334
  insured status and, 31
  maximum, 31, 200–206
  minimum, 31
  money-saving hints, 202–203
  pre-retirement application, 252
  promises, 121–122
  prospectus, 291
  quarters of coverage, 200
  reduction in, 244
  replacement ratio, 154, 205–206, 242–243
  residence and, 256–258
  special minimum, 31, 252
  spouse benefits, 203–206, 241
  supplementation, 153–159, 243–245
  termination, 30
  value of, 222–223
Retirement Insurance, 14
Retirement test. *See* Earnings test
Rhode Island, 233
Role factor, 306, 307

Savings bonds. *See* Freedom Bond Program
Savings incentives, 78–79, 278–279, 306, 307
Savings program, 4, 304
Security risks, 304–305

Self-employment, 182, 224
earnings receipt control, 256
maximum cumulative taxes,
198–199
quarters of coverage, 26, 200
retirement program, 243
sex factor, 149
tax rate, 5, 60, 74, 197
Senior Citizen Benefits, 310–316
dollar amount, 311–312
financing, 312–313, 315
Sex factor, 145–152
Sickness, planning for, 229–231
Sick-pay plans, 233
Sick-pay taxes, 265–266
Social adequacy factor, 154, 182–
183
Social change, 55–56
Social insurance, 182–183
national, 295–296
perspective, 301–308
Social and Rehabilitation
Service, 23
Social Security Act (1935), 13,
62, 107
amendment and repeal, 98
Social Security Administration,
23–24
cost projections, 46–56
district and branch offices, 23–
24, 114
expenditures, 3, 24, 41, 43, 44,
119, 129
information from, 13, 108,
113–119, 228, 248
national headquarters, 24
representative activities, 114
specialized information from,
115–116
staff, 24
Social Security Amendments
(1977), 19, 177, 187

Social Security Disability
Amendments (1980), 66
Social Security Handbook, 13
Social Security program, 14. See
also specific benefit
programs
actuarial deficits, 97
adequacy of, 6, 158, 227–245
alteration vs. abolition, 295–
298
automatic adjustment
provisions, 161–165
benefit security and, 77
changes in, 192
contribution reduction, 77–78
cost allocation, 77, 78
cost-benefit analysis, 127–137
deficiencies, 305–306
discretionary (supplementary)
benefits, 296
financial soundness, 79
Freedom Plan and, 307, 309–
310, 323, 327, 328, 331–332,
334
maturity of, 45–46
private plan comparison, 180–
182, 184–185
private plan integration, 17,
153–159
promises, 296–297, 332
prospectus, 289–293
revision, 307
termination, 103
total income, 4
Social Security taxes, 3–4, 5, 60–
61
actuarial deficit and, 85, 89
benefits relation, 6, 61, 74,
130–132, 168–169, 170, 174,
182–183, 184–185, 199, 222–
225, 306, 307
burden redistribution, 197–198

collection, 23
computation, 70
under Freedom Plan, 335, 337
vs. general revenue financing,
    66–67
incorrectly collected, 263
inflation and, 163–164
maximum cumulative, 198–
    199, 223
minimizing, 262–268
payment method, 263–264
prospectus, 289, 290
rationale, 61–62
reallocation, 63–65
refund, 262–263
resistance to, 197
Social Security Trust Funds
accrued liability, 99
actuarial balance, 84–85, 89
with advance funding, 77–78
assets, 128–129
with current-cost financing,
    71–75
interest, 75, 128–129
investments, 60, 75, 77
management, 5–6
viability, 5–6
Social Security Trust Funds
    Managing Trustee, 23
Society of Actuaries, 48
Socioeconomic factors, 135–136
sexism and, 145–147, 150
Spouse benefits, 20, 33–34, 203-
    206
with disability, 209–212
maximizing, 271
Medicare protection, 254
with retirement, 203–206, 241
as survivor, 213, 214–218, 237
Spouse employment, 4
Standard of living, 162–165

Stand-by pay taxes, 266
State employees, 17–19, 172–173,
    175–179, 191
Student benefits, 34, 35, 204,
    210–211, 214, 216
maximizing, 255
Supplemental retirement plans.
    See Private benefit
    (pension) plans
Supplementary Medical
    Insurance, 14, 21, 23, 37–38,
    230
accrued liability, 100–102
actuarial deficit, 91, 93–96, 97
coinsurance, 38
costs, 65–66
deductible provision, 38
enrollment, 221
financing, 45, 59–60, 64–66, 67,
    74
forecast assumptions, 93
general revenue contribution,
    59–60, 64–65, 74
maximum benefits, 218, 219,
    220
participants, 64
planning, 67
projections, 65, 125
reimbursement system, 38
Supplementary Medical
    Insurance trust fund, 74
accrued liability, 101
assets, 129
Survivor benefits, 4, 20, 34–35,
    181, 203, 237–240, 327–328
automatic increases, 122
beneficiaries increase and, 41–
    42
conditions for, 237
with disability benefits, 209–
    211, 216, 237

Survivor benefits (*cont.*)
  earnings limitation, 139, 141–142, 216
  family maximum, 29, 36
  insured status and, 237–238, 239
  maximizing, 255
  maximum, 212–218
  money-saving hints, 217–218
  promises, 122
  quarters of coverage, 212–213, 237, 239
  reduction, 239
  replacement ratio, 214, 238–239, 240
  spouse benefits, 213, 214–218, 237
  supplementary income, 239–241
  termination, 30, 239
Survivors Insurance, 14

Tax-exempt status, 19
Tax rate, 5, 61, 131, 195–197
  actuarial deficits and, 104
  current-cost financing comparison, 73–74
  projections, 62–64
  scheduled vs. required, 64
Taxation, 57–67. *See also specific taxes*
Teachers, 18–19, 191, 278

Teleservice centers, 24
Texas, 176
Transfer payments, 302
Transitional insured status, 148
Travel, Medicare coverage and, 221, 254
Trust funds. *See also specific programs*
  assets, 127–129
  interest, 128, 129

Unemployment, 305
Unemployment Insurance, 14
  taxes, 264–265

Value-added tax, 290
Values factor, 135–136
Veteran's Administration pensions, 124

Wage level factor, 180–181
Wage-price relation, 163–165
Welfare, 14, 168, 335
Widow's (widower's) benefits, 34–35, 213, 214
  maximizing, 261
  remarriage and, 272
Wife. *See* Spouse benefits
Women. *See* Sex factor
Work option, 270–271
Workers' compensation, 33, 233

This book has been set in 11 point Century Schoolbook, leaded 2 points. Chapter numbers and titles and part titles are 24 point Century Schoolbook Bold Italic. The size of the type page is 26 by 45 picas. The text paper is cream white Finch opaque, sixty pound, offset paper.

About the Author

A. Haeworth Robertson was Chief Actuary of the United States Social Security Administration from 1975 to 1978, the period during which attention was first directed toward the alarming financial problems which lie ahead. He resigned shortly after the 1977 Amendments to Social Security were passed, believing he could more effectively provide the information necessary to bring about further rational change by working on the "outside." During the last six years he has written and lectured widely, giving special emphasis to interpreting and clarifying the financial status of Social Security.

While Chief Actuary of Social Security, he received two awards—the Commissioner's Citation and the Arthur J. Altmeyer Award—for distinguished service in managing the affairs of his office and in explaining Social Security's financial complexities in an easy-to-understand way to the Administration, the Congress, and the public.

Mr. Robertson's actuarial career began in 1953 when, as an officer in the United States Air Force, he served with a special unit of the Department of Defense appointed to prepare an actuarial study of the military retirement system for the 83rd Congress. Since then his entire career has been devoted to personal security programs of one kind or another. In addition to serving as Chief Actuary of Social Security, he worked twelve years as a consulting actuary dealing with private and public pension plans; four years in organizing, operating, and serving as president of a life insurance company; and six years as an international consultant on social insurance programs, which involved assignments in Switzerland, Barbados, Ghana, Lebanon, and the Philippines.

Mr. Robertson received his undergraduate degree in mathematics from the University of Oklahoma in 1951, where he was a Phi Beta Kappa, and his graduate degree in actuarial science from the University of Michigan in 1953. He is a Fellow of the Society of Actuaries, a Fellow of the Conference of Actuaries in Public Practice, and an Enrolled Actuary. He is also a member of the American Academy of Actuaries, the United Kingdom's Institute of Actuaries, and the International Actuarial Association. He is a member of the Board of Governors of the Society of Actuaries and a member of numerous committees and advisory groups dealing with social insurance and private and public employee pension plans.

Mr. Robertson currently resides in the Washington, D.C. area, where he is a Vice President of William M. Mercer, Incorporated, an international firm of employee benefit consultants.